Telling the Stories Right

Telling the Stories Right

Wendell Berry's
Imagination of Port William

EDITED BY

Jack R. Baker and Jeffrey Bilbro

Front Porch Republic *Books*

TELLING THE STORIES RIGHT
Wendell Berry's Imagination of Port William

Copyright © 2018 Wipf and Stock Publishers. All rights reserved. Except for brief quotations in critical publications or reviews, no part of this book may be reproduced in any manner without prior written permission from the publisher. Write: Permissions, Wipf and Stock Publishers, 199 W. 8th Ave., Suite 3, Eugene, OR 97401.

Front Porch Republic
An Imprint of Wipf and Stock Publishers
199 W. 8th Ave., Suite 3
Eugene, OR 97401

www.wipfandstock.com

PAPERBACK ISBN: 978-1-5326-3809-1
HARDCOVER ISBN: 978-1-5326-3810-7
EBOOK ISBN: 978-1-5326-3811-4

Cataloguing-in-Publication data:

Names: Baker, Jack R., editor. | Bilbro, Jeffrey, editor
Title: Telling the stories right : Wendell Berry's imagination of Port William / edited by Jack Baker.
Description: Eugene, OR: Front Porch Republic, 2018. | Includes index.
Identifiers: ISBN 978-1-5326-3809-1 (paperback). | ISBN 978-1-5326-3810-7 (hardcover). | ISBN 978-1-5326-3811-4 (epub).
Subjects: LCSH: Berry, Wendell, 1934- —Criticism and interpretation.
Classification: PS3552.E75 Z9 2018 (print). | PS3552 (epub).

Manufactured in the U.S.A.   MARCH 19, 2018

To Wendell and Tanya Berry. Through your stories, you have given the world no small gift.

Table of Contents

Fiction by Wendell Berry

"The Brothers." *Carolina Quarterly* 8.3 (Summer 1956): 5–11.

Nathan Coulter. Boston: Houghton Mifflin, 1960.

A Place on Earth. New York: Harcourt, Brace & World, 1967.

The Memory of Old Jack. Berkeley: Counterpoint, 1974.

A Place on Earth. Revised edition. San Francisco: North Point, 1983.

Nathan Coulter. Revised edition. San Francisco: North Point, 1985.

The Wild Birds. San Francisco: North Point, 1986.

Remembering: A Novel. San Francisco: North Point, 1988.

Fidelity: Five Stories. New York: Pantheon, 1992.

Watch With Me. New York: Pantheon, 1994.

A World Lost: A Novel. Washington DC: Counterpoint, 1996.

Jayber Crow: The Life Story of Jayber Crow, Barber, of the Port William Membership, as Written by Himself. Washington, DC: Counterpoint, 2000.

Three Short Novels. Washington, DC: Counterpoint, 2002.

That Distant Land: The Collected Stories. Washington, D.C.: Shoemaker Hoard, 2004.

Hannah Coulter. Washington D.C.: Shoemaker & Hoard, 2004.

Andy Catlett: Early Travels. Emeryville: Shoemaker & Hoard, 2006.

A Place in Time: Twenty Stories of the Port William Membership. Berkeley: Counterpoint, 2012.

"The Branch Way of Doing." *The Threepenny Review*, (Fall, 2014). https://www.threepenny review.com/samples/berry_f14.html.

"Dismemberment." *The Threepenny Review*, (Summer, 2015). http://www.threepenny review.com/samples/berry_su15.html

"One Nearly Perfect Day." *Sewanee Review* 123, no. 3 (Summer, 2015): 386–94.

"How It Went." *Sewanee Review* 124, no. 3 (Summer, 2016): 363–69.

The Art of Loading Brush. Berkeley: Counterpoint Press, 2017.

Acknowledgments

WE ARE THANKFUL TO the folks at Front Porch Republic for believing in our work on Wendell Berry—especially Jason Peters who has undertaken the unenviable task of editing this book series. We look forward to many more years of friendship, lively conversation, and good food.

A great joy to us both has been the timely and thoughtful work of each of the contributors to this collection. They have taught us much about Berry's fiction and how the work of imagination can change our lives—our gratitude for them all is profound.

To the librarians of White Library at Spring Arbor University we also owe our thanks, as well as to the university for the release time we both received to work on this project. Our student worker, Alison Westra, helped with the painstaking work of checking citations, formatting the essays, and compiling the index.

Most of all, we give thanks for Kimberly Moore-Jumonville, our department chair, for her tireless support of our many endeavors. Time and again Kimberly has sacrificed her own good for ours—and often without us knowing. She is a remarkable leader and patient encourager. We are grateful to be in membership with her.

I (Jeff) am grateful for my wife Melissa and daughter Hannah and their patience with my writing. I pray that spending time with Berry's fiction is making me not an absent or absent-minded scholar, but a better husband and father, one more faithful and hopeful. It is certainly making me more grateful to dwell with them both in the Room of Love.

I (Jack) find my greatest joy in being both Kelly's husband and Owen, Silvia, and Griffin's father. May we keep telling the stories right as we grow in our love for one another, being sure to visit Port William together, and often.

Introduction

Making Goodness Compelling

ONE OF WENDELL BERRY's most delightful fictional voices is that of Hannah Coulter, a woman who has endured great suffering and loss in her life, but whose memoir is marked by the deep sense of gratitude she feels for this only life she's lived. "This is the story of my life," she recounts, "that while I lived it weighed upon me and pressed against me and filled all my senses to overflowing and now is like a dream dreamed." Despite her lonely upbringing, despite the disappearance of her young husband into the mists of war, despite giving birth to their child in the emptiness of his loss, despite all of her children moving away from her and Nathan's home—despite all her expectations that never came to fruition, Hannah finds a way to narrate the goodness of her life. Her story, then, is the story of a life and a place she has found deeply good: "This is my story, my giving of thanks."[1]

Yet while Hannah gives thanks for her life, she does not pretend it has all been easy. And this tension between gratitude for its goodness and honesty about its sorrows troubles Hannah. In fact, one of the greatest doubts she harbors is whether she and Nathan, her second husband and the father of two of her children, failed to narrate their story in such a way that compelled their children to recognize and care for the good possibilities of life in Port William. Hannah fears the stories she's told her children have been marked by an edge of discontent. As she mourns over their departures for better opportunities in better places, she confides to Nathan, "I just wanted them to have a better chance than I had," to which Nathan replies, "Don't complain about the chance you had." Hannah is struck by the wisdom of Nathan's terse words, and she is changed by them: "Was I sorry that I had known my parents and Grandmam and Ora Finley and the Catletts and the

---

1. Berry, *Hannah*, 5.

Feltners, and that I had married Virgil and come to live in Port William, and that I had lived on after Virgil's death to marry Nathan and come to our place to raise our family and live among the Coulters and the rest of the membership?" The echoes of her question resound throughout her narrative, and she comes to a conclusion that "passed through everything [she] kn[e]w and changed it all":

> The chance you had is the life you've got. You can make complaints about what people, including you, make of their lives after they have got them, and about what people make of other people's lives, even about your children being gone, but you mustn't wish for another life. You mustn't want to be somebody else. What you must do is this: "Rejoice evermore. Pray without ceasing. In every thing give thanks." I am not all the way capable of so much, but those are the right instructions.[2]

Rejoice evermore. Pray without ceasing. In every thing give thanks. These are the instructions for telling our stories right, and stories told in this way compel us to tend the splintered light of goodness that shines through the cracks of our wounded world. But even as Hannah so beautifully comes to terms with the limits of her only life, she yet worries. She is unsettled by the thought that she and Nathan may have narrated their seemingly simple lives in a way that encouraged their children to leave: "But did we tell the stories right? It was lovely, the telling and the listening, usually the last thing before bedtime. But did we tell the stories in such a way as to suggest that we had needed a better chance or a better life or a better place than we had?" Hannah is unwilling to answer her own question, though she must ask it of herself—she must live in her uncertainty. She ponders what would happen if someone, "instead of mourning and rejoicing over the past, [said] that everything should have been different." In the end, she knows that such a line of thinking is the "loose thread that unravels the whole garment."[3] And so Hannah resists a reductive story; she refuses to tug at the loose thread. Instead, despite the imperfect nature of her life's garment, Hannah learns to weave her narrative in gratitude.

The essays that follow are our giving of thanks, our collective attempt at telling the right stories about life and its fictional representations; they are our efforts to trace some of the narrative threads that hold together Berry's Port William stories. We have written in hope that our words can

2. Ibid., 112–13.
3. Ibid., 113–14.

elucidate the workings of Berry's fiction, which makes goodness compelling to so many of his readers. What does it mean to "tell the stories right?" This is a question that haunts not only Hannah and the authors in this collection, but Berry himself.

Yet while Berry identifies himself as "a storyteller," his stories seem to receive less attention than his essays or even his poetry.[4] In talking with those who read and appreciate Berry, we've gathered that people are more likely to have read his essays or poetry than his fiction.[5] Many readers seem to agree with Edward Abbey's assessment that the essay is Berry's primary genre. As Abbey puts it in his blurb on the back of Berry's *Recollected Essays*: "Wendell Berry is a good novelist, a fine poet, and the best essayist now working in America." This ranking of his genres is corroborated by evidence from Google Scholar, which lists the number of times each of his books has been cited. Berry's nonfiction books are cited much more often than either his poetry or fiction: his novels and short story collections are cited, on average, 1.03 times per year, his poetry collections are cited 1.15 times per year, and his essay collections are cited 12.22 times per year.[6] It may seem sacrilegious to subject Berry's oeuvre to big data analytics, and citation count may not correlate precisely with readership, but the large disparity indicated by these numbers confirms our initial hunch that Berry is known predominately as an essayist.

So why do Berry's essays garner the bulk of his readers' attention? Perhaps Berry's essays are provocative in the etymological sense: they call forth responses. Their incisive cultural analyses and uncompromising positions—don't buy a computer, farm with draft horses, accept your inevitable ignorance, don't go to war, foster small farms, stop strip mining—seem to demand responses and engagement. Or perhaps his essays offer a more manageable entry into Berry's complex body of thought than do his novels and short stories, particularly for environmentalists or agrarians who are

---

4. Berry, *Conversations with Wendell Berry*, 187.

5. Others have noted this phenomenon as well. See Mannon, "Leisure and Technology in Port William," 171–72; Major, *Grounded Vision*, 16; Murphy, *Farther Afield in the Study of Nature-Oriented Literature*, 26.

6. We'd like to thank our student, Alison Westra, for painstakingly compiling this data. Alison also used WorldCat to compare library holdings of Berry's different genres. These numbers didn't display the disparity that the citation counts did: on average, libraries hold 1088 copies of each fictional book, 769 of each volume of poetry, and 1054 of each book of nonfiction. So as we note, it's difficult to determine whether Berry's fiction is less-read, or just less-cited than his nonfiction.

most interested in ideas that are immediately practical. As Fritz Oehlsch-laeger surmises in his essay for this collection, those committed to environ-mental causes may be drawn to activist polemics and have less patience for story-telling. Berry's essays sound a strident, provocative note that activists are tuned to hear, while his fiction can seem nostalgic or passé.

Readers of his essays, then, may see Berry primarily as an uncompro-mising advocate for reform, as a crank who advocates against strip min-ing and tractors and who refuses to buy a computer. Viewed through this lens, Berry's fiction can appear to be simply a didactic outworking of his agrarian ideas. Even his fiction teacher, Wallace Stegner, wrote to Berry that he thought *Remembering* was "somewhat didactic, a narrative on the theme of some of your essays."[7] One scholar states this claim more bluntly: "Berry's stories tend to be glosses of his essays." And he goes on to critique this moralizing mode: "No matter how much one sympathizes with Berry's arguments against corporate agriculture, those arguments do not belong in his fiction. The purpose of the novel is to tell a good story, with believable characters engaged in a credible dramatic conflict. When the fiction writer subordinates art to polemics, narrative becomes argumentative discourse and the work lapses into didacticism."[8]

Berry's stories—like his poems—do have a moral edge to them that unsettles our cultural preference for "pure" art, art that resides in some lofty aesthetic realm at a comfortable remove from the pragmatic concerns of our lives.[9] Yet this division between art and life, between beauty and moral-ity, is damaging and false. Part of telling the stories right, then, is telling them in a way that advocates for responsible membership in our places and

7. Stegner to Berry, November 21, 1988. Stegner went on to write, "the theme of your new novel is one I have joined you in more times than one, so it's not the theme I am slightly troubled by, only the translation of that theme into fiction. I guess I kept looking for some Uncle Burley stories." We're indebted to Eric Miller for finding this letter and bringing it to our attention. Ironically, Stegner's own fiction has often been critiqued as too didactic, and both Stegner and Berry aim for stories that are aesthetically whole while also being responsible to their places. See Robinson, *Wallace Stegner*, 110–13. A few years before this letter, Stegner wrote to Jack Shoemaker, Berry's publisher, with a rather different assessment: "It is hard to say whether I like this writer better as a poet, an essayist, or a novelist. He is all three, at a high level. He is, in fact, very special, a sort of national treasure holed up on the Kentucky River. Pilgrimages would not be out of order." Stegner, *The Selected Letters of Wallace Stegner*, 274.

8. Angyal, *Wendell Berry*, 99, 104.

9. For a defense of the didactic poetic tradition that situates Berry's poetry within this mode, see Basney, "Five Notes on the Didactic Tradition, In Praise of Wendell Berry."

communities. At the end of his essay "Imagination in Place," in which he describes how his responsibility to his place fits with his work as a writer, Berry acknowledges the dangers of overt didacticism. Writing on behalf of the health of a place can lead an artist into "a sort of advocacy. Advocacy, as a lot of people will affirm, is dangerous to art, and you must beware the danger, but if you accept the health of the place as a standard, I think the advocacy is going to be present in your work."[10] Yet in his fiction, he advocates not so much for particular issues or stances as for the inherent beauty and goodness of his place and its community.

This advocacy, then, ultimately takes shape in his stories' aesthetic sense of wholeness. When an interviewer asked Berry why he wrote fiction in addition to essays and poetry, he explained, "The reason for writing what we call fiction seems to be the desire to tell a whole story. And to stick strictly to the truth, what we call nonfictional truth—to tell the story that really happened—is invariably to have an incomplete story. Nobody ever knows all the facts. Time passes, gaps come into memories, and so on. The impulse is an artistic one, the impulse toward wholeness."[11] He clarifies the kind of wholeness to which his fiction aspires in an essay on the imagination, "No human work can become whole by including everything, but it can become whole in another way: by accepting its formal limits and then answering within those limits all the questions it raises."[12] The formal wholeness of Berry's fiction is analogous to a larger harmony or pattern— the sense evoked by the Hebrew word *shalom*—into which our lives fit. In our industrial age, it can be nearly impossible to imagine how to lead healthy lives. We are so deeply formed by our culture's consumerist vision of the good life that it is difficult to conceive of living differently. Berry's stories, however, imagine an alternative order, one that attempts to fit together the fragmented pieces of our lives into a beautiful whole.

It is in this way that, while his stories include advocacy, their moral impulse does not compromise but rather flows from their narrative integrity. Hence Stegner writes elsewhere that Berry's life and writing exemplify how "aesthetics and ethics do not have to be kept apart to prevent their quarreling, but [can] live together in harmony."[13] This quarrel is particularly damaging because on its own, didactic polemic is insufficient to change

10. "Imagination," 15.

11. Berry, *Conversations with Wendell Berry*, 188.

12. Berry, "Imagination," 3.

13. Stegner, *Where the Bluebird Sings to the Lemonade Springs*, 211.

people's minds or move them to action. All too often, we humans don't do what we already know to be right. So what we really need is not more moral instruction about the dangers of industrial agriculture, unchecked capitalism, or techno-utopianism; rather, we need stories that will instruct our imaginations and affections so that we can *envision* and *desire* and *embody* the good. This is precisely what Berry's fiction does; as Stanley Hauerwas writes, "Berry's novels do what is next to impossible in our time, and that is make goodness compelling."[14]

As an example of the insufficiency of rational polemic, the philosopher James K. A. Smith recounts an occasion when he found himself reading Wendell Berry in the Costco food court, which is probably "a kind of shorthand for Berry's picture of the sixth circle of hell." This experience brought home to Smith the "gap between my thought and my action—between my passionate intellectual assent to [Berry's] ideas and my status quo action." Smith uses this example to point out that quite often what we need is not better thinking, but better habits and imaginations. As he claims later, human beings are "narrative animals" who are "less convinced by arguments than moved by stories; our being-in-the-world is more aesthetic than deductive, better captured by narrative than analysis."[15] So perhaps reading Berry's fiction and learning to desire the goodness that it portrays shape us on a more fundamental level than does merely nodding in agreement with his essays. Perhaps Berry's stories can lead us out of the Costco food court and through a Purgatorial refinement of our loves and desires.

Structure of the Book

We have arranged the essays in this collection into three somewhat sequential sections. The essays in the first section, Narrative Traditions, work out answers to questions about the forms and traditions in which Berry writes: What kind of a thing is Berry's fiction? What are the traditions and communities to which his fiction responds? Jack Baker, responding to those who see Berry's fiction as overly nostalgic, situates Berry's stories in the *ubi sunt* tradition of Anglo-Saxon wisdom literature. Such elegiac stories mourn over the past not because they long for a return to some simpler time, but because they recognize and honor the good of what has come before.

14. "Foreword," xii.
15. *Imagining*, 8, 108.

The good of the past can be recognized most clearly in the light of eternity. Ingrid Pierce's essay examines some of the many dreams recorded in Berry's fiction and interprets them in the context of medieval dream vision literature. These dreams take characters out of the normal constraints of space and time and reveal an eternal perspective, a glimpse of wholeness, that provides consolation and hope in the midst of suffering and loss.

These glimpses of wholeness reveal a beauty that calls us to work toward its fulfillment in the midst of present brokenness. In her essay, Kiara Jorgenson unpacks Berry's understanding of this calling or vocation. Jorgenson acknowledges that many readers see Berry simply as a critic of Christianity, but she finds continuity between a classic Protestant understanding of vocation and the way that Port William's exemplary characters respond to a religious sense of calling. Such characters answer a call not to some lucrative career, but to work toward a common goal over successive generations in response to the gifts that each one has received.

While these accounts of Berry's fiction as rooted in older literary and religious traditions may give the impression that Berry stands utterly apart from the insular world of contemporary literature, Doug Sikkema reminds us of the ways that Berry remains indebted to his teacher Wallace Stegner and the Stanford writing program. In particular, Sikkema points out that *Jayber Crow* is in some ways a response to Stegner's *All the Little Live Things*, and Berry's novelistic reply to his teacher reveals both affinities between the two as well as important disagreements.

While the first four essays certainly do not exhaust the traditions and communities that shape Berry's fiction, the context they provide prepares readers to better recognize the demands these stories make of them. Like the statue of Apollo in Rilke's famous poem, their beauty confronts readers with a bold declaration: "You must change your life."[16] The second group of essays, Beauty's Instructions, considers some of these counter-cultural demands.

Responding to critiques of Berry's vision as impractical and nostalgic, Jeffrey Bilbro considers how Andy Catlett, with his maimed right arm, might teach us to live as wounded members of a broken world. As Andy learns to make do with only one hand, so we have to learn to get by in spite of our shortcomings and the unjust systems that seem to constrain us. Andy's example challenges us to practice hope despite the many reasons we have to despair.

16. Rilke, *Selected Poems of Rainer Maria Rilke*, 147.

Of course death is one of the primary facts that tempts us to despair, and Ethan Mannon argues that through Berry's rather drastic revision of his first novel, *Nathan Coulter*, he focuses readers' attention on what constitutes a good death. The revised version concludes with the death of Dave Coulter, and Mannon looks at his death as well as the deaths of several others to show how these characters learn to accept death: because these characters die as members of a loving community—a body of which they are a part—the meaning of their lives does not flicker out with their last breath (the echoes of St. Paul's description of the church as Christ's body are crucial here). The Port William membership teaches us how to die well.

This membership is a great gift, yet it entails certain obligations. Fritz Oehlschlaeger traces what Burley Coulter, Berry's eloquent expositor of membership, calls "the requirement" that a community places upon its members. In a culture that is impatient with any constraints on an individual's freedom, understanding love as a joyful requirement seems foreign, and yet Burley and his friends invite us to see love as an unpayable debt we should gratefully accept.

This call to freely give and receive love can be particularly hard for those on the margins of a community. Michael Stevens, however, reveals Berry's keen attention to those our society tends to neglect. Berry's stories include and value the African-Americans who live on the outskirts of the white community, the mentally disabled who never quite fit in, the bitter and warped whose own wounds lead them to hurt others, and the elderly who seem past their usefulness but who nonetheless play crucial roles. Berry's mode of narration instructs us to attend to and value those who all too easily fall through the cracks.

The final section, Responding to the Stories, takes a more personal approach, offering ways that Berry's stories have compelled particular readers to change their lives. While many of Berry's readers continue to shop in the Costco food court, others have been moved to make radical changes. Eric Miller spent two weeks reading archived letters that Berry has received, and he sorts through them for clues to the deep influence Berry has had on so many people. Perhaps, Miller suggests, Berry's writing conveys what Andy Catlett terms "the true world," the world of nature, of prophets, and of poets. The deep magic of this world fills Port William as it fills Middle Earth or the older myths, awakening readers to the possibility of redemption, meaning, shalom. And as these letters attest, the longing for this possibility leads many to walk away from the flattened world of careerism and consumerism.

Gracy Olmstead provides an example of such a journey. She grew up in an Idaho farming community, and after moving across the country for college, she felt rootless. Discovering Berry's novella *Remembering*—and reading it through the lens of Genesis, Dante, and T. S. Eliot—Olmstead gradually learned to resist the lure of cosmopolitan abstraction, to remain faithful to the people and places that shaped her identity, to set roots in her new communities. Exile and homelessness may define much of our lives, and Olmstead still lives far from the Idaho community where she was raised. Nonetheless, by practicing the arts of homemaking and membership that her parents and grandparents modeled, she is preparing for the final homecoming, the one glimpsed by Andy at the end of *Remembering* and by Dante at the end of *The Divine Comedy*.

Reading Berry challenged Olmstead to make a home in a new place, and it led Jake Meador to stay in a place he once wanted to leave. Meador describes the difficulties of growing up in an anti-intellectual, stultifying place—he was lonely, he resented his community, and he wanted to move on as soon as he could. Yet as Meador demonstrates, this tendency to move away from people we don't like exacerbates our cultural and class divides as we sort ourselves out by race, education, and income. Meador finds in *Jayber Crow* both a diagnosis and a cure for our cultural disintegration, and Jayber's willingness to remain in his home, to love even those neighbors he dislikes, inspired Meador and his wife to stay in Lincoln and to anchor their story in the story of their community.

As a preacher's kid in the rural south—growing up in a town that "was like Port William with alligators"—Andrew Peterson also wanted nothing more than to get out of Dodge. So while he was still a teen, he joined a rock band and left for the exciting life of stardom. While his career didn't take off according to his youthful fantasies, he did become a successful musician, and as a singer-songwriter, he saw firsthand the ability of stories to hold an audience's attention, to shape their affections, to tell truth. When he read *Jayber Crow*, Berry's story moved him deeply, and he suddenly found himself *wanting* to garden—the very thing he had despised as a child. Peterson and his family moved from the suburbs to a small farm and began gardening, raising chickens, and keeping bees. When people ask him what caused this profound change in his affections and his way of life, Peterson replies, "I read this story about a barber."

These essays certainly do not provide a comprehensive analysis of Berry's fiction, but they testify to its importance and power. Our hope is that readers of this collection will be encouraged to turn—or to return—to Berry's stories with sharpened vision, better able to recognize and tend the shalom they so beautifully portray. Berry is a polemicist and a poet, but he is also—and we would argue most crucially—a storyteller. And he tells his stories in ways that compel readers to seek the goodness that can be found in our own places.

Bibliography

Angyal, Andrew J. *Wendell Berry*. New York: Twayne, 1995.

Basney, Lionel. "Five Notes on the Didactic Tradition, In Praise of Wendell Berry." In *Wendell Berry*, edited by Paul Merchant, 174–83. American Authors Series 4. Lewiston, NY: Confluence, 1991.

Berry, Wendell. *Conversations with Wendell Berry*. Edited by Morris Allen Grubbs. Literary Conversations Series. Jackson: University Press of Mississippi, 2007.

———. *Hannah Coulter*. Berkeley: Counterpoint, 2005.

———. "Imagination in Place." In *Imagination in Place*, 1–16. Berkeley: Counterpoint, 2010.

Hauerwas, Stanley. "Foreword." In *Wendell Berry: Life and Work*, edited by Jason Peters, xi–xii. Lexington: University Press of Kentucky, 2010.

Major, William H. *Grounded Vision: New Agrarianism and the Academy*. Tuscaloosa: University of Alabama Press, 2011.

Mannon, Ethan. "Leisure and Technology in Port William: Wendell Berry's Revelatory Fiction." *Mississippi Quarterly* 67.2 (2014) 171–192.

Murphy, Patrick D. *Farther Afield in the Study of Nature-Oriented Literature*. New Brunswick: Rutgers University Press, 2000.

Rilke, Rainer Maria. *Selected Poems of Rainer Maria Rilke*. Translated by Robert Bly. New York: Harper & Row, 1981.

Robinson, Forrest G. *Wallace Stegner*. Twayne's United States Authors Series 282. Boston: Twayne Publishers, 1977.

Smith, James K. A. *Imagining the Kingdom: How Worship Works*. Cultural Liturgies. Grand Rapids: Baker, 2013.

Stegner, Wallace. *The Selected Letters of Wallace Stegner*. Edited by Page Stegner. Berkeley: Counterpoint, 2008.

———. *Where the Bluebird Sings to the Lemonade Springs*. New York: Random House, 1995.

———. Letter to Wendell Berry, November 21, 1988. Kentucky Historical Society.

Contributor Biographies

Jack R. Baker is an Associate Professor of English at Spring Arbor University where he teaches medieval literature and Wendell Berry. He and Jeff Bilbro, a friend and colleague, have written *Wendell Berry and Higher Education: Cultivating Virtues of Place* (University Press of Kentucky). He lives in Spring Arbor, Micchigan, with his wife Kelly and their three children, Owen, Silvia, and Griffin.

Jeffrey Bilbro is an Associate Professor of English at Spring Arbor University in southern Michigan. He grew up in the mountainous state of Washington and earned his B.A. in Writing and Literature from George Fox University in Oregon and his Ph.D. in English from Baylor University. He is the author of *Loving God's Wildness: The Christian Roots of Ecological Ethics in American Literature* (University of Alabama Press, 2015) and the co-author, with Jack Baker, of *Wendell Berry and Higher Education: Cultivating Virtues of Place* (University Press of Kentucky, 2017).

Kiara Jorgenson, an instructor of religion and environmental studies at St. Olaf College and a candidate for ordination within the Evangelical Lutheran Church in America, holds a Ph.D. in systematic theology from Luther Seminary in St. Paul, Minnesota. Her recently published dissertation explores the ecological promise of the Protestant doctrine of vocation and calls upon the work of Wendell Berry to illustrate how concepts of calling might be practically recast in our anthropocenic era.

Ethan Mannon is an ecocritic and Assistant Professor of English at Mars Hill University where he teaches American and Appalachian Literature, as well as composition, and coordinates the Regional Studies Program. Along with an article on Wendell Berry in the *Mississippi Quarterly*, he has published on Robert Frost, Michael Pollan, Aldo Leopold, Alain Badiou, Harriette Arnow, and Helena Maria Viramontes.

Eric Miller is Professor of History and Humanities at Geneva College (Beaver Falls, Pennsylvania), where he directs the honors program. He is the author of *Hope in a Scattering Time: A Life of Christopher Lasch* and *Glimpses of Another Land: Political Hope, Spiritual Longing*. His writing has appeared in a range of publications, including *Christian Century, First Things*, and *Christianity Today*. He is currently at work on a study of the rise of localist movements in the United States from the 1960s to the present.

Jake Meador is the editor-in-chief of Mere Orthodoxy and serves as Vice President of the Davenant Institute, a ministry working for the renewal of Christian wisdom. He lives in Lincoln, Nebraska, with his wife Joie, daughter Davy Joy, and sons Wendell and Austin.

Fritz Oehlschlaeger is Professor Emeritus of English at Virginia Tech. He is the author of *The Achievement of Wendell Berry* (Kentucky, 2011), *Procreative Ethics* (Cascade, 2010) and *Love and Good Reasons* (Duke, 2003). He is also co-author, with Peter Graham, of *Articulating the Elephant Man* (Johns Hopkins University Press, 1992).

Gracy Olmstead, an Idaho native and graduate of Patrick Henry College, lives in northern Virginia with her husband, daughter, and Irish Setter. She has written for *The American Conservative, The Federalist, National Review, The Week, Christianity Today, The American Prospect*, and *The University Bookman*.

Andrew Peterson is a singer, songwriter, and author based in Nashville, where he lives with his wife, three children, and 100,000 bees. In addition to his nine albums he's written an award-winning fantasy series called *The Wingfeather Saga*, currently in production as an animated film. He's also the founder of the Rabbit Room, a community of artists and authors committed to telling the truth beautifully. Learn more about Andrew and his work at www.Andrew-Peterson.com.

Though she calls the Blue Ridge Mountains of Virginia home, **Ingrid Pierce** currently lives in West Lafayette, Indiana, where she is working on her PhD in Medieval Literature at Purdue University. While writing her dissertation on sound and hearing in Middle English literature, she teaches composition and World Literature at Purdue. Ingrid has published and presented on authors including Julian of Norwich, Thomas Malory, Geoffrey Chaucer, W.B. Yeats, W.H. Auden, and Ben Jonson. She started seriously reading Wendell Berry after a summer internship on a small farm in Virginia.

Doug Sikkema is currently a Senior Researcher for Cardus, a Christian public policy think tank based in Hamilton, ON, and the managing editor of Cardus's flagship publication, *Comment* magazine. Doug has a B.A. from Redeemer University College, an MA in English Literature from the University of Ottawa, and is currently a doctoral candidate at the University of Waterloo. His research looks at "disenchantment" and traces this notion through several contemporary American writers—Marilynne Robinson, Christian Wiman, and Wendell Berry—to interrogate what this might mean for how we understand mind, language, and ecology in a *post*modern paradigm.

Michael Stevens has taught in the Humanities Division at Cornerstone University since 1997, concentrating on American Literature, various writing courses, and work with students in the 'Great Books' Honors Program. Along the way, he discovered the confluence of nearly all his interests (local communities, gardening, Christian peacemaking) in a certain Kentucky author, and with his colleague and friend Matt Bonzo he wrote *Wendell Berry and the Cultivation of Life* (Brazos Press, 2008). He has been married to Linda since 1992, and they have three children: Ethan, Julia, and Gabriel. They live in Grand Rapids, Michigan.

PART 1: Narrative Traditions

1

Remembering the Past Rightly

Elegy and *Ubi Sunt* Tradition in Wendell Berry's Fiction

Jack R. Baker

"The difference, beloved, ain't in who is and who's not, but in who knows it and who don't. Oh, my friends, there ain't no nonmembers, living nor dead nor yet to come. Do you Know it? Or do you don't?"

—Burley Coulter[1]

Wendell Berry's short story, "The Wild Birds," begins with a rather ominous opening line: "'Where have they gone?' Wheeler thinks. But he knows. Gone to the cities, forever or for the day. Gone to the shopping center. Gone to the golf course. Gone to the grave."[2] And it is probably lines such as these that set Berry at odds with some readers who cast a wary eye at fiction that veers too close to backward-looking polemic. In one fell swoop the narrator paints a grim picture of cities, shopping centers, and golf courses, ending with the full stop of the grave. Lines like these, the critic might say, are proof that Berry's imagination is stuck in the past,

1. Berry, *Hannah Coulter*, 97.
2. "The Wild Birds," in *That Distant Land*, 337–64. Further references to this story will be given parenthetically.

3

propping up the vestiges of an agricultural way of life no longer viable in a modern world. And surely such nostalgia is unhelpful for those of us who live in the ever changing present; the world is mutable, we can't get back to what once was, we must press on, heads high, eyes forward. Indeed, if the critic reads beyond this opening line, he will find that the following pages are filled with further moments of lamentation and nostalgia as Wheeler Catlett looks out from the window of his law office over the landscape of Hargrave and is struck by how different, how desolate, and how devoid of life the world around him has become. And so readers of Berry's fiction must come to terms with the reality that the voice of Port William often calls upon us to cast our vision toward things that have passed away, toward people who have gone to their graves. It is thus understandable that readers may find his fiction to be too concerned with the past, to be suffering from a myopic vision—stuck, like Dante's diviners, with our heads on our shoulders, facing in the wrong direction.

But such would be an unfair critique of Berry's fiction. And despite the somber tone at the outset of the story, it is a tone that is not ultimately pessimistic. Like much of Berry's fiction, "The Wild Birds" is concerned with the passing away of dear things and the thankfulness, forgiveness, and hope those in Port William (and we readers) nonetheless practice.[3] To make sense of this claim, I will situate "The Wild Birds" within the long tradition of literary lamentation that reaches back to some of the earliest surviving poetry in the English language and is poignantly elaborated in the particular example of *ubi sunt* literature. The poetic theme of the *ubi sunt*, which is closely associated with wisdom literature, explores in elegiac tone the limits of our mortality, the goodness of the past we remember, and the power of such to shape us for healthy lives in the present and to inspire in us hope. Thus, it is my argument that the nostalgia in Berry's fiction is in fact teaching us to remember rightly those who have gone before us—not so that we might turn back the clocks to live in the fabled past, but so that we might find hope for today in remembering.

Nostalgia as Homecoming

For some time now in the English language *nostalgia* has been used to describe a sentimentalizing affection for the past—a way of remembering that

3. For a treatment of the Port William community as a *communio sanctorum*, see Brent Laytham, "The Membership Includes the Dead," 173–89.

focuses on the good, but rarely enough on the bad. We might even feel that a person who waxes nostalgic has lost touch with reality. We can't change the past, so dwelling on it is a fool's errand. But at one point in the history of our language, *nostalgia* carried with it a rather positive meaning—"longing for one's home." And I think it is in this vein—when we think of nostalgia not as a quaint emotion, but as a deep desire for homecoming—that we are right to describe Berry's fiction as nostalgic. He is in good company if this is the case; for, the theme of *nostos*, or 'story of homecoming,' was common in Greek literature. Probably the most famous example of such is the *Odyssey*, which is an extended *nostos*, culminating at the great rooted bed around which Odysseus' entire world has been built. Perhaps the most infamous is Aeschylus' *Agamemnon*, which begins with a tragic *nostos* that inverts the virtues of the theme—Agamemnon, returned from war, is slain by his wife Clytemnestra and her lover Aegisthus in his own palace. Berry himself conspicuously ventures into the theme in his short story "Making It Home," which recounts Art Rowanberry's much less eventful return from the war, yet culminates in a beautiful reunion in a field, reminiscent of the parable of the prodigal son. It is to these stories of homecoming, to the image of Odysseus weeping on the headlands of the island Ogygia as he pines for hearth and home, that we might trace the journey of our word *nostalgia*.[4]

If we think of nostalgia, then, as a deep longing for home, a lamentation for a familiar order that has passed away, we are able to save it from the dustbin of shallow sentiment, recovering its long history as a part of those stories in which a protagonist imagines the restoration of something dear that has been lost. Because nostalgia is concerned with imagining the goodness of things as they once were, it is at its core an exercise in the virtues of patience,[5] hope, and gratitude—patience because one must suffer the possibility that all may be lost, hope that though things have changed they might yet reveal their goodness in new and unexpected ways, and gratitude for those who have gone before that we might yet go on after.[6] And so, as Wheeler Catlett looks out his window and suffers the loss of those who have gone before him and the way of life that followed them to

---

4. Berry's extended treatment of homecoming in the *Odyssey* can be found in "The Body and The Earth," in *The Unsettling of America*, 97–140. See especially 120–30.

5. I'm thinking of patience in terms of *passio*, or suffering, not one's ability to wait things out.

6. To be sure, stories of nostalgia do not seek to wrap things up too neatly, to dismiss the real losses we experience in the world; for instance, when Odysseus returns home, he does so alone, without his beloved, loyal men.

the grave, he is also marked by their goodness in the world—a goodness that lives on in him, their inheritor, as it will live on in Danny and Lyda Branch and Andy and Flora Catlett after him.[7] Indeed, stories of nostalgia make us vulnerable; they inflict on us a double wound as we at once feel both the pang of loss for that which we have loved and the pang of joy for having loved it.

The *Ubi Sunt* Tradition

This deeply human theme of "joy and sorrow as sharp as swords"[8] is an ancient one in western literature, especially in English. In medieval literature, particularly medieval poetry, joy and sorrow for things gone is given life in the so called *ubi sunt* formula observable in poems reflecting on the transience of life and the vagaries and finality of death. The words '*ubi sunt*' ("where are they") begin a common poetic formula identifiable in poems across the Middle Ages: "where are those (*ubi sunt*) who have gone before us?" The formula is elegiac and rhetorical, calling the reader to reflect on the passing away of what once was good and beloved, often from the perspective of one who is in a state of suffering or loss.

Though the poetic theme may, on the surface, appear to be a sentimental lamentation for the past, it is something far more nuanced, for it is concerned with patience, hope, and gratitude in the midst of real loss. The *ubi sunt* is typically part of a redemptive cycle in which the poet begins by declaring his grief and suffering in the loss of the life he once knew and concludes in gratitude as the rememberer embraces a consolation which leads to hope that things one day might be made right, or at least that the lost way of life was good. The 13th-century Middle English lyrical poem, "Ubi Sunt Qui Ante Nos Fuerunt" (Where are those who have gone before us?), is a prime example of this poetic theme. Composed of thirty-one stanzas, the lyric begins with the lamentation of the loss of good things, yet ends with the consolation found in placing one's faith in the protection of Mary, Heaven's Queen, a faith that offers the hope of reunion with Christ "In ioye wiþ-outen hende":

> Uuere beþ þey biforen vs weren, (Where be they who before us were,)
> Houndes ladden and haukes beren (Who led hounds and bore hawks)

---

7. See Berry, "The Inheritors," in *That Distant Land*, 428–40.

8. Tolkien, "On Fairy-stories," 27.

And hadden feld and wode? (And owned field and wood?)

Þe riche leuedies in hoere bour, (The rich ladies in their bowers,)

Þat wereden gold in hoere tressour (Who wore gold in their tresses)

Wiþ hoere briȝtte rode, (With their bright faces)

Eten and drounken, and maden hem glad; (Who ate and drank, and made glad together;)

Hoere lif was al wiþ gamen .I.-lad, (Their life was all with games filled,)

Men keneleden hem biforen; (Men knelt before then;)

Þey beren hem wel swiþe heye; (They bore themselves well so high)

And in a twincling of an eye (And in a twinkling of an eye)

Hoere soules weren forloren. (Their souls were forlorn.)

…

Mayden moder, heuene quene, (Virgin Mother, Heaven's Queen,)

Þou miȝt and const, and owest to bene (Thou art able and know how, and ought to be)

Oure sheld aȝein þe fende: (Our shield against the Fiend:)

Help ous sunne for to flen, (Help us, sin, to flee,)

Þat we moten þi sone .I.-seen, (That we might Thy Son see,)

In ioye wiþ-outen hende. Amen! (In joy without end. Amen!)[9]

As R. D. Fulk notes, this poem represents "a long literary standing, to be found in Boethius' *Consolatio philosophiae* ("Ubi nunc fidelis ossa Fabrici manent?") and at several places in OE literature, most memorably in *The Wanderer* [ll.] 92–96."[10] In such poems there is a working out of the individual's need to come to terms with a deep sense of loss, which is part of their lasting quality. We can trace this thread of loss through to later English elegies: "The Old English poems do have a kinship with later English elegies of a broader kind, for example with *Gray's Elegy*, which treats themes of death and transience in a general way, and even with Tennyson's *In Memoriam*, which, though far longer than the Old English poems, resembles them in consisting of rather various reflections prompted by the need to come to terms with a sense of loss."[11] Thus the elegy, which at times contains the

9. Fulk, *An Introduction to Middle English*, 227–31. See also Carleton Brown, ed., *English Lyrics of the XIIIth Century*, 85–87.

10. Ibid., 227.

11. Klinck, *The Old English Elegies*, 11.

formulaic expression of *ubi sunt*, has a long history in English literature, offering us glimpses into the human condition across time and within a shared language.[12]

The tradition is far reaching and poignant, and has perhaps its fullest expression in the elegiac poetry of the Anglo-Saxons, a corpus characterized by themes of "exile, loss of loved ones, physical hardship, desolate landscapes and seascapes, contemplation of ruins, meditation on the inevitability of decay and the transience of all earthly things."[13] Anne L. Klinck has described the voice of these poems as "discourse arising from a powerful sense of absence, of separation from what is desired, expressed through characteristic words and themes, and shaping itself by echo and leitmotiv into a poem that moves from disquiet to some kind of acceptance."[14] Both Klinck and Fulk note that the poignant nature of the *ubi sunt* formula is rather at home in the elegiac poetry of the Anglo-Saxons—poetry that is morose, whose voice is profoundly bereft of joy, and which is often bookended with Christian hope. As David Lyle Jeffrey has so beautifully articulated, we find in Old English literature

> an elegiac recognition of the frailty and transience of human life (in Old English, a recurrent expression is *lif is læne*, "life is fleeting"). In many Anglo-Saxon lyrics a deep yearning for enduring peace is set against the dark realities of violence and terror, which are often in these poems explicitly connected with the legacy of the Fall. In Beowulf, the marauding Grendel is an age-old exile from human community, said to be *"Caines cynne,"* of the lineage of Cain, and the bright light and warm comforts of Hrothgar's hall are threatened by an evil *sheadu* representative of the dark and fallen wilderness beyond. "The Wanderer" and "The Seafarer" capture hauntingly experiences of exile (OE *ut-lagu*, lit. "outside the law") and a longing for homecoming to the *hlaf-weard* (loaf-guardian, the origin of ME *lauerd* and then our contracted modern English word lord). The Anglo-Saxon speaker in these poems is not a happy wanderer, but one who keenly seeks a return to the Lord, and his reconciling embrace. At another register we might say that these poems typically express a deep desire for closure, for a turn to meaning that might transform the chaos of the fallen experience into a new day of grace and peace.[15]

12. It is worth noting that the first poem in Berry's *New Collected Poems* is an elegy.

13. Lapidge, *The Blackwell Encyclopaedia of Anglo-Saxon England*, 164.

14. Ibid., 246.

15. Jeffrey and Maillet, *Christianity and Literature*, 149–50.

In no clearer place is the elegiac "deep yearning for enduring peace . . . , closure . . . , and a new day of grace and peace" felt than in the *ubi sunt* section of the Old English poem "The Wanderer."

The Wanderer and Ubi Sunt

The Wanderer, an Old English elegiac poem found in the *Exeter Book*, is marked by the virtues of patience, gratitude, and hope despite the somber state of the Wanderer himself. The poem opens with a man who is alone, sorrowful, and wandering across the *hrimcealde sæ* ("frost-cold sea" l. 4) as an exile. His situation is among the worst imaginable to the Anglo-Saxon warrior ethic,[16] for he is separated from his social structure, that order upon which his entire life is built. He has no home, and so nostalgia—a longing for homecoming—is its central theme. But it is this very longing for home that the Christian poet seeks to redirect, for we and the Wanderer must accept that his home is no longer to be found in an earthly kingdom, but with the "Father in Heaven" (l. 115). In an important way, the poem is an artifact of the period of transition in England from secular tribalism to Christianity. As one scholar has noted, we should read *The Wanderer* as a poem expressing the transformation of a man who is yet bound "to the whole societal construct that he feels he has lost."[17]

The poem is bookended with Christian consolation and hope as the narrator tells us that the Wanderer awaits the grace and mildness of the Maker (ll. 1–2) and only finds true consolation in the embrace of the "Father in Heaven": "*Wel bið þam þe him are seceð, / frofre to fæder on heofonum, þær us eal seo fæstnung stondeð*" ("Well it will be for one who seeks grace, a consolation from the Father in heaven, where for us all stability stands" ll. 114–15). Yet, as the Wanderer himself is given a voice, we learn from him the depth of his sorrow and loss, which is epitomized in his poignant description of the bereavement he's experienced at the departure of all his companions—a passage commonly referred to as the *ubi sunt* portion of the poem:

> Hwær cwom mearg? Hwær cwom mago? Hwær cwom maþþum-gyfa? (Where has gone the mare? Where has gone the young man? Where has gone the treasure-giver?)

---

16. Cf. *Beowulf, The Battle of Maldon, The Battle of Brunanburh, The Seafarer*, etc.

17. Bjork, "Sundor æt Rune," 316.

Hwær cwom symbla gesetu? Hwær sindon seledreamas? (Where have gone the seats of feasts? Where are the hall-joys?)

Eala beorht bune!   Eala byrnwiga! (O bright cup! O byrnie-warrior!)

Eala þeodnes þrym!   Hu seo þrag gewat, (O glory of a king! How the time passed away,)

genap under nihthelm,   swa heo no wære! (grew dark under the helm of night, as it never were before.)[18]

Despite the rather dark outlook expressed in the *ubi sunt* passage, we learn in the poem's closing lines that such lamentation is a sort of acceptance marked by hope. The Wanderer's plight does not require him to forget his past; much like an exile who must leave behind all that he has formerly known in order to construct a new identity, he will not forget from whence he came, his past is not erased. Instead, who he was is integral in shaping who he will become.

In this poem, then, it would seem that the poet is not making a moral assessment of the Wanderer's past life, but rather crafting an elegy that attempts to give thanks for the way things were while acknowledging that those ways have passed. Thus, the Wanderer ends his speech with the realization that the old has, indeed, passed away:

Eall is earfoðlic eorþan rice; (All is full of hardship in the kingdom of earth,)

onwendeð wyrda gesceaft weoruld under heofonum. (the working of Wyrd changes the world under heaven.)

Her bið feoh læne, her bið freond læne, (Here is wealth fleeting, here is friend fleeting,)

her bið mon læne, her bið mæg læne. (here is man fleeting, here is kinsman fleeting.)

Eal þis eorþan gesteal idel weorþeð.[19] (All the foundation of this earth will become empty!)

Here the "*eorþan rice*" and "*weoruld*" are placed in contrast and submission to the workings "*under heofonum;*" through this subjugation of the

---

18. Klinck, "The Wanderer," ll. 92–105. Translation is my own. See again Berry's poem "Elegy" in *New Collected Poems*, 5. Much like "The Wanderer," the poem navigates between shadow and light throughout: "Spring tangles shadow and light, / . . . . / From the cloud to the stone / The rain stands tall, / Columned into his darkness. / The church hill heals our father in. / Our remembering moves from a different place."

19. Ibid., ll. 106–10.

kingdom of man, the poet is not only pointing out the transitory nature of the world, but also he is reaffirming the joy that can be found in the stability of Christianity—one that is driven by the hope of the kingdom of heaven.[20] After the Wanderer's closing remarks, the narrator notes that the Wanderer is now *"snottor on mode"* ("wise in [his] mind" l. 111). He has come out of his suffering in grief and into a place of gratitude and hope and consolation. We may thus read the Wanderer as a man who has wrestled with the loss of his past (and still does, as he *"gesæt him sundor æt rune"*—"sat himself apart in secret [thought]" l. 111), but has found *"frofre to fæder on heofonum, þær us eal seo fæstnung stondeð"* ("a consolation from the Father in heaven, where for us all stability stands" l. 115).

"The Wild Birds" and *Ubi Sunt*

It is my suggestion that in "The Wild Birds," Wheeler (like the Anglo-Saxon Wanderer) is a man bound "to the whole societal construct that he feels he has lost."[21] He is the rememberer, the protector of the membership, as Andy comes to be in his own time and way. It is thus appropriate that "The Wild Birds" begins with the very "powerful sense of absence" so common in OE elegies as Wheeler reflects upon all that has passed away in his life: "'Where have they gone?' Wheeler thinks. But he knows. Gone to the cities, forever or for the day. Gone to the shopping center. Gone to the golf course. Gone to the grave" (337). *Ubi sunt qui ante nos fuerunt,* Wheeler wonders in the silence of Hargrave's vacant downtown. It is important that the story *begins* this way, for it ends in the hope of consolation.

The story, like elegies of old, is shaped by "echo and leitmotiv" (as is much of Berry's fiction) as it "moves from disquiet to some kind of acceptance."[22] As we'll see, automobiles serve as leitmotifs throughout Berry's fiction; in Wheeler's case, his car reminds us of his ever vigilant watchfulness in his place among the Port William membership.[23] Another

---

20. See Wendell Berry, "Two Economies."

21. Bjork, "Sundor æt Rune," 316.

22. Lapidge, *The Blackwell Encyclopaedia of Anglo-Saxon England*, 246.

23. In many of the stories of Port William, automobiles are symbols of mobility and division—cf. Jayber Crow's car, Elton Penn's early lessons in driving in "Nearly to the Fair," and Hannah Coulter's recounting of Burley and Big Ellis's experience with the detachable steering wheel. But Wheeler uses his car differently, and I've often wondered if we shouldn't appreciate a pun in his name.

leitmotiv is the division between darkness and light, which comes to play a prominent role in "The Wild Birds" as Wheeler and Burley navigate the territory between the wayward and the better way in both their friendship and lives.

What Wheeler Has Lost

After lamenting the loss of those who have gone before him, Wheeler turns to work away at a speech he's writing, addressing how the economy has "thrived by the ruin of the land" (339). As he does so, his mind wanders to things he'd rather be doing as a "fidelity older than his fidelity to word and page began to work on him" (340). In the midst of the present troubles of the world on which he ruminates in his speech draft, his mind calls him back to the work he intends for his feed barn, and further back to the work of his father, Marcellus, who built that very barn "to replace an older barn on the same spot" (340). He gives himself over to the distraction of this memory: "His mind, like a boy let out of school, returned to those things with relief, with elation. His thoughts leapt from his speech to its sources in place and memory, the generations of his kin and kind" (340). Thus, the speech is itself a signifier because it alone bears no meaning unless one follows its threads to its source in the signified—a home economy that reaches back through place in time—imbuing both his farm and memory with meaning and value that grow out of his lament over the greater diminishment of such things in his world.

As a man of habit, Wheeler appears in many stories with his automobile. He is wont to drive about his fields and through Port William at dusk after a long day of work at the office in Hargrave. In the short story "The Boundary"[24] it is on one of these excursions, as he drives along with Elton Penn and Nathan Coulter, that he and the men stumble upon Mat Feltner who has fallen amidst his confusion and exhaustion. Resting, but "still as a stone," Mat sees the men driving near him as the sun sets and the dew begins to settle on him. And Mat "knows that Wheeler found Nathan and Elton, wherever they were, after he shut his office and drove up from Hargrave, and they have been driving from field to field ever since, at Elton's place or at Nathan's or at Wheeler's, and now here."[25] Mat recognizes that this is their habit; he hasn't counted on it, but he is thankful for it in this

24. In *That Distant Land*, 289–307.
25. Berry, "The Boundary," 306.

moment. He observes as "Wheeler drives the car slowly, and they look and worry and admire and remember and plan" (306).

Wheeler is also a man of the ordered way who does not waiver in his convictions once they are settled. He sees himself as one of the shepherds of the Port William membership—a warden of those who have gone before and those who remain. In "The Wild Birds," once his mind had shifted from his speech writing to the work of his home, his work in the office was over: "his mind had begun a movement that would not stop yet. His mind's movement, characteristically, was homeward. What he hungered for was the place itself" (340). These changes are not new to Wheeler, he has been faithful to such ways for years. It is this fidelity to habit, fidelity to his people and place, that makes him a bulwark for those in the Port William community, both the living and the dead. And he is, if anything, consistent in such loyalties: "This sudden shift of his attention is so familiar to him as almost to have been expected, for in its fundamental structure, its loyalties and preoccupations, Wheeler's mind has changed as little in forty years as his office" (340).

For Wheeler, change is a reality of his daily life; yet, it is not what matters to him. What matters to him is the ordered way which includes making a difference in the lives of those he serves, in the life of the land he serves: "If change happens, it happens; Wheeler can recognize a change when he sees one, but change is not on his program. Difference is. His business, indoors and out, has been the making of differences" (340). Wheeler's loyalty to his people and place acknowledges change but is not persuaded by it. Instead, his loyalty is to his responsibility as protector and rememberer of the membership that is fading from Port William and Hargrave. And so he works for a chance to make a difference in their lives and land by preserving that passing way of life. But, as he soon learns, his desire for the right order of things is about to be challenged by the waywardness of his dear friend Burley Coulter.

The Order of Things and Waywardness

The central tension in "The Wild Birds" is Burley's insistence upon acknowledging Danny Branch as his rightful heir, and he's brought Hannah and Nathan Coulter along with him to Hargrave to be sure Wheeler understands Burley's intent.

Wheeler, however, perceives himself as a protector of his people and place across time, and so he cannot accept what he believes to be another instance of Burley's waywardness; for, in willing all that he owns to Danny and Lyda Branch, he is doing a grave disservice to Hannah and Nathan Coulter who have worked tirelessly to preserve his farm and way of life as his ability has lessened. They are, in Wheeler's estimation, the rightful inheritors—and this is the right order of things. If anything, Wheeler is a man of the "orderly handing down" of things:

> If Burley has walked the marginal daylight of their world, crossing often between the open fields and the dark woods, faithful to the wayward routes that alone can join them, Wheeler's fidelity has been given to the human homesteads and neighborhoods and the known ways that preserve them. Through dark time and bad history, he has been keeper of the names that bear hope of light to the human clearings, and an orderly handing down. He is a preserver and defender of the dead, the more so, the more passionately so, as his acquaintance among the dead has increased, and as he has better understood the dangers to their living heirs. How, as a man of law, could he have been otherwise, or less? How, thinking of his own children and grandchildren, could he not insist on an orderly passage of these frail human parcels through time? (349)

Yet, for all of their differences, Wheeler and Burley's affections are drawn to the same hope in the membership that is fragile and threatened—that the waywardness of the world will be overcome by love for people and place, that those who have gone before them are still with them. They happen to disagree, however, when it comes to what this love for the past home requires them to do now, in the present. For Burley, this love manifests itself in his making things right by acknowledging Danny as his son; for Wheeler it manifests itself in the preservation of Nathan and Hannah as the rightful heirs.

What Wheeler is initially unable to comprehend is that Burley has come to acknowledge his waywardness once and for all. Burley has lived a double life that has been marked by his meandering between his two loves, "not always compatible" (348). He has "loyally kept place and household," yet also journeyed through the "nighttime woods and the wayward ways through the dark"—never fully being accountable to either. And, though Burley's waywardness was a great source of humor among the Port William membership, he has come now to Wheeler to make amends for his moral wanderings. He has come also to hold Wheeler accountable for being among those who found his waywardness humorous. For, it is the community's willingness to find Burley's waywardness humorous that has allowed him to abscond from acknowledging Danny's paternity. They have failed to love him enough to hold him accountable, and such a failure has allowed him to live as though he were a bachelor though he is, in fact, an absentee father who has never openly acknowledged Danny as his rightful heir; surely such secrecy has been a source of shame for Danny.

But Wheeler's insistence upon the right order of things blinds him to Burley's intent. In his perspective, Nathan and Hannah Coulter are the rightful heirs of Burley's land because Nathan has been like a son to Burley, and he and Hannah have been faithful to his farm. In his exacting mind, they deserve it because they have worked that land, because they are known kin; after all, Burley's paternity of Danny is only a rumor. What Burley would like to make clear, though, is that it is only a rumor because no one—Wheeler included—has found it necessary to hold him account-able by asking him whether or not the rumors are true.

Thus, Burley understands himself to be the protector of what is right in the way of his inheritors. Danny has suffered the shame of the rumors, and for this Burley is sorry; for this he must depart from the wayward and embark on the orderly way. Yet Wheeler, whose view of the orderly way differs from Burley, understands himself to be the protector of Nathan and Hannah who he sees as the inheritors of the old way of life, the way lived by those who have gone before him: "The wayward is a possible way—because, for lack of a better, it has had to be. But a better way is thinkable, is imagin-able, and Wheeler, against all evidence and all odds, is an advocate of the better way" (349). His desire to invest his energy to fight for the better way is not only forward looking—in fact, his obligation to the better way comes very much from the debt he feels toward those who have gone before him, those who have cared for the land and kin he himself inherited. Much like the poets of old, he finds himself defending an almost indefensible posi-tion—he must take his stand for an old way in the midst of a new way. Yet he is perhaps succumbing to a simplistic, sentimental nostalgia; he wants the past handed down formally, legalistically, but sometimes honoring the past requires more creativity and imagination and, of course, forgiveness:

> He does not forget . . . that he is making his stand in the middle
> of a dying town in the midst of a wasting country, from which
> many have departed and much has been sent away, a land wast-
> ing and dying for want of the human names and knowledge that

could give it life. It has been a comfort to Wheeler to think that the Coulter Place, past Burley's death, would live on under that name, belonging first to Nathan, whom Wheeler loves as he loves Burley, and then to one of Nathan's boys. That is what he longs for, that passing on of the land, in the clear, from love to love, and it is in grief for that loss that he is opposing Burley. But this grief has touched and waked up a larger one. How many times in the last twenty years has Wheeler risen to speak, to realize that the speech he has prepared is a defense of the dead and the absent, and he is pleading with strangers for a hope that, he is afraid, has no chance? (349–50)

Wheeler's position is defensible because he believes Burley's position means the orderly way will die with him and will not be passed on to a Coulter as it should, "from love to love." He is suffering in his newfound grief that the way of life he so cherishes is passing away, and he is bereft of hope.

However, in his desire to enact his exacting view of the orderly, Wheeler has failed to see that Burley is likewise a protector of the old way. It appears that Wheeler is not omniscient after all. Burley rises up in Wheeler's law office and himself takes on the role of protector of the dead as he gives Kate Helen the standing she deserved years before—a failure for which he confesses to the law man Wheeler: "There is a tenderness in Burley's voice now that Wheeler did not expect, that confesses more than he is yet prepared to understand, but it gives Kate Helen a standing, a presence, there in the room, one among them now, who will not lightly be dismissed" (352). As Burley openly acknowledges his love of Kate Helen for the first time to Wheeler, sitting among them all as "her protector" (353), Wheeler begins to feel "under his breastbone the first pain of a change" (353). To this point, Wheeler has been driven by his desire for the better way—the way that eschews the wayward. This way is orderly, according to law, regular. Yet, when Burley "confesses" his love for Kate Helen, he does so in a way familiar to Wheeler—a way Wheeler himself knows well as "a preserver and defender of the dead" (349)—and Wheeler begins to be persuaded.

Wheeler's failure is two-fold: he has failed faithfully to hold Burley accountable to his waywardness and he has failed to imagine how Danny, as Burley's rightful heir, is a member of their way of life:

> I'm saying that the ones who have been here have been the way they were, and the ones of us who are here now are the way we are, and to *know* that is the only chance we've got, dead and living, to be here together. I ain't saying we don't have to know what we

ought to have been and ought to be, but we oughtn't to let that stand between us. That ain't the way we are. The way we are, we are members of each other. All of us. Everything. The difference ain't in who is a member and who is not, but in who knows it and who don't. What has been here, not what ought to have been, is what I have to claim. (356)

Those who have gone before them, those who ought to have been with them, and those who deserve a standing among them rise up now in Wheeler's imagination, taking shape for the first time in the story. At the outset, Wheeler's imagination is constrained to those who have gone before him, and he suffers for it without hope. But now Burley has opened up an orderly way that follows a more expansive, more complex order than Wheeler's legal mind could initially image—one that includes Danny Branch as Burley's inheritor—and he is moved to the hope of consolation.

The Hope and Consolation in Forgiveness

Near the end of the story, Wheeler has come to the place where he accepts Danny as Burley's inheritor, and not begrudgingly—"Danny Branch now turns up in Wheeler's mind, admitted or not, put there by the words of his would-be lawful father, after the failure of all events so far to put him there, and his face now takes its place among the faces that belong there" (361). It's not that Danny was kept apart from the Port William membership; it's that Wheeler has failed to imagine him as such—he has had to gain a clear vision, one that can see that Danny is now clearly among the membership.

But Wheeler's transformation is not yet complete—this man who so loves the regular, better way. For he has yet to go through the pain of coming to terms with his own failure among the membership: his failure to hold Burley to the same exacting standards of the better way after which he imagines he so carefully patterns his own life. As Burley explains, "If we'd been brothers, you wouldn't have put up with me . . . . As it was, [my doings] could be tolerable or even funny to you because they wasn't done close enough to you to matter. You could laugh" (362). Wheeler is stunned. And he knows that Burley is right. For all his blustering about rightful heirs and the better way, Wheeler has himself failed Burley, Kate Helen, and even Danny because he has found Burley's way amusing. In this way, he is a coconspirator of sorts implicated in Burley's waywardness.

At this moment in the narrative a "great cavity" opens "at the heart of a friendship, a membership, that not only they here in the office and the others who are living but men and women now dead belong to, going far back, dear as life. Dearer. It is a cavity larger than all they know, a cavity that somebody . . . is going to have to step into, or all will be lost" (362). But Wheeler remains frozen, dumbstruck at the realization of his guilt in this all, and he has "become as a little child" (363).

As a smile appears on Burley's face, though, it becomes clear that he has stepped into the cavity yawning between their friendship, filling it with forgiveness: "'Wheeler, if we're going to get this will made out, not to mention all else we've got to do while there's breath in us, I think you've got to forgive me as if I was a brother to you.' He laughs, asserting for the last time the seniority now indisputably his, and casting it aside. 'And I reckon I've got to forgive you for taking so long to do it.'" The tables have been turned on Wheeler who, at the beginning of the story, imagined himself as the orderly one. Now he is both forgiving and seeking forgiveness. And it is out of Burley's moment of confession and grace that the "deep dividing valley" that has appeared within their friendship "has been stepped across": "To Wheeler, it seems that all their lives have begun again—lives dead, living, yet to be. As if feeling himself simply carried forward by that change, for another moment yet he does not move" (363).

The power of forgiveness manifests itself in a profound and unexpected way for Wheeler. And in this moment of mutual forgiveness he experiences gratitude and consolation, perceiving that such forgiveness takes them beyond time and is both temporal and eternal. Forgiveness connects him not only to the membership of those present in the room, but also back to those who are dead and gone and forward to the hope of those who are "yet to be" (363).

As the men reconcile their differences, Wheeler comes to have a new vision of things in the world—"his sight has changed" (363). He has gained a clarity that allows him to see beyond his own small way of imaging the world, imagining the better way. As they sit in the silence of this moment, the "office is crowded . . . with all that they have loved, the living remembered, the dead brought back to mind," and a "gentle, forceless light" is with them: "There in the plain, penumbral old room, that light gathers the four of them into its shadowless embrace" (363). As they sit in Wheeler's shadowy office, they are embraced by light that does not force itself upon them. I believe this is the same light that surrounds Jayber at the end of

Jayber Crow—the all-encompassing presence of the Divine that casts away all shadows, and from which we are unable to hide. It is a revealing light. It is a healing light. It is light that is out of time yet within time. It is the light of patience, hope, and gratitude. It is the light of forgiveness that chases away the "*sheadu* . . . of the dark and fallen wilderness beyond,"[26] a consolation that gathers us all together, the living and the dead—those who will come after us, those who walk with us, and those who have gone before us.

Where Are Those Who Have Gone Before Us?

Just as the *ubi sunt* tradition calls us "from disquiet to some kind of acceptance," so does Berry's short story "The Wild Birds" move Wheeler, Burley, and us from the disquiet of the mutable Port William community to the acceptance of its continuation in people like Danny Branch and Nathan and Hannah Coulter, even in the midst of the possibility of its disappearance from the face of the earth.

To appreciate what Berry accomplishes in the rather somber moments of his fiction, we do well to position him as one member in a long line of English writers who is able to navigate the undulating waters of human transience, steering us to harbors that are marked by joy and sorrow. He is himself, like the poets of old, "a preserver and defender of the dead . . . as he has better understood the dangers to their living heirs" (349).

Berry's fiction teaches us not that the past is perfect and preferred to the present or future, but that we can look to the goodness of things in the past as a source of hope, with gratitude, while simultaneously lamenting their passing. As we do so, we become—like Wheeler and Burley and Andy—rememberers, protectors and defenders of the orderly way, which includes even the wayward and wild and fallen, which is transcendent and immanent, which is of both time and eternity, which is a source of consolation. The nostalgia practiced in Port William includes us; we learn along with its members how to acknowledge our own faults, how we might come to forgive the failings of others so we can tend our inevitably wayward homes.

In the end, we are bound to our past as we are bound to our present, and remembering all that has passed away does not make us people who live in the past to the detriment of the present or at the expense of the fabled future. Instead, remembering the goodness of the past connects us

26. Jeffrey and Maillet, *Christianity and Literature*, 150.

to the human community through time and shapes us into members of our people and places for our time too, even for the hope of the future. Where are those who have gone before us? They are in us and with us—so let us give thanks through remembering.

Bibliography

Berry, Wendell. "The Body and The Earth." In *The Unsettling of America: Culture & Agriculture*. San Francisco: Sierra Club, 1986.

———. *New Collected Poems*. Berkeley: Counterpoint, 2012.

———. "Two Economies." In *Home Economics*, 54–75. New York: North Point, 1987.

Bjork, Robert E. "Sundor æt Rune: The Voluntary Exile of The Wanderer." In *Old English Literature: Critical Essays*, edited by R. M. Liuzza, 315–27. New Haven: Yale University Press, 2002.

Brown, Carleton, ed. *English Lyrics of the XIIIth Century*. Oxford: Clarendon, 1932.

Fulk, R. D. *An Introduction to Middle English: Grammar and Texts*. Peterborough: Broadview, 2012.

Jeffrey, David Lyle and Gregory Maillet. *Christianity and Literature: Philosophical Foundations and Critical Practice*. Downers Grove: IVP Academic, 2011.

Klinck, Anne Lingard. *The Old English Elegies*. Montreal and Kingston: McGill-Queen's University Press, 1992.

Lapidge, Michael et al., eds. *The Blackwell Encyclopaedia of Anglo-Saxon England*. Oxford: Wiley-Blackwell, 2000.

Tolkien, J. R. R. *On Fairy-stories*. Edited by Verlyn Flieger and Douglas A. Anderson. London: HarperCollins, 2008.

2

Dreaming in Port William

Foreknowledge, Consolation, and Medieval Dream Vision Literature

Ingrid Pierce

SCATTERED THROUGHOUT THE PAGES of Wendell Berry's fictional accounts of the town of Port William are moments when characters fall asleep and dream. In such moments, Berry takes us into his characters' dreams, describing the strange and evocative things they experience. Many residents of Port William have dreams, including Jayber Crow, Hannah Coulter, Old Jack, Mat Feltner, and Andy Catlett, and Berry pays close attention to what they encounter in their dreams and how their dreams affect them. Often artful and poetic, these dream sequences create a story within a story, the dream reflecting or defining the larger narrative. Berry's dreamers often find themselves existing outside the normal bounds of space and time, in a version of Port William that is wondrous and sometimes frightening. Berry uses the device of the dream to begin and end his novels, search the inner lives of his characters, or craft moments of revelation. Through these dreams, he explores the power of what Old Jack experiences when, as Berry puts it, "he rises up in his mind."[1] In particular, as this essay proposes,

I am grateful to Jeffrey Bilbro, Jack Baker, and Larry Pierce for their insightful suggestions during the process of writing this essay and to the other contributors for helping me to see more deeply into Berry's fiction.
    1. Berry, *The Memory of Old Jack,* 190.

a number of the dreams in Berry's fiction provide world-worn characters with consolation through visions of Port William's future redemption.

These redemptive dreams in Berry's fiction strikingly resemble medieval dream vision literature—a genre in which a narrator recounts a memorable dream, often taking great care "to telle [the dream] aryght."[2] Although it is impossible to fit the dreams in Berry's fiction into any rigid mold, they often mirror noteworthy conventions of medieval dream poems such as a feeling of wonder, a lush natural setting, a heightened sensory experience, and a journey through space and/or time. In addition to these similarities, the dreams in Berry's fiction explore two timeless questions that underlie many medieval dream poems: What happens after death? How can a person find consolation in a world of suffering?[3]

The first of these questions—What happens after death?—fascinated medieval writers, who often pondered whether dreams could convey revelation about the future.[4] Macrobius's commentary on the *Dream of Scipio*, a popular work during the Middle Ages, proposes a method for discerning the trustworthiness of dreams. Macrobius sets out five kinds of dreams, calling them the oracular dream, the prophetic vision, the enigmatic dream, the nightmare, and the apparition. According to Macrobius, the first three types are "reliable" as sources of truth: the oracular dream contains an authoritative figure or guide who "clearly reveals what will or will not transpire"; a prophetic vision is a dream that "actually comes true"; and the enigmatic dream "conceals with strange shapes and veils with ambiguity the true meaning of the information being offered, and requires an interpretation for its understanding."[5] For Macrobius, these three kinds of dreams—oracle, vision, and enigma—can convey something about the next life.[6] Versions of these three dream types appear in Berry's fiction,

2. Chaucer, *The House of Fame*, line 79. This concern about telling a dream correctly recalls Hannah Coulter's desire to "tell the stories right." Berry, *Hannah Coulter*, 113. All references to Chaucer are taken from *The Wadsworth Chaucer*.

3. Wendell Berry's prose and poetry demonstrate his familiarity with medieval literature, including the works of Dante, Chaucer, and William Langland. For example, find references to medieval literature in "Poetry and Place," collected in *Standing by Words*, "The Presence of Nature," collected in *A Small Porch*, and "Dante," in *Given*, 8.

4. As Malcolm Andrew and Ronald Waldron observe, "The dream vision is a medium singularly well suited to revelation, in that through it the protagonist may be simultaneously in touch with the actual world and (in some sense) out of it." *The Poems of the Pearl Manuscript*, 13.

5. Macrobius, *Commentary on the Dream of Scipio*, 90.

6. It is important to note that in medieval dream poems, as in Berry's fiction, any

which is similarly interested in envisioning the future as a way of shedding light on the meaning and fate of Port William's community.[7]

While the dreams in Berry's fiction look to the future to find redemption, they also remain grounded in the real struggles of life in the present. The dreams in his fiction explore how a person can find consolation in a world of suffering—specifically, within a community vulnerable to deterioration.[8] The writer Boethius addresses a similar question in his *Consolation of Philosophy*, a sixth-century work that had a profound influence on medieval dream vision literature. In the *Consolation*, Boethius languishes in prison, unjustly accused and condemned to death. To help revive him, Lady Philosophy appears, "a woman of majestic countenance whose flashing eyes seemed wise beyond the ordinary wisdom of men."[9] Through poetic speech and rational argument about the nature of true happiness, she eventually helps him achieve tranquility despite his adverse circumstances. A number of Middle English dream poems written in the late fourteenth century represent this same human need for consolation. Their restless dreamers are, as one of Chaucer's narrators puts it, "fulfyld of thought and busy hevynesse."[10] From the grieving father in *Pearl* to the melancholy insomniac in *The Book of the Duchess*, these dreamers wrestle with painful human problems and find varying degrees of comfort from their dreams. Though the dreamers find themselves visiting otherworldly realms in their dreams, these experiences often inform their lives in the real world.

Looking at the dreams in Berry's fiction in light of this medieval tradition helps us to better understand both their meaning for individual characters and their message about Port William's community. Three dreams in particular explore how knowing the future can provide consolation—Andy Catlett's oracular dream, Jayber Crow's prophetic vision, and Mat Feltner's enigmatic dream. These three dreamers experience flashes of insight in which they grasp, at least in part, the symbolic significance of their dreams, thus becoming both dreamer and interpreter. These dreamers

---

dream might contain aspects of different types, and it is sometimes hard to distinguish between them. As the narrator in Chaucer's *House of Fame* puts it, "Why this a drem, why that a sweven ... Why this a fantome, why these oracles, / I not," lines 9, 11–12.

7. For more on medieval dream poetry, including a fuller discussion of Macrobius's dream categories, see Spearing, *Medieval Dream-Poetry*.

8. For an extended discussion of consolation in medieval poetry, see Zak, "The Ethics and Poetics," 36–62.

9. Boethius, *The Consolation of Philosophy*, 3.

10. Chaucer, *The Parliament of Fowls*, line 89.

provide glimpses of the fate of the fictitious Port William community; though ravaged by time and tragedy, Port William is not beyond the hope of redemption.

Andy Catlett: The Oracular Dream

Andy Catlett's dream in *Remembering*—an encounter with a mysterious figure who leads him to a sight of Port William's future—clearly reflects features of a medieval dream vision. This is an oracular dream, where the dreamer encounters an authority figure who provides revelation. The structure of Andy's dream—he finds himself in a dark valley, meets a guide, and goes on a journey to a place filled with light—strongly resembles Dante's *Divine Comedy*, as some have noticed.[11] And, as I propose, Andy's dream of paradise also resembles the Middle English oracular dream poem *Pearl*, a story about a grieving father who catches a glimpse of the celestial city across a flowing river. As in *Pearl*, Andy's dream is set in a beautiful natural landscape and concerns his vision of a membership of redeemed people living in an eternal city. Both dreams emphasize a love for the world and earthly community.

To understand Andy's dream, we first need to briefly consider the nightmare at the novel's beginning. The two dreams frame the novel and function as two visions of Port William, one of destruction and the other of redemption. At the beginning of the story, lying alone in a hotel in San Francisco, Andy dreams that his home in Port William is destroyed by a bulldozer, an enormous causeway being erected in its place. The old forest is now gone, along with the birds, fields, farmsteads, neighbors, and graveyards. The dream embodies Andy's "old terror . . . the end, simply, of all he knew and loved."[12] Upon waking, Andy's thoughts focus uncomfortably on the stump of his right wrist, where he lost a hand in an accident with a harvesting machine. The book begins, then, by associating the fragmentation and destruction of the land with the fragmentation of Andy's own body. For Andy, losing Port William is like losing a limb—the tearing apart of something that once was whole, whose former presence is particularly poignant in its absence.

11. See, for instance, Donnelly, "Biblical Convocation," 275–96; Manganiello, "'Dante, e poi Dante,'" 184–89; and Manganiello, "Dante and Wendell Berry's Modern Book of Memory," 115–25.

12. *Remembering*, 4. Further references to *Remembering* will be given parenthetically.

By way of contrast, the dream at the end of the book is a vision of Port William's healing and redemption. It comes just after a turning point in Andy's narrative; after wandering in the city, brooding over the loss of his hand, he returns home and walks out among the trees. Growing weary, he falls asleep "at the foot of a large oak" (100).[13] He then has a vision of Port William's future. A nameless figure, simply called "the dark man," leads Andy through this dream world and shapes his experience of it (102). In this way, Andy's dream is like *Pearl*, in which a maiden appears to guide the dreamer through a natural landscape toward the heavenly city.

Before Andy sees the guide, he feels the touch of his hand on his shoulder. As the dream begins, Andy is immersed in primordial darkness and "the sounds of crying and of tearing asunder" (100).[14] Then, suddenly, there is a change: "But now from outside his hopeless dark sleep a touch is laid upon his shoulder" (100). What appeared to be a nightmare becomes something quite different—an act of creation. The touch on his shoulder brings transformation and he is filled with light and life. Berry echoes the language of Adam's creation in Genesis, where God breathes life into him— "Breath and light come into him" (100). Andy's lost hand is restored: "He feels his flesh enter into mind, mind into flesh . . . [and] is whole" (100). This moment of restoration prepares Andy for the end of the dream, in which he lifts his newly restored hand in a gesture of farewell: "He lifts toward them the restored right hand of his joy" (103). Like Boethius's Lady Philosophy, who heals Boethius's mind with her soothing music and reasoned words, this guide is a healer, though he uses touch rather than words. Andy begins to see that the landscape has also undergone a transformation: "He is where he was, in the valley, on the hillside under an oak, but the place is changed" (100). A stream that was dry has begun to flow, flowers bloom, and birds sing. Just as, in his initial nightmare, the destruction of the land mirrored the loss of his right hand, Andy now sees that his own healing happens in concert with the healing of the land.

13. This image of a man sleeping at the foot of a tree is a recurring motif in Berry's writing. For example, at the end of "A Native Hill," Berry lies down among the falling leaves and has a reverie about death, *The Art of the Commonplace*, 30–31. Similarly, when Jack dies in *The Memory of Old Jack*, he envisions himself sitting at the root of a walnut tree, 192. See also the image of a "sleeper at the rowan's foot" in Kathleen Raine's "Northumbrian Sequence," quoted in Berry, *Imagination in Place*, 127. This motif of people sleeping under trees recalls a scene in the Middle English poem *Sir Orfeo*, where the queen falls asleep under a tree and learns that she is in danger of death, though she is saved at the end.

14. This is an echo of the first words of the novel: "It is dark." *Remembering*, 3.

When Andy sees the mysterious man for the first time, he learns that he is to embark on a journey. The man becomes his guide: "He sees that a man, dark as shadow, is walking away from him up the hill road, not far ahead" (100). Then, Andy has the first of several flashes of understanding within the dream. He comprehends instinctually that this is the one whose touch restored his flesh and who, while Andy languished in darkness, had "leaned and looked at him face-to-face" (121). The man remains silent and his face stays hidden, but he exerts power and authority. The man shows the way forward through the darkness while, again, acting as a creative force. The ground itself, Andy says, seems to take form when the man sets his foot down: "The ground underfoot is dark, seeming not to exist until his foot touches it" (101). Andy is watching regeneration take place.

While watching the dark man lead the way through the forest, a memory from childhood springs to Andy's mind. He realizes that the dark man is like one of the experienced hunters who used to lead him through the woods at night: "Burley Coulter and Elton Penn and the Rowanberrys, men who knew the way, who *were* the way of the places they led him through" (101). Men like Burley Coulter carry the memory of the paths through the woods. Like these old hunters, the guide in Andy's dream has intimate knowledge of this place and the way of traveling through it. The guides in medieval oracular dreams commonly are figures of authority and stature. Andy's guide adds to these qualities an aura of divinity: Andy instinctively knows to treat him with devout reverence. When they reach their destination, for instance, Andy respectfully remains "several steps behind" (102). As a creator with power over the land, a healer who restores Andy's body, and the one who shows "the way" (101), this guide is a dream-version of Christ, the son of God who comes to save the world. Like Christ, he is as human as he is divine, an incarnate God whose form and manner identify him with the Port William community. He is an old hunter, a deeply familiar and earthly figure who also possesses supernatural power. Although Andy's dream world is mystical and wondrous, it leads him back to the familiar place of Port William; his dream is an adventure at the same time as it is a homecoming.

The dream guide never speaks, yet through his silence, he teaches Andy to listen intently to the world around him. The guide's muteness is the quality that most distinguishes him from medieval dream poems, wherein the guide normally carries on a dialogue with the dreamer. By contrast, the guide in Andy's dream only walks and gestures. Andy's sense of hearing is heightened as he follows behind the guide. He hears strange music filling the countryside, "whether of voices or instruments, sounds or words, he cannot tell" (101). In a flash of insight, he realizes that the music is the sound of light: "he is hearing the light; he is hearing the sun" (122). This light, as Andy realizes, emanates from his guide—"the dark man giving light" (101). As sunlight floods the scene, every plant and animal sings in harmony. Like his newly-healed body, the earth is now whole, reverberating with cosmic music: "The world sings. The sky sings back. It is one song, the song of the many members of one love, the whole song sung and to be sung, resounding, in each of its moments. And it is light" (101). This description of a singing world recalls the medieval concept of the music of the spheres—the idea that all the stars and planets move in perfect balance that creates a harmonious sound.[15] In striking contrast to his nightmare, which earlier seemed to presage the fragmentation and disintegration of the world, this final dream points to a time when the world will be made whole. The music in this scene helps Andy understand this wholeness and feel it with his senses.

At the climax of the dream, the guide leads Andy to a marvelous sight: the restored town of Port William. He offers no explanation, but simply stops and points:

> The dark man points ahead of them; Andy looks and sees the town and the fields around it, Port William and its countryside as he never saw or dreamed them, the signs everywhere upon them of the care of a longer love than any who have lived there have ever imagined. The houses are clean and white, and great trees stand among them and spread over them. The fields lie around the town, divided by rows of such trees as stand in the town and in the woods, each field more beautiful than all the rest. Over town and fields the one great song sings, and is answered everywhere; every leaf and flower and grass blade sings. And in the fields and the town, walking, standing, or sitting under the trees, resting and talking together in the peace of a sabbath profound and bright, are people of such beauty that he weeps to see them. He sees that

---

15. A reference to the music of the spheres appears, for instance, in Chaucer's *Parliament of Fowls*, when he recounts Scipio's vision:

And after that the melodye herde he
That cometh of thilke speres thryes thre,
That welle is of musik and melodye
In this world here, and cause of armonye. (lines 60–63)

these are the membership of one another and of the place and of the song or light in which they live and move. (102)

The dreamer in *Pearl* glimpses the New Jerusalem, a city as bright as the sun where the redeemed sing to God, dressed in white robes. In the above passage, Andy looks into heaven, only to realize that he is looking at Port William. This vision is noteworthy for the way it combines mystical elements—the marvelous song that sounds over the town and the transcendently beautiful people—with ordinary elements such as the white houses and the fields divided by rows of trees. This is the ideal version of Port William, characterized by purity, order, and beauty. It is a place of sabbath rest, everyone and everything in its place and deeply interconnected. This sight answers and dispels Andy's old fear that "all he knew and loved" in the world would end, existing only in "the little creature of his memory" (4). The final dream reveals that this beloved place and its people will find resurrection: "He sees that they are dead, and they are alive. He sees that he lives in eternity as he lives in time, and nothing is lost" (102). In this dream, Andy's glimpse of heaven transforms his understanding of Port William; his insight is that Port William itself will take part in eternity.

Ultimately, the dream directs Andy back toward his present life in the physical world. He thinks at one point that he is dying, and, in fact, his dream looks similar to Old Jack's dream-like journey that actually does usher in his death. But the dark man turns Andy away and sends him back to his life in the waking world. Similarly, in *Pearl*, the dreamer longs to enter paradise but is sent back to his earthly life instead. Captivated by the spectacle of heaven's glory—"For luf-longyng in gret delyt" (line 1152)—he tries to ford the river to get to the holy city when a voice calls him to stop, awakening him from his dream.[16] Like the dreamer in *Pearl*, Andy is filled with longing for this place and its people but is not allowed to remain: "He would go to them, but another movement of his guide's hand shows him that he must not. He must go no closer" (102). Andy receives a hopeful vision of eternity where "nothing is lost" (102), but does not consummate that vision. In fact, both *Pearl* and *Remembering* end with this paradise of joy and wholeness still out of reach. Both dreams evoke a poignant sense of expectation and suggest the necessity of patiently waiting for redemption.

Beyond poignant expectation, the dream vision also offers guidance for the rest of life, for there is more work to be done. Berry writes of Andy,

16. All quotations from *Pearl* come from Andrew and Waldron, *The Poems of the Pearl Manuscript*.

"He must go back with his help, such as it is, and offer it" (102). Although scholars disagree over the sincerity of the dreamer's response at the end of *Pearl*,[17] it is significant that he turns the audience toward the Eucharist, the tangible sacrament of Christ's real presence in daily life. Both dreamers, then, find a degree of consolation through their dreams that, in turn, informs their lives in the real world. The dream vision has the potential to motivate the life of the dreamer by supplying a vivid mental picture of what he is working toward—the promised resurrection of humanity and creation. Andy returns to his life in the waking world with the dream "singing in his mind" (103).[18]

Andy's dream, then, is focused on worldly and not otherworldly things. Though it follows medieval dream visions in many other ways, his dream does not follow the pattern in which the guide urges the reader not to focus on the world but to contemplate higher realities.[19] Instead, this dream is a revelation about the permanence of the world. Andy learns to hear the music emanating from every living thing on earth—the wholeness of creation. He learns that Port William and the land around it and the people who live in it are eternal. In this way, Andy's dream resonates deeply with Christian eschatology, which offers hope in the resurrection of the dead and the restoration of creation.[20] At its core, this dream conveys hope in redemption—that nothing in the world, not even small towns like Port William, will ultimately be lost.[21] It is, as Andy later reflects in the short story "Dismemberment," a "foreknowledge of wholeness."[22] This

17. For an account of this disagreement about how to interpret *Pearl*, see Aers, "The Self Mourning," 54–73.

18. In his essay in this collection, "Re-membering the Past Rightly: The *Ubi Sunt* Tradition in Wendell Berry's Fiction," Jack Baker reveals how looking to the past in Berry's fiction can enable characters to live a good life in the present. As my essay shows, characters in Berry's fiction also find meaning for their present lives in dream visions of the future.

19. For instance, in the Dream of Scipio, the guide berates the dreamer for staring down at the earth and instructs him to look up at the stars and galaxies instead. See Macrobius, *Commentary*, 72–73.

20. See Rom. 8:22–23 and 2 Cor. 5:17. See also a discussion of the Christian view of last things in Alistair McGrath, *Christian Theology*, 540–63.

21. Andy's dream can, of course, also be seen as a prophetic vision, since Andy sees a vision of "his abode after death and his future condition," Macrobius, *Commentary*, 90.

22. Berry, "Dismemberment." For a fuller discussion of "Dismemberment," see Jeffrey Bilbro's essay in this collection, "Andy Catlett's Missing Hand: Making Do as Wounded Members."

foreknowledge involves more than simply knowing the future. The vision is about Andy receiving consolation; like Boethius in *The Consolation of Philosophy* and, perhaps, the dreamer in *Pearl*, he is lifted from the despair he feels at the beginning of the novel when the world seems overtaken by evil. The final dream vision allows Andy to transcend this despair and continue to love Port William, knowing that the community exists in eternity and that its pains and losses—such as his missing right hand—will be made whole.

Jayber Crow: The Prophetic Vision

In the novel *Jayber Crow,* the story of a bachelor barber, we encounter a prophetic vision that, without the help of a dream guide, points to the meaning of Port William's community through time. From his vantage point in the barber shop, Jayber has much occasion to observe the people of Port William: "Port William repaid watching. I was always on the lookout for what would be revealed. Sometimes nothing would be, but sometimes I beheld astonishing sights."[23] Sometimes, these "astonishing sights" appear to him in dreams.

One day, shortly after taking up the job of church janitor and grave digger, Jayber falls asleep in the church and has a dream. This is no ordinary dream; Jayber himself calls it "my vision" (205). The traditional dream vision, as defined by Macrobius, is a dream that foretells the future. Jayber's dream is more expansive. It is a vision of the members of Port William from past, present, and future gathered together in one place:

> I saw them in all the times past and to come, all somehow there in their own time and in all time and in no time: the cheerfully working and singing women, the men quiet or reluctant or shy, the weary, the troubled in spirit, the sick, the lame, the desperate, the dying, the little children tucked into the pews beside their elders, the young married couples full of visions, the old men with their dreams, the parents proud of their children, the grandparents with tears in their eyes, the pairs of young lovers attentive only to each other on the edge of the world, the grieving widows and widowers, the mothers and fathers of children newly dead, the proud, the humble, the attentive, the distracted—I saw them all. I saw the creases crisscrossed on the backs of the men's necks, their

---

23. 5. Further references to *Jayber Crow* will be given parenthetically.

work-thickened hands, the Sunday dresses faded with washing. (164–65)

Jayber's vision transcends time. He can see the people "in all the times past and to come" (164–65). People from every stage of life are there. He describes the people in painstaking detail, from the creases in the back of men's necks to the faded Sunday dresses. This is not an ideal picture of Port William, like Andy's vision; Jayber sees tears in the eyes of the grandparents.

The scene evokes a sense of unity, not through joyful music like in Andy's dream, but in a collective silence. The whole group sits there without making a sound: "They were just there. They said nothing, and I said nothing" (165). This shared silence recalls Jayber's description of the church service in which a preacher would call for "a moment of silence": "And then the quiet that was almost the quiet of the empty church would come over us and unite us as we were not united even in singing" (164). There is a speechless recognition of the tie that binds them all together, and the silence stirs Jayber's awareness of his love for the community: "I seemed to love them all with a love that was mine merely because it included me" (165). It is a powerful moment of inclusion, especially for Jayber who, as the confirmed bachelor of Port William, "was in a class by myself" and "remained a sort of bystander a lot longer than I remained a stranger" (123). When he wakes from this deeply communal dream, Jayber's face is stained with tears.

Insofar as it is a vision of the interconnectedness among members of a community, Jayber's dream resembles *Piers Plowman*, an allegorical dream poem written in Middle English by William Langland in the late fourteenth century. In this poem, the dreamer, Will, falls asleep by a stream and dreams about a field full of people, "A fair feeld ful of folk . . . Of alle manere of men, the meene and the riche, / Werchynge and wandrynge as the world asketh."[24] Like *Jayber Crow*, and Berry's works in general, *Piers Plowman* is concerned with the question of how to create a good society, and in his dream Will confronts problems of community life related to food production, labor, social contracts, poverty, and the need for spiritual renewal. Although society in *Piers Plowman* is falling apart, the poem continues to uphold the value of human bonds.[25] To comprehend this communal bond, *Piers Plowman*, and Jayber's dream in the church, envision what it would look like for the whole community to gather together in one place and at

24. Langland, *The Vision of Piers Plowman*, lines 17–19.

25. As Emily Steiner has written, "*Piers Plowman* promises that salvation lies in community," *Reading Piers Plowman*, x.

one time. It is a picture of the "membership"—the term Burley Coulter often uses and Jayber adopts.[26]

Later in the novel, Jayber refers back to the dream in the church and indicates that his earlier vision has been reshaped: "What I saw now was the community imperfect and irresolute but held together by the frayed and always fraying, incomplete and yet ever-holding bonds of the various sorts of affection" (205). This, he recognizes, is "the membership of Port William and of no other place on earth" (205). Like Andy Catlett, he finally envisions the inhabitants of Port William enjoying a restored and renewed existence: "I saw them all as somehow perfected, beyond time, by one another's love, compassion, and forgiveness, as it is said we may be perfected by grace" (205). Jayber's vision indicates a Port William membership that lasts through time—a membership that holds together; this enduring bond of affection serves as a consolation for the sorrows among Port William members.

Mat Feltner: The Enigmatic Dream

In *A Place on Earth*, Mat Feltner has an enigmatic dream—one in a series of dreams mourning his son Virgil, who has been reported missing from a WWII battlefield.[27] While in Andy and Jayber's dreams, learning about the future is a hopeful experience, Mat believes that "the mercy of the world is you don't know what's going to happen."[28] Indeed, his dream is more grief than revelation, though it hints at the possibility of resurrection.[29]

26. For a discussion of Burley Coulter's concept of "membership," see Fritz Oehlschlaeger's contribution to this collection, "Living Faithfully in the Debt of Love in Wendell Berry's Port William."

27. When revising *A Place On Earth* for the later version, Berry condenses this dream sequence in a way that enhances its enigmatic quality. For instance, in the first version he writes, "He can see his own hands holding the reins, the black rumps and heads of the team of mules," while in the second version he removes the detail about the mules to make the moment more nebulous: "He can see his hands holding the reins as he drives the long, slowly shortening rounds of the field." Berry, *A Place on Earth*, 369; Berry, *A Place on Earth [Revised]*, 224. Further references to *A Place on Earth [Revised]* will be given parenthetically. For further discussion of how Berry revises his fiction, see Ethan Mannon's essay in this collection, "The Gift of Good Death: Revising *Nathan Coulter*."

28. In a painful dream about Virgil as a five-year-old boy, Mat looked at the boy and "knew everything that was to come," *Jayber Crow*, 149. Compare with Berry, "The Inlet" in *Given*, 12.

29. For another discussion of Mat's dream, see Bilbro, "A Form for Living," 97.

Mat's oracular dream is characterized by uncertainty and ambiguity. Having been told nothing more than that Virgil is "missing," he struggles between the fear that his son is dead and the hope that he is alive.[30] This resembles Chaucer's *Book of the Duchess,* a dream poem about a man grieving his wife's death. It is, as Kathryn Lynch writes, "the story of a grief that struggles to know and define itself, of a man whose attempts to name that grief properly lead nowhere until he returns to the very object grieved for."[31] Mat's dream in *A Place on Earth* also dramatizes a mental and emotional tension between uncertainty and certainty.

Waiting in the hospital while Virgil's wife Hannah delivers their baby, right on the verge of new life, Mat falls asleep and dreams about death. The pain of Virgil's absence returns: as Berry puts it, the "familiar ache sits on his shoulder now like a red bird, not moving" (224). With this strange image of the bird, the dream begins:

> He dreams he is at work, harrowing a broken field. He can see nothing. He can see a cloud of bright dust rising thickly from the disks of the harrow. He can smell and taste the dust. His eyes are gritty with it. And then the dust seems to draw in and around him until he can no longer see it. He becomes aware of the compactness of his body. He can see his hands holding the reins as he drives the long, slowly shortening rounds of the field. He can see all the surface of the worked earth. He is aware of a point like an eye in the center of the field that his circling will finally bring him to, and where it will end. The dust rises around him again, blotting his sight, to become what next he does not know. (224)

The dream is made up of familiar things, such as the sight of his hands holding the reins, but these things become nightmarish in the swirling dust. His vision flickers, obscured by the dust. The repetitive quality of the language creates a hypnotic rhythm, increasing the sense of strangeness: "He can see . . . He can see . . . He can see . . . " (224). Yet, the dream is about not being able to see. The dust thickens, thins, and thickens again, like watching a camera fade in and out. In a flash of understanding, he recognizes that the "point like an eye" in the middle of the field represents his destination. But the eye is quickly overcome by the dust "blotting his sight" (224).

---

30. *Jayber Crow* describes Mat's struggle with the news about his son: "Mat had the worst of it, maybe. In loyalty to his boy he had to try to believe that 'missing' meant *alive somewhere.* And yet lengthening time insisted, like a clock ticking, that it meant *dead.*" Berry, *Jayber Crow,* 148.

31. Lynch, *Chaucer's Philosophical Visions,* 57.

Eventually, Mat understands fully the heart-breaking reality of his son's death. He realizes that he is sitting on top of a moving machine, and at this moment, everything becomes clear:

> And then there comes a little more light and he *does* see. With the blade of a bulldozer he is trying to scrape up enough dirt from a frozen, rocky slope to fill a grave. The grave is as big as a field. Young men, soldiers, lie in rows in it, awaiting the covering earth. They lie on their backs, unspeakably submissive to the approach of the great machine. He has a hurt in his shoulder, but whether it is a wound or the claws of a red bird perched there, he cannot tell. He knows with sorrow who he is. He knows that there is a face among all those of the dead that he cannot bear to see. The engine pulses steadily on. (224)

In Chaucer's *Book of the Duchess,* the dreamer's "grasp of death is vivid, immediate, horrifying," and, to some degree, "fleeting."[32] It is similar to Mat's sudden understanding of the intimate connection between himself, the fate of his son, the fates of many other young men, and the fate of the soil. Startlingly, Mat realizes that he is filling a grave with the bulldozer, burying the young men. His grave-digging is also the work of planting; the young men's bodies are like seeds in the earth—"young men, soldiers, lie in rows in it" (224). His work takes part in death and, somehow, in the farmer's expectation of new life. Planting brings the possibility of resurrection. The crucial moment comes when he imagines the face "that he cannot bear to see" (224), his son Virgil, not in a battlefield far away, but in his own field in Port William, lying beside his companions. This dream makes death tangible and local. In this dream, Virgil's death binds together the community, the land, the grieving father, and even the machine. His understanding comes from his experience of tasting the gritty dust, hearing the sound of the engine, feeling the rain, and seeing the face of his beloved son.

Comparing the medieval enigmatic dream with Mat's dream helps us appreciate the tension with which it holds together understanding and ambiguity, hope, and despair. Mat distances himself from the too-painful truth. He knows that there is "a face" out there that means more to him than any other, but he never looks at Virgil's face up close. He feels a vague pain in his shoulder, but he does not know if it is "a wound or the claws of a red bird" (224).[33] And when his wife asks him about the dream after he wakes,

---

32. Lynch, *Chaucer's Philosophical Visions*, 56.

33. The figure of the red bird in this dream sequence is obscure, though it seems to

all he can bring himself to say is, "I can just remember it was a bad one" (225). Mat's dream helps him imagine his son's death, difficult to grasp as it is. Like Andy in his dream, Mat senses the presence of something he cannot fully accept. Indeed, it is not until later that Mat finally says, "Virgil is dead. He's not going to come back" (235).

Despite its focus on death, Mat's dream is not without hope. The image of planting in the field suggests the potential for new life, which is fulfilled only moments after Mat awakens: "He turns, blinking to accustom his eyes to the dimness, and sees, lying upright in the doctor's gloved hands, naked and red, still wet from the womb, a newborn child . . . The joy he heard in Margaret's voice swells in Mat now, leaving hardly room for breath" (226). Mat's dream about Virgil's death serves as the prelude to the celebration of the birth of Virgil's child. Placing the dream at precisely this moment in the narrative, Berry suggests that, like in the agricultural cycle of planting and harvesting, death and life follow hand in hand. Later in his story as he sits in a reverie at the foot of a tree, Mat makes peace with this fact. As Berry writes, "He has come into a wakefulness as quiet as a sleep" (321).

Dreams and Imagination

The dreams in the stories of Andy Catlett, Jayber Crow, and Mat Feltner help us understand what Berry means when he explains in *Imagination in Place* that his aim as a writer is to "make a thing that is whole."[34] His dreams are visions of wholeness, binding the past to the present and the future and showing how the membership of Port William endures through time, "clear and whole in the mind's eye."[35] In this regard, Berry's fiction operates like the fourteenth-century poem *Piers Plowman,* which uses dreams to "create the effect of total vision" and "conjure up the image of a society in its totality."[36] Similarly, Berry crafts visions of redemption that console people living in the fractured world that Andy laments in *Remembering.*

serve as a symbol for the abiding ache of grief that Mat feels in his body. Just before falling asleep, Mat ponders the pain that surrounds him in the hospital "in ever-widening circles" and associates this with the nighthawks he hears over the roof: "Over the roof the nighthawks circle and cry, their voices like small stones striking together under water." Berry, *A Place on Earth [Revised],* 223.

34. Berry, *Imagination in Place,* 3.

35. Berry, *Imagination in Place,* 3–4. Compare Phillip J. Donnelly's discussion of convocation as central to Berry's writing in "Biblical Convocation," 275–96.

36. Steiner, *Reading* Piers Plowman, 12 and 13.

We can see Berry's dreams, then, as microcosms of his fiction, fostering hope through reviving the imagination. Like Mat Feltner, none of us knows the future, and yet, as Berry's fiction suggests, our dreams of redemption can guide us through life.

Bibliography

Aers, David. "The Self Mourning: Reflections on *Pearl*." *Speculum* 68.1 (1993): 54–73.

Andrew, Malcolm and Ronald Waldron, eds. *The Poems of the Pearl Manuscript: Pearl, Cleanness, Patience, Sir Gawain and the Green Knight*. Exeter: University of Exeter Press, 2007.

Berry, Wendell. *The Art of the Commonplace*. Edited by Norman Wirzba. Washington D.C.: Shoemaker & Hoard, 2002.

———. *Given: Poems*. Emeryville, CA: Shoemaker & Hoard, 2005.

———. *Imagination in Place*. Berkeley: Counterpoint, 2010.

———. *A Small Porch: Sabbath Poems*. Berkeley: Counterpoint, 2016.

———. *Standing by Words*. Berkeley: Counterpoint, 1983.

Bilbro, Jeffrey. "A Form for Living in the Midst of Loss: Faithful Marriage in the Revisions of Wendell Berry's *A Place on Earth*." *The Southern Literary Journal* 42.2 (2010): 89–105.

Boethius. *The Consolation of Philosophy*. Translated by Richard Green. London: Macmillan, 1962.

Chaucer, Geoffrey. *The Wadsworth Chaucer*, formerly *The Riverside Chaucer*. Edited by Larry D. Benson. Boston: Wadsworth, 1987.

Donnelly, Phillip J. "Biblical Convocation in Wendell Berry's *Remembering*." *Christianity and Literature* 56.2 (2007): 275–96.

Langland, William. *The Vision of Piers Plowman: A Critical Edition of the B-Text Based on Trinity College Cambridge MS B.15.17*. Edited by A.V.C. Schmidt. London: Everyman, 1995.

Lynch, Kathryn L. *Chaucer's Philosophical Visions*. Cambridge: D.S. Brewer, 2000.

Macrobius. *Commentary on the Dream of Scipio*. Translated by William Harris Stahl. New York: Columbia University Press, 1952.

Manganiello, Dominic. "'Dante, e poi Dante': T.S. Eliot, Wendell Berry and 'Europe's Epic.'" In *T.S. Eliot, Dante, and the Idea of Europe*, edited by Paul Douglass, 184–89. New Castle upon Tyne: Cambridge Scholars Publishing, 2011.

———. "Dante and Wendell Berry's Modern Book of Memory." *Studies in Medievalism* 15 (2006): 115–25.

McGrath, Alistair. *Christian Theology: An Introduction*, 2nd Ed. Cambridge and Oxford: Blackwell, 1997.

Spearing, A.C. *Medieval Dream-Poetry*. Cambridge: Cambridge University Press, 1976.

Steiner, Emily. *Reading Piers Plowman*. Cambridge: Cambridge University Press, 2013.

Zak, Gur. "The Ethics and Poetics of Consolation in Petrarch's *Bucolicum carmen*." *Speculum* 91.1 (2016): 36–62.

3

Called to Affection

Exploring the Ecology of
Christian Vocation in Port William

Kiara Jorgenson

IN 2013 THE AMERICAN Academy of Religion recognized Wendell Berry's influence in religious studies, awarding the prolific American writer the Martin E. Marty Award for the Public Understanding of Religion. A decade ago, such acknowledgement would have seemed unlikely for, as many of Berry's commentators and critics have noted, his agrarian ideal is often articulated in contrast to baptized economic forces that undermine and destroy nature's resiliency. "The certified Christian," Berry remarked in a 1992 essay, "seems just as likely as anyone else to join the military-industrial conspiracy to murder creation."[1]

Yet, as I will seek to demonstrate here, Berry's unfolding tales of the Port William Membership ultimately reject cliché ecological indictments of religion in general and Christianity in particular. Rather than forsaking the traditions and theological resources of Christianity, as with good cause many an ecologically-minded writer has done, Berry innovates. As Lawrence Buell and others have suggested, to read Berry and to read him well is to engage and understand something about the creedal traditions of Western Protestantism.[2]

---

1. Berry, "Christianity and the Survival of Creation," 94.

2. Lawrence Buell goes so far as to suggest that Berry's writing is more emphatically creedal and denominational in manner than many other American environmental

This essay will explore one important Christian concept explicit in much of Berry's nonfiction and latent throughout the Port William fiction—vocation, or the religious sense of calling. As a doctrine, vocation (from the Latin *vocare*, meaning "to call" or "to voice") has its roots in the Hebrew verb *qara* and Greek *kaleo*. In the Hebrew Bible calling is verified by election. Israel is itself *qahal*, or the "called out ones" who exist to love Yahweh and fulfill the stipulations of His covenants. In this sense calling is a duty or a task and involves obedience on a personal and corporate level. With the New Testament's emphasis on Gentile inclusion, *kaleo* takes on a different nuance. Here one is called because he or she is "invited" to utilize the gifts of the Spirit for the benefit of the neighbor. To be the church or *ekklesia* (a cognate from *kaleo*), therefore, is to receive such gifts and multiply them.

Up until the 4th century, Christian vocation was understood in these terms—as task and gift—but with the gradual syncretization of Christian teaching and imperial power the doctrine's emphasis became increasingly spiritualized and privatized. Through the early 16th century, only clerics, priests, or monastics were said to be called; their lives of contemplation were prized above those of the laity. However, the ecclesial and theological reforms of the Protestant Reformation interrogated such divisions and radically revised the doctrine. Rather than continuing as an elite concept, calling was democratized in the work of Luther, Calvin, and their early progeny and began to refer to the external work of one's hands *and* the spiritual orientation of one's heart and mind. Vocation became a deeply embodied and fundamentally relational reality, a doctrinal linchpin of sorts between themes of creation and redemption.

It is this early Protestant rendering of calling that Berry draws upon in his fiction. As we shall see, for Berry vocation is a given goal shared among intergenerational community members where the needs of the neighbor are paramount and individual fulfillment is necessarily held in check. Because vocation is always discerned within community and ideally pursued in a manner that tethers one to it, Berry's depiction of calling proves decidedly Protestant. When read alongside his nonfiction, calling in the Port William narrative reifies Berry's unspoken resolve to investigate imperial

---

writers, such as Willa Cather, Henry Thoreau, John Muir, Robinson Jeffers, Ralph Waldo Emerson, and James Fenimore Cooper. See "Religion and the Environmental Imagination in American Literature," 219.

forces inherent in Christendom while also excavating the fecundity of the Christian Gospel.

In his 2012 National Endowment for the Humanities Jefferson Lecture, Berry defined vocation as the responsibility each person has to participate in a neighborly and conserving economy. Understanding economy in simple and classical terms, Berry qualifies authentic economy by "terms of thrift and affection, our connections to nature and to one another."[3] The Christian doctrine of vocation is also a matter of appropriate and responsible relationship, a triadic relationship between God, self, and other, and as such speaks to the whole of life. While frequently rendered as work or occupation, calling in the Christian tradition (and particularly in Protestantism) is never merely a question of what a person produces, the work that is accomplished, or even the philanthropic gifts one gives.[4] Vocation is defined, rather, by what a person freely receives from God through the needs of the neighbor and in the act of work itself. While Berry is scathingly critical of many historical applications of work, the Christian doctrine of calling, as understood in terms of a triadic relationship, remains foundational to Berry's envisaged authentic culture.[5] To make clear Berry's appropriation of Christian concepts of vocation, some preliminary attention

3. Berry, "It All Turns on Affection," 20.

4. Berry is critical of philanthropy or charity that has little to no relational connection to the receiving subject. Furthermore, he demonstrates the frequency with which charitable gifts are given from the proceeds of monies earned in harmful and unjust ways. To this end, he highlights James L. Duke, the philanthropic founder of Duke University, in "It All Turns on Affection." Berry argues that Duke, while undeniably financially generous, made his money on the backs of small tobacco farmers by monopolizing the markets and pigeonholing families into tenant farming contracts.

5. Berry's critique of the historical application of the doctrine of vocation largely relates to the nature and purpose of work. In "The Gift of the Good Land," for example, Berry laments how Christianity has always emphasized the spiritual at the expense of the physical, thereby devaluing what he calls "earthy work," 267. Over a decade later, Berry remarks, "If you are going to destroy creatures without respect, you will want to reduce them to 'materiality;' you will want to deny that there is spirit or truth in them, just as you will want to believe that the only holy creatures, the only creatures with souls, are humans—or even only Christian humans." "Christianity and the Survival of Creation," 104. Criticisms of disembodied theology surface throughout the Port William fiction, particularly through the musings of the young-seminarian-turned-town-barber, Jayber Crow, who often wondered why "Everything bad was laid on the body, and everything good was credited to the soul." *Jayber Crow*, 49. The essay "God and Country" also criticizes Christianity for its tacit approval of (and enmeshment with) capitalism. In Berry's opinion, the malformed ecology of capitalism misconstrues anthropology and cheapens the dignity of work.

to methodology is warranted, with particular attention paid to similarities and differences between Berry's working embodied ethic and overtly theological work.

Many have argued against locating Berry in the realm of theological ethics given that he never proposes any cohesive ecological ethic in the way philosophers of science or ecotheologians do. And to be sure, while capable of reaching similar moral outcomes to that of philosophy and theology, Berry's collective work makes different attempts and uses different tools. It does not seek to provide answers to existential questions in the same way that most philosophy does; but rather, it demonstrates possibilities through narrative. It shows rather than tells. And while theology by definition iteratively emerges in the life of a faith community, the Port William narrative reimagines what those very communities might be, and as such questions the public usefulness of theology. Indeed, despite his expressed discomfort with the realms of philosophy and theology, Berry often finds himself being described as an American moral prophet or Christian literary ethicist. "I'm no moralist," Berry said to a small group of Christian graduate students gathered in his hometown of Port Royal, Kentucky, "and even less so a theologian or Christian writer. What I *am* is a storyteller who has a mind to pay attention to the world around him."[6] Yet, as with a good amount of ethical writing with proven staying power, Berry's narrative appeals to the classical ontological categories of goodness, beauty, and truth. In the aforementioned Jefferson Lecture, Berry mentions these categories outright, suggesting that we give our affection to things embodying such principles rather than to those which destroy and corrode. What marks Berry's voice as unique among other transcendentalists, particularly in contrast to those hailing from the Platonic tradition, is his insistent location of such properties in the fleshy and authentic experience of everyday life.

When we enter the Port William story we bear the fortune of taking on this embodied working ethic. As characters and circumstances unravel, we are engaged in a sort of literary paideutic, or an artful learning venture, not unlike the Christian Gospels that Berry testifies to having always appreciated.[7] As in the synoptic parables or Johannine anecdotes, where the story

6. Taken from the unpublished notes of a personal interview at the annual Au Sable Graduate Fellows retreat in Port Royal, KY on January 20, 2014.

7. One of Berry's most theologically astute characters, Jayber Crow, makes similar remarks: "I saw the Bible as pretty much slanting upward until it got to Jesus, who forgave even the ones who were killing Him while they were killing Him, and then slanting down again when it got to St. Paul. I was truly moved by the stories of Jesus in the Gospels. I

serves to both describe and implore, we the reader become an externalized observer and a moral agent simultaneously. For example, in Jayber Crow's descriptions of differences between wise, old farmer Athey Keith and his foolishly proud son-in-law, Troy Chatham, he not only paints a picture of sustainable farming in contrast with industrialized land abuse—a contrast of personal character over vain ambition—but also invites the reader to examine such polarities and possibilities within one's self. The story teaches as much as it entertains, exhorts as much as it chronicles.

And just as agrarianism focuses on the particularity and locale of ethical questions, ultimately concerning itself with the life one actually lives not only the one imagined, so Berry's ethic is revealed in the palpable realities of Port William's relationships rather than through theoretical or universal musings.[8] If anything, Berry's created world demonstrates how experiences shape and inform beliefs.

Explicit Definitions of Vocation in Berry's Nonfiction

Berry's most explicit commentary on calling is found in his nonfiction, where vocation is largely expressed apophatically—i.e., in relationship to the negative effects of human degradation. Though the Jefferson Lecture speaks of vocation in a cataphatic way—as affectionately participating in a thrifty and authentic economy that values "the many human households to the earth's many ecosystems and human neighborhoods"—much of his nonfiction links work to an alternative rendering of economy, an industrial one. Here the relationship one has with land and neighbor is cast as pillage and indifference, the result being the fracturing of the *oikos*. Lamenting these reigning conceptualizations of economy, Berry observes how economists "rarely if ever mention the land-communities and the land-use economies. They never ask, in their professional oblivion, why we are willing to do permanent ecological and cultural damage to "strengthen the economy?"

---

could imagine them. The Nativity in the Gospel of Luke and the Resurrection in the Gospel of John I could just shut my eyes and *see*. I could imagine everything until I got to the letters of Paul." *Jayber Crow*, 50.

8. This is in contrast to other American environmental writers, such as Barry Lopez, whose migratory stories paint a picture of elsewhere and aggressively address anthropocentrism more than the practiced ethics of place. See, for example, "Renegotiating the Contracts."

Yet, to Berry's eye this is the critical contemporary question, for one's vocation or calling is never merely a question of industry. As nearly all of Berry's writing depicts (and as we shall see in greater detail below), earn and strive as we humans will, what we ultimately depend upon—land and relationship—is given. The competing economies of our present day, one oriented toward production and the other rest, depend equally upon the endowed "Great Economy" of biological life, although only the latter recognizes and adheres to the inherent limitations therein. For Berry, when vocation is properly understood as an obligation to receive gifts and honor creation's limitations, work

> moves virtue toward virtuosity—that is, toward skill or technical competency. There is no use in helping our neighbors with their work if we do not know how to work. When virtues are rightly practiced within the Great Economy, we do not call them virtues; we call them good farming, good forestry, good carpentry, good husbandry, good weaving and sewing, good homemaking, good parenthood, good neighborhood, and so on.[9]

In contrast to the tenets of American exceptionalism, in which people are thought destined to greatness by virtue of association and the longstanding ideology of the "self-made-man," Berry construes the outcomes of good work as gifts. Rather than work becoming a vehicle for pride, wherein the mind is easily incapable of wonder and subject to loneliness, work ought to grace us with health and heal us with grace. In Berry's words, work as vocation "preserves the given so that it remains a gift."[10] Unlike capitalism, which measures and values natural goods and relationships as commodities according to a fabricated monetary bottom line, Berry's agrarianism suggests that if more communities viewed productivity as a gesture of return then "the economy would have to accommodate the need to be worthy of the gifts we receive and use."[11] The obvious result would be a lifestyle more read-

9. Berry, "Two Economies," 73–74.

10. Berry, "Healing," 9–10.

11. Berry, "The Agrarian Standard," 27. Here we see how Berry, like other Agrarian thinkers, fundamentally rejects the reigning capitalist logic of "tradeoffs," wherein ecological integrity and the well-being of the poor are sacrificed for maximized economic growth. As Willis Jenkins explains in a recent chapter on economies of desire in *The Future of Ethics*, on the whole, agrarianism is disgusted by the impoverishment wrought by globalizing capitalism, and it denies the claim that human development must inevitably encroach upon ecology and exploit the poor. "Economic reasoning is not about making choices among rivalrous goods to maximize benefit," Jenkins summarizes, "but about

ily characterized by constraint rather than consumption, gratitude rather than greed. Thus practically speaking, Berry's working concept of vocation is thoroughly Protestant in the way it engenders thankfulness to God on the one hand and responsibility to the neighbor on the other, as made manifest in one's affection for place and people, land and culture.

The place in which a person finds oneself, their particular locale, is central to one's vocation. In Berry's mind a person's embodied memory—one's home—is not where thoughts settle, cease or rest, but rather, where they begin. And not only is calling to a particular place an important theme throughout Berry's writing, but it's also proved an important element in his biography. As anyone even vaguely familiar with his story knows, Berry and his wife, Tanya, have repeatedly declined prestigious invitations to work and teach outside of their beloved Kentucky.[12] Even Berry's brief tenures at the University of Kentucky proved challenging, as he grew to despise the commute and what he perceived even then to be a growing chasm between academic life and farm life. In prose and lifestyle alike, Berry's working definition of vocation underscores the importance of being rooted in a place, of being in relationship to the land of the place and of entering into community with the people of the place.[13] In one of his autobiographical essays, "A Native Hill," Berry shares how being grounded in place has shaped his vocation as a writer: "I knew that because I was a writer the literary world would always have an importance for me and would always attract my interest," he writes, "[b]ut I never doubted that the world was more important to me than the literary world; and the world would always be most fully and clearly present to me in the place I was fated by birth to

---

cultivating forms of wealth that satisfy an entire membership. An economy could develop differently, producing habitat for others while producing food for humans. Economy should be the skillful art of blessing, not the dismal math of scarcity," 270.

12. Tanya grew up in northern California, but eventually moved to Kentucky when her father took a position in the Art Department at the University of Kentucky. Having moved around most of her life, she speaks about Kentucky becoming her home upon marrying Wendell. Laura and Jef Sewell capture her sentiments on this well in their recent documentary on the couple, *Look & See*: "I had no clue what I was getting into," Tanya admits, "but I've been lucky because of him, because he's the kind of person he was, and he's been lucky because of me, because I believe in the continuity of the home and the family."

13. Edmondson, *Priest, Prophet and Pilgrim*, 70.

know better than any other."[14] He would be, in the words of his beloved teacher, Wallace Stegner, a "sticker" rather than a "boomer."[15]

Pictures of Vocation in Berry's Port William Fiction

The importance of commitment to and affection for place and people is most evident in the fiction of Berry's Port William Membership. In these novels and short stories we meet an array of persons, "stickers" and "boomers" alike. There are some who, by contributing to the local economy while preserving the greater one, enliven the ecology of their respective vocations. There are others who fail to do so, and often at the expense of the community at large. In their book, *Wendell Berry and the Cultivation of Life*, J. Matthew Bonzo and Michael Stevens helpfully highlight six categories of interaction in Berry's hospitable world, ranging from those who are born into the Port William membership but leave in search of better options, to those who are born outside the community yet invest in it and are welcomed as full members, to those who are born and remain members but are always dwelling along the margins.[16] As Bonzo and Stevens suggest, no single character type is dominant in the narrative; there is no signature hero in Port William, no signature villain. For example, Jayber Crow and Hannah Coulter—aliens by birth to the community—are as critical to its well-being as are its life-long residents, Andy Catlett or Mattie Chatman. The Port William membership is a dynamic, yet stable, community with bounded space for mutuality and accountability.[17] In a real sense, Berry's protagonist is the community itself, with individuals' respective callings understood relative to the myriad relationships they inhabit within the community.

To understand better how Berry recasts the Christian concept of vocation in a manner both true to the doctrine's original emphasis and in contrast to contemporary conceptions of work, I would like to consider three aspects of vocation in the Port William narrative. First, Berry tethers

14. Berry, "A Native Hill," 173–75.

15. "It All Turns on Affection," 10–11. In short, "boomers" typify people on the take, those primarily concerned with making a profit at the expense of people and land. "Stickers," on the other hand, cultivate affection for a place and seek to preserve and strengthen it.

16. See the introduction of *Wendell Berry and the Cultivation of Life*. For a further consideration of such marginal characters, see Michael Stevens's essay in this collection, "Hiding in the Hedgerows: Wendell Berry's Treatment of Marginal Characters."

17. Ibid, 143.

vocation to place by emphasizing the importance of a common and shared goal. Second, vocation is depicted as something given rather than discovered or earned. And third, Berry employs an intergenerational sense of calling, noting how lives "dead, living and yet to be" influence one's present work.[18]

Vocation and A Common Goal

We begin with the story of the Catlett men—Wheeler and his two sons, Henry and Andy. The Catlett men are unique in Port William for their advanced, formal education and professional careers; Wheeler and Henry are both lawyers, and Andy is an agricultural journalist. As Berry implies time and again, these men could have easily led more fiscally comfortable lives elsewhere. But what makes the Catletts unique is how they utilize their skills and abilities in service to the shared and common life of the Port William community. Take, for example, Henry Catlett's aiding and abetting role in the abduction of old Burley Coulter from a Louisville hospital in the short story "Fidelity." Knowing that Burley's bastard son, Danny, wished his bachelor father to die in surroundings that he loved, Henry uses his legal prowess and status to deter a legalistic detective and preserve the broader ecology of a communal vocation.

Andy Catlett's prodigal story of return, captured primarily in *Remembering*, also defines vocation in relationship to the needs of community. While presenting the difficulties of small farmers like those in Port William in a paper at a national conference attended by many who had been "off the farm" for decades, Andy has a conversion-like experience. Unlike his literary colleagues, he is burdened by the mounting injustices related to corporate agricultural practices and doesn't wish to be, or think himself able to be, a writer who records the course of farming outside of an actual farming community.[19] Andy, the most autobiographical of Berry's characters, returns from San Francisco to Port William seeking reconciliation with those he left and begins to write on behalf of his beloved community.

Interestingly, we see a counter example of this story in the life of Caleb Coulter. Using the language of calling, Hannah Coulter describes how "farming was what [Caleb] played before he could work at it."[20] From her

18. *The Wild Birds*, 363.

19. Berry, *Three Short Novels*, 137–140.

20. Berry, *Hannah Coulter*, 126.

vantage, Caleb's call to farm seemed evident. However, as sure as Caleb may have been of such a vocation, he is depicted as being equally certain of the expectations laid upon him. His young adult life, heavy with the yoke of potential, was not only Caleb's to live—and so began what Hannah refers to as "the distancing." While in school, Caleb was urged to make more of himself than a farmer. Hannah imagines the voices saying, "There's no future for you in farming" and "Why should you be a farmer yourself when you can do so much for farmers?"[21] Ultimately these voices did shape Caleb's perceived calling. He earned a Ph.D. in agriculture, finding some semblance of solace in teaching others about the art of keeping land. To be sure, Berry's fairly neutral depiction of Caleb makes clear that, unlike his colleagues, who championed the ways of booming agribusiness, Caleb remained tethered to the Port William community in his own removed way, promoting responsible participation in small economies. To this end, Caleb's academic vocation is authentic by Berry's standards and undoubtedly serves as a deliberate alternative to the way of the ivory tower that Berry himself entertained and left behind.

And yet, in Berry's novel, *Hannah Coulter*, we learn of Caleb's deep dissatisfaction. Seemingly stuck in a laboratory while invariably yearning to break soil of his own, his mother describes his existence as "always trying to make up the difference between the life he has and the life he imagines he might have had."[22] Here Berry illustrates the dangers of universality over particularity. Caleb's hidden anguish uncovers a tension in Berry's working concept of vocation: the significance of a community's perceived needs and guidance on the one hand and a person's own still, small voice on the other.

Vocation as Given

This location of the individual in the context of community gives way to a free sense of vocation, as briefly mentioned above. In numerous cases, Port William members come into their calling by way of gift. Berry evokes images of apprenticeship and priesthood repeatedly in his unfolding tale, juxtaposing the wisdom of less-than-credentialed characters with those who are teachers and pastors in name only. A clear example of this can be found in the story of Elton and Mary Penn. Initially poor tenant farmers on the outskirts of town, the Penns exhibit genuine interest in the life of

21. Berry, *Hannah Coulter*, 128.
22. Ibid., 131.

the community and are welcomed with open arms, learning the skills of housewifery and husbandry from their neighbors.[23] These relational gifts lead not only to increased knowledge and skill, but also to a recognized identity, indeed a vocation, as good and faithful farmers. After Old Jack Beechum resigns himself to the reality that his only-daughter, Clara, and her banker husband, Gladston Pettit, have no intention of caring for his beloved farm, Jack bequeaths a portion of it to the Penns and, with the additional aid of senior lawyer Wheeler Catlett, the Penns become farmers in their own right. When pressed about his generosity, Wheeler democratizes the situation, establishing his position as similar to that of his beneficiary: "I mean you're a man indebted to a dead man. So am I. So was [Jack]. That's the story of it."[24] Here the given precedes the giving. Elton and Mary Penn's calling came by what was given—the knowledge of the trade and possession of property. Likewise, Wheeler Catlett's vocation as social advocate and community philanthropist comes to be through what was first given him: "It's not accountable," Wheeler remarks at the end of the story,

> we're dealing in goods and services that we didn't make, that can't exist at all except as gifts. Everything about a place that's different from its price is a gift. Everything about a man or woman that's different from their price is a gift. The life of a neighborhood is a gift . . . . So there is to be no repayment. Because there is to be no bill.[25]

We also see vocation as given in the storyline between Jack Beechum and his nephew, Mat Feltner. In "Pray without Ceasing," the young Mat ponders revenge in response to the murder of his father, Ben. While sometimes regarded as a bitter curmudgeon in the Port William community, it is Jack Beechum that saves young Mat from such a fate. Unlike the disembodied pastoral figure of Brother Preston, who Berry describes as having "washed his hands of the whole world," Jack sees and understands the vulnerability of Mat's flesh.[26] Like a true priest, he recognizes the beauty and significance of Mat's pain and embodies a kenotic compassion for his nephew. Jack never consciously takes on such a role, nor does he feign importance amidst the tragic circumstances. Rather, he faithfully and silently accompanies Mat, never wholly detached and yet unobtrusive and in so doing is given the vocation of ministry to the entire Feltner family. The role is fruit of Jack's keen

23. Ibid., 201.
24. Berry, "It Wasn't Me," 284.
25. Ibid., 288.
26. Berry, *A Place on Earth [Revised]*, 32.

attention to a particular person in a particular place at a particular time; and because it's given, Jack's calling extends to multiple generations, as evidenced in the relationship forged with Hannah Feltner (Coulter) some thirty years later. The vocation of priesthood in the Port William Membership, like any worthwhile vocation, is "apprenticed to those who are observant and willing to adapt their own lives to the demands of others."[27]

The Intergenerational Nature of Vocation

This brings us to the third component of Berry's working concept of vocation, the intergenerational. As Brent Laytham has shown, Berry's Port William fiction exhibits a reverence for example by highlighting stories of past righteousness and neighborly concern.[28] Rather than one being replaced after they die, "cast out of place and out of mind . . . to be alone at the last maybe and soon forgotten," as is the case in most modern work environments, one's vocation in a communal membership extends beyond their lifetime. In Andy Catlett's words to Hannah Coulter, membership "keeps the memories even of horses and mules and milk cows and dogs."[29] There is, as Laytham has observed, an almost ecclesial quality to the Membership, wherein those gone before constitute part of the *Communio Sanctorum*.

Because it is linked to those who have gone before, calling is equally associated with those yet to come. In the short story "The Wild Birds," for example, we learn of Burley Coulter's desire to bequeath his farm to Danny Branch, not only out of a sense of obligation, but also because Danny has proven able to steward the land just as Burley responsibly tended what was given to him. Here the validity of vocation has everything to do with what it yields in generations to come, a particularly important aspect of Berry's working concept of vocation in today's environmentally perilous times.

Conclusion

In conclusion, it can be said that, despite his many critiques of Christianity, Wendell Berry's envisaged culture is deeply informed by Christianity's dialogical relationship between God, self, and other. As I've sought

27. Edmondson, *Priest, Prophet and Pilgrim*, 132.
28. Laytham, "The Membership Includes the Dead," 174.
29. Berry, *Hannah Coulter*, 133–134.

to demonstrate, receiving and acting upon one's vocation is critical to membership in the Port William community. A life well lived is attentive to place, mindful of gifts past and present, and oriented toward a material future. It is these qualities, among others, that make Berry's fictional work relevant in our actual contemporary communities. Will we, like the Coulters, Catletts, Beechums, and Branches, care for one another well? And will we, like the best of them, responsibly carry out human relationships with great affection for the land that sustains them?

Bibliography

Berry, Wendell. "The Agrarian Standard." In *The Essential Agrarian Reader: The Future of Culture, Community, and the Land*, edited by Norman Wirzba, 23–33. Lexington: University Press of Kentucky, 2003.

———. "Christianity and the Survival of Creation." In *Sex, Economy, Freedom & Community*, 93–116. New York: Pantheon, 1992.

———. "The Gift of Good Land." In *The Gift of Good Land: Further Essays Cultural and Agricultural*, 267–81. Berkeley: Counterpoint, 2009.

———. "God and Country." In *What Are People For?: Essays*, 95–102. New York: North Point, 1990.

———. "Healing." In *What Are People For?*, 9–13. San Francisco: North Point, 1990.

———. "It All Turns on Affection." In *It All Turns on Affection: The Jefferson Lecture & Other Essays*, 9–39. Berkeley: Counterpoint, 2012.

———. "A Native Hill." In *Long-Legged House*, 170–213. New York: Shoemaker & Hoard, 2004.

———. "Two Economies." In *Home Economics*, 54–75. San Francisco: North Point, 1987.

Bonzo, J. Matthew, and Michael R. Stevens. *Wendell Berry and the Cultivation of Life: A Reader's Guide*. Grand Rapids: Brazos, 2008.

Buell, Lawrence. "Religion and the Environmental Imagination in American Literature." In *There Before Us: Religion, Literature, and Culture from Emerson to Wendell Berry*, edited by Roger Lundin, 216–38. Grand Rapids: Eerdmans, 2007.

Dunn, Laura, and Jef Sewell. *Look & See: A Portrait of Wendell Berry*. Documentary, 2016.

Edmondson, Todd. *Priest, Prophet and Pilgrim: Types and Distortions of Spiritual Vocation In the Fiction of Wendell Berry and Cormac McCarthy*. Eugene: Pickwick, 2014.

Jenkins, Willis. *The Future of Ethics: Sustainability, Social Justice, and Religious Creativity*. Washington, DC: Georgetown University Press, 2013.

Laytham, Brent. "The Membership Includes the Dead: Wendell Berry's Port William Membership as *Communio Sanctorum*." In *Wendell Berry & Religion: Heaven's Earthly Life*, edited by Joel James Shuman and L. Roger Owens, 173–89. Lexington: University Press of Kentucky, 2009.

Lopez, Barry. "Renegotiating the Contracts" in *This Incomperable Lande: A Book of American Nature Writing*, edited by Thomas J. Lyon, 381–88. Boston: Houghton, 1989.

4

Between the City and the Classroom

Stanford, Stegner, and the Class of '58

Doug Sikkema

Two Roads Diverged

THERE ARE BASICALLY TWO paths to publication today. Some writers may travel both, but it's a rare few who travel neither. At least that's the story Chad Harbach tells in *MFA vs NYC: The Two Cultures of American Fiction.*[1]

As he understands it, the first path leads would-be writers to one of the thousands of MFA programs that have popped up all over the United States since the mid-twentieth century. In this arrangement, the wild-and-free[2] writer admits herself to the confines of the Ivory Tower (or, at least an anchoress' cell appended to it). Here apprentices to the craft are nurtured, but always within earshot of academia. So MFA fiction, for better or (often) for worse, bears an academic self-consciousness that can start to grate on a general readership untrained with theoretical jargon.[3] American fiction

---

1. Harbach, *MFA vs NYC.*

2. In case it wasn't clear, this is said with tongue firmly in cheek. If anything, Harbach and the various voices he gathers for this essay collection dispel the notion that writers (maybe excepting Hemingway) have ever been so wild or so free. Just think of the top ten writers you know. Odds are likely they are the product of some elite educational institution or another.

3. For a more complete treatment of this, I would recommend looking at the book which prompted Harbach's own essay and proceeding collection: McGurl, *The Program Era* (It should be noted that one of McGurl's central concerns is how many writers have

today is so indebted to this organizational arrangement that whether a writer attended an MFA or not, she has most likely been fed a steady diet of contemporary literature written by those who have.

The second path leads one to the cocktail-swilling inner circles of the New York City trade publishing circuit. There is obvious overlap between the NYC worlds and the MFA worlds: Many NYC insiders have spent time in MFA programs, and most of the fiction they'll receive will be the products of such programs. The mark of the NYC publisher, though, is his status as gatekeeper to a certain set of NYC-centric attitudes and predilections. They not only take the pulse of the culture, they set its pace—or so they claim.

To be sure, neither MFA programs nor NYC publishers are as monolithic as this gloss might suggest;[4] yet the fact remains: any writer of note today has been formed by one or both of these institutions.

Except for Wendell Berry. Or so I thought the first time I read him. Unlike many who first come to Berry through his essays, my introduction to the Kentucky sage was through his fictional world of Port William. It was 2007 and *Jayber Crow* was the last on a list for some 6000-level graduate course in English Language and Literature. (At the time I was finishing up my MA at the University of Ottawa.[5]) After slogging through James Joyce and David Foster Wallace,[6] it was a welcome relief to end our sojourns with the quiet ruminations of Jayber, a bachelor-barber in Port William, some no-man's-land in central Kentucky. Unlike most of the contemporary writers I'd come across as a grad student, Berry seemed not just oblivious,

---

become navel-gazers. McGurl posits that much postwar writing in the "program era" is about writing [e.g. the ward in Ken Kesey's *One Flew Over the Cuckoo's Nest* can be read as an analogue to the writer's workshop]).

4. And I'd suggest reading essays throughout Harbach's collection to see how true this is. Especially George Saunders's "A Mini-Manifesto" for what MFA programs are and, more importantly, are not; and Jim Rutman's "The Disappointment Business" to see how fickle, diverse, and complex the NYC publishing world really is.

5. That I read this in graduate school should have been an obvious sign Berry was working *within* the strictures of the MFA/NYC pattern. I was young(er).

6. Of course Joyce is *not* an American writer let alone a late twentieth-century one; however, *Portrait of the Artist* as *a Young Man* and (more so) *Ulysses* and (much more so) *Finnegan's Wake* are the epitome of the kind of modernist writing that hopes to be overheard by the burgeoning literary "professionals." As Joyce famously said: "I've put in so many enigmas and puzzles [in *Ulysses*] that it will keep the professors busy for centuries arguing over what I meant, and that's the only way of insuring one's immortality." David Foster Wallace's *Infinite Jest* is perhaps the example *par excellence* of this phenomenon.

but openly hostile, to the goings on within the "two headed monster" of American publishing.

Just read the opening preface of *Jayber Crow,* which warns:

> Persons attempting to find a "text" in this book will be prosecuted; persons attempting to find a "subtext" in it will be banished; persons attempting to explain, interpret, explicate, analyze, deconstruct, or otherwise "understand" it will be exiled to a desert island in the company only of other explainers. BY ORDER OF THE AUTHOR.[7]

The irony—which, I admit, I completely missed back then—is that such a warning is just *another* form of academic self-consciousness. (This kind of preface is graduate-student fly-paper.) Yet the simplicity of Berry's prose offered sweet release from the mind-altering complexity of writers like Joyce, who was keenly aware of the burgeoning formalists who held his reputation under their gaze, or Wallace, who knew that scads of post-theoretical-turn academics and publishers held his.[8] Berry, though, seemed not to care about post-Marxist paradigms, deconstruction, or any other theoretical sledgehammers. *Finally,* I thought, *this wasn't another "professional" man of letters: Berry was a farmer who just happened to be able to write.*

It didn't take too much digging to realize that Berry is actually no exception to Harbach's general thesis. He is no lone voice, crying in the wilderness, as first-time readers might think. As I thought. He did not develop *outside* the MFA or NYC worlds, but *within* them, particularly the MFA world. He was really a trained writer—just one who could also farm.

This is not a reason to love Berry nor is it a reason to hate him. My main argument is that knowing more about Berry's MFA and NYC backgrounds helps to better understand the ways in which his fiction was formed by the community of writers in which he found himself. In many ways, Berry's work is a good case study in just how the formation of the American literary tradition in the late twentieth century through MFA programs and NYC publishers worked. Writers responded to one another in close geographic and temporal proximity. They championed and eviscerated each

7. Berry, *Jayber Crow,* 1.

8. This is not to denigrate such writers. Full disclosure, I love the writing of both Joyce and Wallace. They do, however, provide a much different experience of reading than a Berry or a Stegner. I also do not think Joyce or Wallace wrote in their idiosyncratic styles solely because they were concerned with their reputation and longevity. It's simply a matter of the audience they envisioned as they wrote, which are those who shared a formation in the ivory tower.

other. They turned each other into literary characters and riffed off one another's themes and structures. And reading Berry with such a context in mind is helpful because it leads inevitably to Wallace Stegner and Ken Kesey and the unique dynamic born out of the Stanford creative writing program of 1958.

Of Stanford and Stegner

The "Program Era" of American writing began because of the work of people like Wallace Stegner. After a childhood spent restlessly moving around America's "last" frontier at the whims of an opportunity-chasing, "boomer" father, Stegner's creativity, intelligence and hard work launched him into some of the most elite academic institutions in the country as a student and later as an instructor. However, it was at Stanford where he indelibly left his mark with the formation of an ambitious creative writing program.

It was 1945 and Stegner was thirty-six years old. Having lived in the East for a while, Stegner was well-versed in the biases and assumptions of the NYC publishing industry. "I knew," he told his biographer Jackson Benson, "that literary careers cut off from New York tend to wither over the years."[9] So with his signature ingenuity and effort, he drafted a proposal to create prizes, fellowships, anthologies that would find publication through the University press, and a whole network of writers who would visit, mentor, and teach emerging writers at Stanford. Impressed by what the Iowa Writers' Workshop[10] had set up in 1936, Stegner believed the West needed its own version, and Stanford could be the ideal place to house it.

By 1947, Stegner took his plans to the department chairman R.F. Jones whose brother E.H. Jones was so taken up by the vision that he decided to fund it for the first five years.[11] It was also decided during these fledgling years to create an M.A. level program where a limited number of "Stegner Fellows" could come for one year apprenticeships. Through the years such notable writers as Ken Kesey, Sandra Day O'Connor, Edward Abbey, Ernest

---

9. Benson, *Wallace Stegner*, 164.

10. Wilbur Schramm, the founder of the Iowa Writers' Workshop in 1936 was actually one of the most formative influences on Wallace Stegner. But that's another story.

11. There is a peculiar irony that although E.H. Jones was a medical doctor, he actually never practiced medicine because the oil found on his Texas property made him a phenomenally wealthy man. See Benson, 165.

Gaines, and, of course, Wendell Berry would be formed within the tight knit community.

Through the late 1940s and early 1950s Stegner maintained his seemingly mythical work ethic, traveling widely to speak, rereading novels and stories for his weekly lectures, poring over student work and providing detailed commentary, keeping office hours each afternoon, and pecking away at his typewriter every morning for over four hours.[12] But in the program's early years—before Wendell Berry's arrival in 1958—Stegner was also undergoing a rigorous, self-directed education in environmentalism, ecology, and conservation. As he knew firsthand, these were increasingly urgent topics in mid-century, post-frontier West.

During this time Stegner became a guiding light (and hired pen) for the burgeoning environmental movement.[13] With the publication of *Beyond the Hundredth Meridian*—began in the 1940s and released in 1954—Stegner helped revive the story of geologist John Wesley Powell not simply as one of the last men to know the American frontier, but as a man who embodied the values and principles Stegner believed Americans would need to cultivate if they were to live well with each other and the land long into the future. In Powell, Stegner found a man who met the frontier with "courage, leadership, and cooperation, rather than a rugged individualism."[14] And these virtues provided Stegner (and later Berry) with a heroic prototype who resisted the unbridled materialism, competition, exploitation, and decadence that threatened to undo both the social and natural fabric of America.[15]

As he chipped away on the Powell book, Stegner was also working with the Sierra Club and other local conservation organizations, fighting against the Washington-backed industries that were making profits today even though it meant stealing the inheritance of tomorrow. The principles Stegner was formulating in all these projects reach something of a climax in the "Wilderness Letter," penned in 1960 to David E. Pesonen. The letter has become a manifesto of sorts for conservationists the world over and, in

---

12. Ibid., 174.

13. A role Stegner both cherished and resented, since it led many in the NYC establishment in later years to pigeonhole Stegner.

14. Ibid., 211.

15. Marian and Joe Allston in *All the Little Live Things*, Jayber Crow, Athey Keith, and Burley Coulter in *Jayber Crow* are just a few. Significantly, Andy Catlett's seatmate on his flight home in *Remembering* is reading *Beyond the Hundredeth Meridian*, and Andy calls it "a book that [he] knows, by a writer he loves." *Remembering*, 83.

addition to beautifully capturing the value of wild places, it yields a glimpse into Stegner's increasing animosity towards the cultural epicenter of the East Coast that was rejigging the American imagination in self-destructive ways.

In one of several similar passages from the short letter, Stegner's defense of the wilderness suggests a certain romanticized Luddism that echoes Henry David Thoreau and John Muir:

> Without any remaining wilderness we are committed wholly, without chance for even momentary reflection and rest, to a headlong drive into our technological termite-life, the Brave New World of a completely man-controlled environment. We need wilderness preserved—as much of it as is still left, and as many kinds—because it was the challenge against which our character as a people was formed. The reminder and the reassurance that it is still there is good for our spiritual health even if we never once in ten years set foot in it.[16]

As Stegner argues, the protected wildness of the country not only made humans distinctly human, but Americans distinctly American. Land protected from human domination (not, mind you, human *interaction*) required wisdom, local knowledge, and, above all, a disciplined restraint. But such virtues, Stegner believed, were lacking in many modern people.

And he feared the abuse of land was only bound to get worse because the current manifestations of ecological destruction in the 1950s were but a symptom of the deeper cultural diseases of self-indulgence, consumption, and competition. To compound the problem, American writers were no longer performing their proper duty in calling their fellow citizens back to such a life of responsibility and virtue but were actively feeding this diseased imagination. Stegner's letter continues:

> As a novelist, I may perhaps be forgiven for taking literature as a reflection, indirect but profoundly true, of our national consciousness. And our literature, as perhaps you are aware, is sick, embittered, losing its mind, losing its faith. Our novelists are the declared enemies of their society. There has hardly been a serious or important novel in this century that did not repudiate in part or in whole American technological culture for its commercialism, its vulgarity, and the way in which it has dirtied a clean continent and a clean dream.[17]

16. Stegner, "Wilderness Letter."
17. Ibid.

While Stegner's "Wilderness Letter" is often read through an environmental lens, this subtle undercurrent of rage at the countercultural literary establishment taking off in the 1960s is often missed. Yet this is the heart of the issue. The battle to be fought was not solely through politics and policies (although Stegner fought those battles), but through the imagination. Americans required a literature that could teach them how to live—and die—well.

Yet this call for a literature that hadn't lost its mind or its faith still begs the question: faith in *what* exactly? There are several answers that Stegner might have given to such a question, but none of these would include faith in any kind of metaphysical reality, afterlife, or the Christian understanding of a transcendent God separate from the created order. And the reason I mention this is because Wendell Berry, the student who resolved to take up Stegner's challenge and write such a literature, disagreed with his Stanford mentor on precisely this point.

But one can imagine Wendell Berry, as a youngish man at the time, reading these words from Stegner and accepting his challenge. And of course, it's easy to imagine this because with the privilege of hindsight we know that's exactly what he did.

Class of '58: Ken Kesey

But not all of Stegner's pupils championed the virtues that Stegner valued. Some of them gave voice to the very sickness against which he warned. In fact, it's difficult to read Stegner's disparaging comments about contemporary American literature without hearing a rather pointed swipe at his most notorious student: Ken Kesey.

Although a much less prodigious (and disciplined) writer, the young Kesey eclipsed Stegner's popularity with his debut novel *One Flew Over the Cuckoo's Nest* (1962). Crafted in part during his time at Stanford through a Woodrow Wilson Fellowship,[18] Kesey became a voice of the disaffected, anti-establishment youth of the 1960s in a way that Kerouac and Salinger had in the 1950s. The story's irreverent protagonist, Randle Patrick McMurphy, became a cult icon for an emerging counterculture bent on its Dedalusian flight beyond the constraints of authority and traditional mores.

It's little wonder that Wallace Stegner's writing had little resonance with such a generation. Even among his literary peers, such as Updike or

18. Although he applied multiple times for a Stegner Fellowship, Stegner denied him.

Vonnegut, Stegner did not participate in the decade's *zeitgeist*; he refused to tell readers "that authority is corrupt and should be ignored or resisted, that pleasure can be an ultimate good, and self-indulgence is fine, that freedom is something that can be exercised without responsibility, that lives lived according to the traditional values of self-sacrifice, courage, and self-discipline are wasted and spent foolishly."[19] And while his fiction consistently cast this as the vision of a life well lived, he sacrificed the literary celebrity the NYC world might have bestowed upon him had he compromised and used his gifts to give people what they wanted to hear.[20]

While Stegner was vocally sceptical of Kesey's ideas—calling them "half-baked"[21]—the feelings were mutual. In Stegner's conduct was an adherence to social convention and custom that the counterculture could not abide. And Kesey's animosity extended to the whole MFA structure for creative writing—a structure into which (ironically? hypocritically?) he enrolled. Nevertheless, Kesey believed such a rigid, bureaucratic format clipped the wings of writers and kept them from really experiencing (and experimenting) with life. His most scathing critique of his mentor was that by the 50's and 60's, the great and powerful Stegner was merely "writing to a classroom and to his colleagues."[22] What Chad Harbach and Marc McGurl would write about decades later, Kesey was already concerned about: the entire MFA structure was problematic for creative expression.[23] So Kesey

19. Benson, *Wallace Stegner*, 4.

20. Of course, one might rightfully say, "Thou dost protest too much," since Stegner did, in fact, win a Pulitzer for *Angle of Repose*. Such a prestigious award suggests a certain "celebrity" I may be willfully ignoring. However, as Jackson Benson, and even Stegner in his conversations with Etulain, points out, he was one of the most maligned and ignored Pulitzer prize winners ever. Even the obligatory review of *Angle of Repose* was buried in the backpages of the *New York Review of Books*, and several other of his later books were not even given attention in NYC circles.

21. The double-entendre was definitely implied.

22. Benson, *Wallace Stegner*, 252. Jackson Benson's biography of Stegner, while remarkable on many counts, often reads more as hagiography of Stegner, which is a fault of many biographies. The case Benson brings against Kesey is particularly grating on this score since it never takes seriously the claims Kesey brings against the whole creative writing structure. And the fact that Stegner denied Kesey the Stegner Fellowship multiple times bears much more attention than Benson gives it.

23. That is, "creative expression" as narrowly defined by Kesey. Stegner would rejoin (as would others in Harbach's wonderful book), that creative expression best happens *within the* bounds of such a guild of practitioners who are steeped in the craft and in the tradition. For Stegner, the MFA format was an embodiment of Eliot's ideal about how the individual talent melded with the Tradition. Berry, as we'll see, understood this moreso

and his band of Merry Pranksters formed an anti-seminar in a bohemian neighbourhood near Stanford where they would gather to read their work and explore the last frontiers of their minds, experimenting with narrative voice and LSD.

But Kesey's love of a rugged individualism and his blatant disregard for authority were, despite their popularity, not the virtues Stegner believed people could live by—at least not for long. These ideas were diseased. These were the vices against which Stegner wrote his whole life. And in *All the Little Live Things*—the novel Stegner was writing as Kesey came through Stanford in '58—the character Jim Peck bears a remarkable resemblance to Stegner's precocious student. Peck is a college dropout who establishes his own anti-academy on the property edge of the retired, curmudgeonly literary agent Joe Allston. (Allston is the epitome of a New York City publishing insider.)

In his 1990 conversations with Richard Etulain, when asked to explain whether or not *All the Little Live Things* was merely a "grumpy criticism of the hippie generation," Stegner suggests that the Peck narrative was an almost unintentional add-on:

> The hippie just wandered into it by accident and became a rather half-witted Principle of Evil. . . . The hippie is only a kind of dumb bystander. That was my feeling about hippies in general at that point. I've changed to some extent since, but the ones that I knew then were dumb bystanders who didn't have any notion of what went on but thought they did.[24]

In the story, Peck (at least through Allston's eyes) remains "half-witted" throughout the story largely because he does not understand the evil of death lurking within all those "little live things" in the California Eden where he's camped. So he lives with a foolish and naive abandon. The orgies that take place on his compound know no restraints, the nights of revelry are followed by a wake of destruction as a teenaged neighbour becomes pregnant. Peck's conduct also causes the land to suffer. After a short time, the tiny camp(us) becomes a wasteland of garbage and refuse, a harsh counterpoint to the beauty and abundance of Joe Allston's carefully stewarded property. Self-indulgence might be built on a foundation of individualism, but when the edifice crumbles, the damage ripples out to the society

---

than his rebellious classmate.

24. Stegner and Etulain, *Conversations with Wallace Stegner,* 75.

and the natural world.[25] Or as Stegner put it a 1965 essay, "[T]his sort of emancipation is actually imprisonment, obsession; we have broken down inhibitions to achieve disorder."[26]

After Peck has moved on, Joe Allston remains haunted by the young bohemian and all he signifies and foreshadows, much the way I imagine Stegner must have felt after Kesey moved on from Stanford:

> When we first met Peck in the bottoms I should have come away cackling and clutching my brows, crying, "A fool! A fool! I met a fool I' the forest, a motley fool!" Instead I came away implicated, entangled, and oppressed, and I knew exactly why. He was like a visitation—beard, motorcycle, and all, and his head rattled with all the familiar loose marbles. He angered me in a remembered way, he made me doubt myself all afresh. And there was a threat in him, a demand that he and his bughouse faiths be somehow dealt with or they would undermine peace forever.[27]

The Peck subplot on one level is the comedic release valve to an otherwise dark story. But it is also Stegner's attempt to write back against Kesey, and to "somehow deal with" the rising counterculture he was witnessing on America's West Coast. There is no doubt Stegner deeply felt the threat of what Kesey and his followers stood for and the implications such a philosophy could have on American society and the landscapes in which they were embedded. Yet these values would largely be trampled underfoot by the rising mass of American writers whose "emancipation" from the old constraints had just begun.

Class of '58: Wendell Berry

Yet if Kesey was trampling upon these "Stegnerian" values as he sauntered on to the literary celebrity that eluded Stegner late in life, Wendell Berry

---

25. Intriguingly, this is the central theme of Pope Francis's encyclical *Laudato Si'* (2015). Social and ecological realities are embedded. The Pope, however, sides more with Wendell Berry by connecting both of these realities to the divine: If we don't properly love and know God, we won't know and love each other or the created world. Stegner would never make *that* move.

26. Stegner, "Excellence and the Pleasure Principle," 53.

27. Stegner, *All the Little Live Things*, 10.

proved to be a student who would quietly[28] and consistently take a stand for them.

As Berry has pointed out, Stegner (as a good teacher) refused to demand his creative writing students to believe what he believed: "He did not pontificate or indoctrinate or evangelize. [Students] were not expected to become Stegnerians."[29] Yet, Berry goes on, "although I do not think that Mr. Stegner thinks of himself as my teacher, my awareness of him as a teacher has grown over the years. And I think myself more than ever his student."[30]

After his 1958/1959 year as a Stegner Fellow, Berry followed the NYC route that respectable American writers who wanted to be a "somebody" were expected to travel. The years from 1959 to 1964 saw Berry and his wife Tanya travel and work in both Europe and New York City until Berry landed back at the University of Kentucky, returning to his native community in Kenucky's Henry County where he has lived and worked ever since.[31]

Of all Stegner's former pupils, Berry receives some of his teacher's highest praise and attention. In "The Sense of Place," for example, Stegner writes: "Berry is a writer, one of our best who belongs to an honourable tradition, one that even in America includes some great names: Thoreau, Burroughs, Frost, Faulkner, Steinbeck—lovers of the known earth, known weathers, and known neighbors both human and nonhuman."[32] While Stegner leaves his own name off this list, he is the obvious linchpin connecting Berry to this great community of American writers.

Given the trajectory of Berry's career since his time under Stegner's tutelage, it's hard to overstate the influence Stegner has had on the Kentucky man of letters. Berry is Stegner's protégé in so many ways: He has championed conservation and written beautifully in its defense; he has advocated for strong local communities and has lived in and cared for one his whole life; he practices the disciplines (or arts) of good farming that stem from a loving affection balanced by knowledge, humility, and restraint; and his realist fiction, published with a prodigiousness as daunting as his mentor's,

28. "Quietly" in the sense of not being a NYC sensation. No one who reads (or listens to) Berry would accuse him of lacking fire.

29. Berry, "Wallace Stegner", 52.

30. Ibid., 54.

31. The story of this is recounted in several of Berry's essays, but most notably in *The Long-Legged House*.

32. Stegner, "The Sense of Place."

has gained him a large following today. Echoing his teacher, Berry has raged against a world where everything is for sale and where the almost unstoppable powers of the State and the Economy[33] run roughshod over individuals. And he has lamented a world where people live so self-indulgently that they can bring Hell to Earth instead of turning it into a Heaven.

Stegner also modeled the courage of having unpopular convictions and not compromising those for the sake of literary acceptance. Perhaps it took Berry a few years to settle down and live into such a role himself, but Berry soon learned how to live precariously as a member of the literary establishment, not getting discouraged by disagreeing voices,[34] and never writing in search of adulation. Berry felt the sting of the NYC literary community for his choice to become a "regional" writer. But Berry also has stinging words for those NYC-based writers who "write so exploitively, condescendingly, and contemptuously of their regions and their people" that they become a catalyst for worse forms of exploitation and destruction. Such regionalists, Berry scoffs, write from their NYC offices without any real affection for the communities and places for whom they speak. By leaving the self-proclaimed center of the universe, Berry followed in Stegner's footsteps to become the type of regional writer "who does not only write about his region, but also does his best to protect it."[35]

Yet this defensive posture was one that could inhibit community. And Berry seems to have realized this more than Stegner. In a letter written in April of 1970 to Ed McClanahan,[36] Berry reflects on how "[t]hat class [at Stanford in 1958] failed to be any kind of meeting ground" and how "his own contribution to its failure was a scared conviction that life was a contest and that [he], having wandered out of [his] league, was about to get done in."[37] Yet the letter is also written by a man who has changed, who is now less guarded and defensive, more confident in his role as regional writer and Henry Country poet. That is, as one who craves the community

---

33. Often given "scare-capitals" in Berry's prose.

34. For an example of this charitable dialogue, I would recommend reading Berry's correspondence with Gary Snyder, another "hippie" Stegner wanted little to do with. These movingly charitable letters between very different writers can be found in Chad Wriglesworth's, *Distant Neighbors*.

35. "Wallace Stegner," 56–57.

36. This was written after Ed, Ken Kesey, and several of the "Merry Pranksters" went to Henry County to visit Berry at Lane's Landing.

37. Berry, "Kentucky River Junction, 70.

of those with whom he disagrees. In fact, he ends the letter by penning a beautiful poem to Kesey and the Pranksters in honour of their visit.[38]

But the risk Stegner faced in training his students to find their voice and cultivate independent thought that would challenge the status quo is that sometimes even the teacher becomes a target for some "uncomfortable" truths. And although Berry greatly respected his Stanford master, he had no reservations in taking Stegner's thought further and deeper. Despite their many similarities, Berry and Stegner differed radically. And if Stegner wrote *All the Little Live Things*, in part, to show the limits of Ken Kesey's individualism, there's an equally strong case to be made that Berry wrote *Jayber Crow*, in part, to show the limits of Stegner's humanism.

Reflecting on his year in Stanford, Berry recalls:

> One sunny afternoon he read us a piece of work of his own—a chapter, I think, from *All the Little Live Things*—and then graciously paid attention to all we said to him about it. I remember that I made an extensive comment myself, and I am tempted to wish I could remember what I said. Probably I should be glad to have forgotten. I would be glad, anyhow, to know that he has forgotten.[39]

We'll never know the critique the young Berry offered, but it seems that something about Stegner's work-in-progress stuck with him for many years; and I believe that Berry's thoughts (and dissatisfactions) with his teacher's book find their full articulation many years later in *Jayber Crow*. The high degree of structural and thematic similarity suggests that *Jayber Crow* is a sustained reflection on—and of—*All the Little the Live Things*.

Both novels are written from the perspective of an older man struggling to find membership, both socially and ecologically, in a place in which he was not born; both stories center upon a rather unconventional relationship between the elderly narrators and much younger women who become impossible objects of desire (for Jayber Crow it is Mattie Chatham, for Joe

---

38. To contrast Berry and Stegner, just listen to the reaction Stegner had upon reading Berry's poem to Kesey: "I got to your poem to Ken Kesey and Ken Babbs, and I said, in the idiom of my time, Shit, what can Wendell be thinking of, commemorating that garbage? He's too good to be raking around among that old two-holer privy. Then I thought, Maybe he's composting it. On that comfort I rest. But you stopped me reading, and I haven't got past that page. Prejudice, no doubt. But if it's really being composted, I forgive you." *The Selected Letters of Wallace Stegner*, edited by Page Stegner, 198.

39. "Wallace Stegner," 51.

Allston it is Marian Catlin[40]); both novels end with the untimely death of these women to cancer; and, finally, both stories reach their crisis point against a backdrop of ecological destruction, in each story the final scene involves the bulldozers of development destroying a pristine landscape that was of particular significance to the dying woman. Such blatant parallels, particularly in the last chapters, are just too uncanny to be coincidental.

Yet the primary divergence of Berry's text is that it provides a completely different attitude towards death than does Stegner's, and the reason for this can be traced to the differing beliefs of both writers.[41]

In his 1952 manifesto, "This I Believe," Stegner confesses that "About God I simply do not know; I don't think I can know. That limits my beliefs to the conduct of this life."[42] And a little further in the short essay, he confirms: "I believe in conscience, not as something implanted by divine act but as something learned since infancy from tradition and the society which has bred us. . . . I shall sometimes fail miserably to live up to my conscience, but I shall not mistrust its word, even when I can't obey it."[43] Stegner, in other words, is more a classical humanist and agnostic. For Stegner, the virtues he lived by need not rely on any sacred source, nor was there any judgment or afterlife for which one had to hope. His religion was very *this*-worldly.

And while this essay came earlier in his career, Stegner consistently maintained these views late into life. In one of the last pieces he wrote, a very moving letter to his deceased mother, Stegner maintains that despite wanting to, he can't believe she's in heaven, or that he'll ever be reunited to her there.[44] Stegner's world is one of absurd courage in the face of the nihilism death brings. It is more akin to Camus than to Kierkegaard.[45] In

40. Are the same "J" and "M.C." initials a coincidence? I'll let you decide.

41. In Kenneth Burke's famous essay, "Literature as Equipment for Living," he makes the claim that the purpose of fiction is to equip readers with strategies and attitudes that help us to live well. We learn what to love and cherish, and what to hate and despise. The truth of the parable is the truth of all literature: stories are equipment for living wisely in a time and a place. I think in both of these novels, though, Berry and Stegner are trying to provide us with "Equipment for Dying." For more on Berry's reflections about how to die well, see Ethan Mannon's essay in this collection, "The Gift of Good Death: Revising *Nathan Coulter.*"

42. Stegner, "This I Believe," 3.

43. Stegner, "This I Believe," 4.

44. Stegner, "Letter, Much Too Late."

45. Or, if we use one of the main intertexts of *Jayber Crow*: Stegner = Virgil; Berry = Dante.

his conversation with Richard Etulain, Stegner acknowledges the influence of Teilhard de Chardin's strictly materialistic conception of death on the novel. For Teilhard, death was merely the return of one's molecules back into the earth from which new life forms would grow and evolve.[46]

This is embodied in the seeming absurdity of Marian Catlin's death in *All the Little Live Things*—an absurdity compounded by the fact that as she is about to die, many of the central characters (Peck, Allston, Thomas) find themselves having to bludgeon a horse to death to put it out of its misery. Really, death is at the center of *All the Little Live Things*. Joe knows that keeping his place in the ecological community requires him to actively kill gophers and spray insecticides. That death brings life is no metaphysical mystery, it's communicated in the natural world all around us. As he explains to Marian, "You can't ignore the struggle for existence. There are good kinds of life and bad kinds of life." To which Marian rejoins: "Bad is what conflicts with your interest"[47] and then again, much later, "The same thing that's in a mushroom spore so small you need a microscope to see it, or in gophers, or poison oak, or anything else we try to pave under, or grub out, or poison. There isn't good life and bad life, there's only life. Think of the *force* down there, just telling things to get born!"[48] Marian is both pregnant and infected with cancer as she says this, and only after Marian and her unborn child die, can Allston finally manages a response:

> God is kind? Life is good? Nature never did betray the heart that loved her? Then why the parting that she had? Why the reward she received for living intensely and generously and trying to die with dignity? . . . I do not accept, I am not reconciled. . . . *Think of the force down there, just telling things to get born, just to be!* I had no answer for her then. Now I might have one. Yes, think of it, I might say. And think of how random and indiscriminate it is, think how helplessly we must submit, think how impossible it is to control or direct it.[49]

Yet if he could have the God-like power to do so, Allston is resolved that he would never choose to forego meeting Marian just to save himself the heartbreak of her passing. Marian Catlin's death has made his life richer.

---

46. Stegner and Etulain, *Conversations with Wallace Stegner*, 75.

47. *All the Little Live Things*, 64.

48. Ibid., 87.

49. Ibid., 343–344.

His pain and sorrow have also yielded wisdom and a new awe for the sacredness, beauty, and, ultimately, fragility of life.[50]

Wendell Berry, however, shows a decided dissatisfaction with Stegner's rather Manichean approach to life and death, good and evil. To live in such a way would be to give death the final word. For Berry, the world is not simply the forces of good and evil (life and death) battling it out indiscriminately, forcing humans to take a noble path of conduct in the face of whatever befalls them. Berry's fictional world is decidedly cast through a Christian lens. Death and evil in the world are never just matters of fact, but the twisting and breaking of what was once originally good. Humans, therefore, can choose to participate in evil, and perpetuate disease and death, or they can participate in life and work to recover the wholeness and holiness of the world. Of course, for the man of faith, the audacious hope in such goodness is often hard, if not impossible, to live by. It involves trust in something we can't fully see: "Faith," Jayber says near the end of his life, "puts you out on a wide river in a little boat, in the fog, in the dark."[51]

This changes the attitude toward life and death, but also toward good work, ecological preservation, and heroism in Berry's fiction.[52] In Stegner, death has the final say. Even while Joe Allston might have been made stronger in this life through the death of Marian, his death is also coming. And for him it will be final. Such finality, Berry knew, could lead to despair.

---

50. Stegner's views find an echo in Nietzsche's fragments on eternal recurrence, where he writes, "Your whole life, like a sandglass, will always be reversed and will ever run out again, —a long minute of time will elapse until all those conditions out of which you were evolved return in the wheel of the cosmic process. And then you will find every pain and every pleasure, every friend and every enemy, every hope and every error, every blade of grass and every ray of sunshine once more, and the whole fabric of things which make up your life. This ring in which you are but a grain will glitter afresh forever. And in every one of these cycles of human life there will be one hour where, for the first time one man, and then many, will perceive the mighty thought of the eternal recurrence of all things: —and for mankind this is always the hour of Noon." *Complete Works*, 250. Bernd Magnus and Kathleen Higgins argue that Nietzsche's talk of the eternal recurrence was more a thought experiment for living boldly in a world where God was dead. If you could, Nietzsche seems to ask, would you take all the pain and the suffering of your life and do it all again? For the person who has lived well, the answer should be an unreserved "yes!" (Magnus and Higgins, "Introduction to Nietzsche's Work," 8).

51. *Jayber Crow*, 356. Imagine Dante and Virgil rowing through the Inferno, and you'll catch the subtext.

52. I would recommend reading "Christianity and the Survival of Creation," or "Two Economies" to get a sense of how Berry's "enchanted" universe provides a radically different motivation for conservation than Stegner's.

And for this reason *Jayber Crow*, although it is also about the death and pain of losing a loved one (and a loved place), refuses to forego hope and is ultimately "a book about Heaven."[53]

Even though men like Troy Chatham, driven by lust and greed, will ascend in power; and even though well-stewarded farms and wilds will be bulldozed and razed for profit; and even though a virtuous woman like Mattie Chatham will die too soon; Berry's consolation is not simply in what such death does to the living, but in the hope that even death is a small circle within a greater one that is eternal life and light. Jayber writes:

> Listen. There is a light that includes our darkness, a day that shines down even on the clouds. A man of faith believes that the Man in the Well is not lost. He does not believe this easily or without pain, but he believes it. His belief is a kind of knowledge beyond any way of knowing. He believes that the child in the womb is not lost, nor is the man whose work has come to nothing, nor is the old woman forsaken in a nursing home in California. He believes that those who make their bed in Hell are not lost, or those who dwell in the uttermost parts of the sea, or the lame man at Bethesda Pool, or Lazarus in the grave, or those who pray, "*Eli, Eli, lama sabachtani.*"[54]

Such hope is nestled in a humility that there is ultimately more at work than the work of our hands. Even Stegner's faith and hope in virtuous conduct and a stoic apprehension of death only brings us so far. And while Berry rages against the forces of evil and misconduct presently at work in our industrialized age, he finds rest—albeit uneasy rest—in the faith that even our participation (willing or not) in diseased ways of thinking and acting are not beyond the scope of a God who wants it otherwise, has the power to make it so, and asks his followers to work, in faith and hope, accordingly.

Talent and Tradition

The current anxiety over whether MFA or NYC or both are wielding too much power over the American literary tradition today is perhaps an anxiety that is ultimately misplaced. As Berry's own maneuvering in and out of these worlds suggest, the (naïve) belief that better writing might be crafted in some new arrangement is next to impossible to prove. And Berry is far

53. *Jayber Crow*, 354.
54 Ibid., 357.

from some backwoods naif writing from his Kentucky shed. He is in community and communication with some of the leading writers and thinkers in America today, not to mention the whole "democracy of the dead"—Dante, Virgil, Eliot, Milton—who continue to influence his writing.

Would Berry's work have been better had he never attended Stanford? Would it have improved had he never traveled to NYC or Europe and developed literary friendships? We can't know the answer, but odds are his writing would be unrecognizable from what he's given us so far.

Writers have always required communities in which to dialogue with one another and infrastructures (with all their attendant gatekeepers) to disseminate those works. As a Christian Kentucky regionalist, Berry has managed to situate his talent within the American literary tradition, and only time and future generations will tell how significant that place actually is. But whether Berry reaches canonical status or not, the trajectory and scope of his work was not shaped despite the constraints of the Stanford classroom or the predilections of New York, but because of them. *Jayber Crow* is not the same novel without *All the Little Live Things*, and it even loses some of its vitality when it is not read against this backdrop. The same can be said of *One Flew Over the Cuckoo's Nest* in the context of the Stanford program. No writer and no text exist in isolation. And when we are able to understand the individual's place within the larger whole, we better grasp the ecological interdependence of this living, ever-changing tradition.

Bibliography

Benson, Jackson J. *Wallace Stegner: His Life and Work*. New York: Viking, 1996.

Berry, Wendell. "Kentucky River Junction: A Letter and a Poem." In *Spit in the Ocean: All about Ken Kesey*, edited by Ed McClanahan, 70–73. New York: Penguin, 2003.

———. *The Long-Legged House*. Berkeley: Counterpoint, 1969.

———. "Wallace Stegner and the Great Community." In *What are People For?* Berkeley: Counterpoint, 1999.

Berry, Wendell and Gary Snyder. *Distant Neighbors: The Selected Letters of Wendell Berry and Gary Snyder*. Edited by Chad Wriglesworth. Berkeley: Counterpoint, 2014.

Burke, Kenneth. "Literature as Equipment for Living." In *The Philosophy of Literary Form*, 293–304. Berkeley: University of California Press, 1973.

Harbach, Chad, ed. *MFA vs NYC: The Two Cultures of American Fiction*. New York: Faber and Faber, 2010.

Magnus, Bernd and Kathleen M. Higgins. "Introduction to Nietzsche's Work." In *The Cambridge Companion to Nietzsche*. Cambridge: Cambridge University Press, 1996.

McGurl, Mark. *The Program Era: Postwar Fiction and the Rise of Creative Writing*, Cambridge: Harvard University Press, 2011.

Nietzsche, Friedrich Wilhelm. *Complete Works.* Edited by Oscar Levy. Translated by Anthony M. Ludovici. Vol. 16. Edinburgh: T. N. Foulis, 1911.

Stegner, Page ed. *The Selected Letters of Wallace Stegner.* Berkeley: Counterpoint, 2007.

Stegner, Wallace. *All the Little Live Things.* New York: Penguin, 1962.

———. "Excellence and the Pleasure Principle." In *One Way to Spell Man.* New York: Doubleday, 1982.

———. "Letter, Much Too Late." In *Where the Bluebird Sings to the Lemonade Springs: Living and Writing in the West.* New York: Random House, 2002.

———. "The Sense of Place." In *Where the Bluebird Sings to the Lemonade Springs: Living and Writing in the West.* New York: Random House, 2002.

———. "This I Believe." In *One Way to Spell Man.* New York: Doubleday & Co., 1982.

———. "Wilderness Letter," The Wilderness Society, accessed 21 Nov. 2016, http://www.colorado.edu/AmStudies/lewis/west/wilderletter.pdf.

Stegner, Wallace, and Richard W. Etulain. *Conversations with Wallace Stegner: On Western History and Literature.* Revised Edition. Salt Lake City: University of Utah Press, 1990.

PART 2: Beauty's Instructions

5

Andy Catlett's Missing Hand
Making Do as Wounded Members

Jeffrey Bilbro

ANDY CATLETT IS THE most autobiographical character in Wendell Berry's fictional Port William. Both Andy and Berry were born in 1934, both have fathers who practice law on behalf of farmers, both graduate in 1956 and marry the following year, both leave Kentucky and become writers, both return in 1964 to cultivate marginal farms.[1] Yet one rather glaring difference between the two stands out: Andy loses his right hand to a corn picker in 1974 while Berry still has the full use of both his hands. Berry cautions readers against identifying his "fictional characters with actual people," but

I am indebted to the Issachar Fund Writer's Retreat for the time and space to write this essay and to Joe Wiebe for his thoughtful comments on an earlier draft.

1. Bernard Baker traces these parallels most explicitly: "the parallels between Andy Catlett's life and Berry's own are unmistakable. Both are born in 1934 in rural Kentucky to a father who is a lawyer; they each have a brother . . . who will join in the father's practice; they both graduate college in 1956, marry in 1957, and then move to urban areas, making their livings by writing. Both return home in 1964 with their wives and two children, buy a small run-down farm and begin to re-claim it. They re-discover their links to tradition and community and find in their farming a clearer vision which informs their writing. Both become uncompromising critics of American economic policies which devalue life as they see it" ("Responsibly at Home," 170 n. 11). See also Janet Goodrich, *The Unforeseen Self in the Works of Wendell Berry*, 74–75; Jason. Peters, "Imagination and the Limits of Fiction," lxxxvi–lxxxvii; Eric T. Freyfogle, *Agrarianism and the Good Society*, 141; P. Travis Kroeker, "Sexuality and the Sacramental Imagination," 123. In a personal conversation, Berry referred to one of the Andy Catlett stories, "Andy Catlett's Early Education," as mostly autobiographical.

given the parallels between his own life and Andy's, this missing hand remains conspicuous.[2] Despite the seeming significance of Andy's maimed limb, after the short novel *Remembering*, which revolves around Andy's struggle to accept the loss of his hand, none of the many Port William stories narrated by Andy mention his disability.[3]

In his 2015 short story "Dismemberment," however, Berry returns to the subject of Andy's lost right hand, framing its significance in ways that indicate the parallel wound Berry himself bears. Andy comes to see his various prosthetic devices as symbolizing the "inescapable dependence of the life of the country and his neighborhood upon mechanical devices." Berry goes on to develop this metaphor in ways that clearly apply not only to Andy and Berry, but also to all of us who live in a modern economy:

> The absence of his right hand has remained with him as a reminder. His most real hand, in a way, is the missing one, signifying to him not only his continuing need for ways and devices to splice out his right arm, but also his and his country's dependence upon the structure of industrial commodities and technologies that imposed itself upon, and contradicted in every way, the sustaining structures of the natural world and its human memberships. And so he is continually reminded of his incompleteness within himself, within the terms and demands of his time and its history, but also within the constraints and limits of his kind, his native imperfection as a human being, his failure to be as attentive, responsible, grateful, loving, and happy as he ought to be.
>
> He has spent most of his life in opposing violence, waste, and destruction—or trying to, his opposition always fragmented and made painful by his complicity in what he opposes.[4]

Andy's maimed arm makes visible a wound that he and his community already carried—their dependence on industrial technologies that exacerbate their "native imperfection[s]." This is a wound we all share: even if, like Berry and Andy, we strive to live in healthy, sustainable ways, we remain complicit in systems we oppose. But the ways that Andy learns to "splice out" his right arm offer insight into how we can learn to make do as wounded members of a diseased world.

2. "Imagination in Place," 3.

3. One story even seems to imply that Andy still has his right hand, although the reference is somewhat ambiguous. See Bilbro, "The Ecology of Memory," 341 n. 10.

4. Berry, "Dismemberment."

In what follows, I reflect on how the metaphors Berry develops in "Dismemberment" might help us imagine ways of making do in spite of our dependence on and complicity in these systems. Through his story, Berry responds to the two most common critiques of his vision. The first critique is that he is self-righteous or impractical: just because he's managed to live a sustainable, agrarian life, he preaches that everyone else should be like him. The second is that he nostalgically desires society to return to a simpler time (one that never actually existed) when humans lived in harmony with each other and with nature.

Berry responds to these critiques by imagining how we might "make do," a phrase I use to indicate two overlapping senses. First, in its common usage, to make do simply means to get by, to make do with what we have. The French Jesuit scholar Michel de Certeau adds another facet to this phrase in his book *The Practice of Everyday Life*. For Certeau, making do means to subvert a system oriented toward control and mechanization, using its structures to serve more healthy, life-giving ends. These two senses of making do correspond to Berry's twin responses to his critics: he imagines Andy, himself, and all of us as maimed people who have to learn how to get by in our wounded state. Furthermore, he imagines how people like Danny Branch, Andy's faithful friend, don't seek to return to some simpler time so much as they learn to creatively make do—in Certeau's sense—with the implements of an unjust system, finding subversive ways to tend the health of their places.

Berry has received plenty of criticism, as should be expected by any writer who takes unpopular, counter-cultural stands. In principle, he welcomes disagreement. As he writes in one essay, "If you tell me, dear reader, that you agree with me completely, then I must suspect one or both of us of dishonesty."[5] However, many of the criticisms leveled at Berry's ideas misapprehend his claims, often because they respond only to his essays and fail to consider the additional perspectives that his poetry and fiction provide.

One such critique is that Berry's vision is impractical and that he himself is hypocritical or self-righteous. Among those who find him hypocritical, Bruce Bawer caustically summarizes Berry's work, "Proprietor of a Kentucky farm that's been in his family for generations, Berry has produced an *oeuvre* (novels, short stories, nonfiction) whose central conviction is that the optimum lifestyle choice for *homo sapiens* is—ahem—running a farm

---

5. Berry, "Preface: The Joy of Sales Resistance," xix.

that's been in your family for generations."[6] Andy Crouch similarly claims that "the moral force of [Berry's] anti-technological vision is undercut by internal contradictions." He goes on to explain that "Berry, famously, does not own a computer, but he seems untroubled by the machine-readable bar codes on the back of his own books. And if I, unlike Berry, have no patrimony in rural Kentucky to retire to and tend with my hands, what do I do? A poet, not a philosopher, Berry has little to say about these problems."[7] Even those who don't think Berry himself is hypocritical find his agrarian vision impractical. Ursula Heise states local agriculture is "not [a] viable path" for most Americans, and she argues that Berry and other proponents of small-scale, local change are naive to think local solutions are adequate in a globalizing world.[8]

These are indeed serious charges, or they would be if they were accurate. As Berry points out in a reply to Bawer, he and his wife did not inherit their farm, and, more to the point, Berry has repeatedly urged young people *not* to go into farming given the challenges that the current farming economy poses.[9] Beyond these factual errors, the central question remains: are Berry's apparently uncompromising, extreme positions on technologies like computers and tractors realistic in our modern world? Andy Catlett's struggle to learn how to relate to his wounded right arm may provide insight into this question.

When Andy was wounded, he refused to "get over the loss of his hand" and desperately sought some "prosthetic device" that would make him whole again: "He was forever trying to piece himself whole by mechanical contrivances and devices thought up in the night, which by day more often than not would fail, because of some unforeseen complication or some impossibility obvious in daytime. He worked at and with the stump of his arm as if it were inanimate, tying tools to it with cords, leather straps, rubber straps, or using it forthrightly as a blunt instrument."[10] But all these attempts

6. "Civilized Pleasures," 143. I'm grateful to Joe Wiebe for sending me a list of critical responses to Berry he has compiled, which included Bawer's review.

7. Crouch, "Eating the Supper."

8. Heise, *Sense of Place* 48. Ketey Castellano—who is otherwise sympathetic to Berry—parallels this line of thought: "Clearly, the vast majority of Americans do not have a family farm to which they might return, and in this way Berry's agrarian practice is rooted in white privilege" ("Romantic Conservatism," 86).

9. In addition to his reply to Bawer—Berry, "Letter to the Editor," 525—see also Berry, "The Making of a Marginal Farm," 338; Berry, "The Whole Horse," 121; Berry, "Nature as an Ally."

10. "Dismemberment." Berry's metaphorical link between technology and Andy's

fail. It is only when he accepts his wound and accommodates himself to the new limits it imposes on him that Andy learns to make do: "So long as he regarded it as merely a tool, as merely a hook or a claw or weak pliers, he used it readily and quietly enough." If we look to the wonders of modern industry to make us whole, if we think that Facebook and FaceTime will provide deep community, that Google will enable us to remember everything needful, that UPS or FedEx can deliver whatever we want to our front door, that some new social program will magically fix our culture's racial or economic divisions, we are doomed to frustration. In other words, if we idolize modern industry, thinking it will bring about the New Jerusalem, we will find ourselves, like Andy, isolated within "the hardened carapace of his self." If, however, we accept these "wonders" as mere tools, we can learn to make do with them.

This is essentially the point Berry makes in his essay "Why I Am Not going to Buy a Computer"; computers are just tools.[11] They won't make us suddenly write better. Humans have used styli, quills, pencils, and typewriters to write good books and bad books, and the computer won't magically enable us to write masterpieces. If I am frustrated by my inability to articulate my thoughts in clear words, it is probably not due to any fault in my writing implements but to my own limitations.[12] As Berry writes about chainsaws, a modern technology that he does use, "I knew a man who, in the age of chainsaws, went right on cutting his wood with a handsaw and an axe. He was a healthier and saner man than I am. I shall let his memory trouble my thoughts."[13] Thus Berry's uncompromising stands on particular issues, like not buying a computer, function as examples that should trouble those of us—like myself—who do use computers. As Berry puts it in a letter to Gary Snyder about using tractors and chemicals in farming,

---

prosthetic hand may draw on Marshall McLuhan's interpretation of technologies as "extensions" of our bodies in *Understanding Media*.

11. Berry, "Why I Am Not Going to Buy a Computer," 170–77.

12. Ethan Mannon offers a similar response to critics (like White, "'Are You an Environmentalist or Do You Work For a Living?,'" 171–85) who claim Berry praises archaic farming practices while demonizing modern tools. Mannon demonstrates that "Berry does not uniformly celebrate archaic labor; nor does he automatically criticize contemporary agriculture because it utilizes modern technology. . . . Berry levels his ultimate critique . . . not at technology per se, but at capitalism's intrusion into an arena (agriculture) that should be informed by natural limits rather than focused solely on market production. . . . The technology Troy uses is but a symptom of his flawed way of thinking" ("Leisure and Technology," 185).

13. Berry, "Feminism," 196.

"All right, I think, to look on compromise as a necessity; dangerous to make it a virtue."[14] Berry's extreme stances, then, remind us that all those devices we think are so necessary can never make us whole; they are only tools, and we remain most in need of those virtues that humans have always struggled to practice, "attenti[on], responsib[ility], grat[itude], lov[e]."

Learning such virtues is an ongoing process; we can't strap on gratitude like a new prosthetic hand. Four times in this brief story Andy relates an emotion or experience that he says made him "better": he laughs at his clumsiness, he weeps in tender affection for his patient horses, he accepts the help of his neighbors, he repents of his shame and self-imposed loneliness. Each of these events makes him "better," but none of them cures him. Berry articulates this ongoing process by distinguishing between being healed and being whole: "[Andy] became, containing his losses, healed, though never again would he be whole." To adapt a phrase from Jayber Crow's professor, Dr. Ardmire, Andy is learning to live out his wound a little at a time, and this process may take the rest of his life or even longer.[15]

The process of healing is never complete; Andy will always be wounded. This is perhaps the most important point missed by those who find Berry to be self-righteous or impractical. Berry does not claim that by being a small-scale farmer or installing solar panels outside his home he can somehow escape the moral quandaries of an unjust economy. As Andy realizes, his missing hand signifies the ways in which he is wounded by and dependent on the industrial technologies that he opposes. Andy lost his hand to a corn picker, an emblem of mechanized farming, and the various prosthetics he relies on are products of modern manufacturing. We are all wounded by and implicated in injustice, and no individual efforts to work

14. The context of this quote is Berry's response to Snyder about whether he would be justified in buying a tractor: "I regret tractors . . . [They can], however, be well used. . . . I'm dependent on a tractor myself to get my hay baled, and occasionally for some other purpose. I don't expect it to be immediately clear how to get altogether free of these dependences. If you see a way to improve your land by use of a machine, I say use it! I'd say the same thing to anyone wondering about using chemical nitrogen to start a grass cover on a starved or strip-mined hillside. . . . To get 'organic' phosphate and potash I'd have to order a carload to get a little. So later this summer I'll top dress some alfalfa fields with chemical P and K. It's a trap I hope to work my way out of but it'll take a while. That's compromising with the enemy, dragging our skirts in the mire, etc. But how are we going to escape that and *do* much of anything? . . . All right, I think, to look on compromise as a necessity; dangerous to make it a virtue." Berry and Snyder, *Distant Neighbors*, 62–63. See also Berry's essay on the moral complexity around the issue of growing tobacco, "The Problem of Tobacco," 53–68.

15. Berry, *Jayber Crow*, 54.

toward healing—foregoing a computer or planting a garden or biking to work or shopping at a farmer's market—absolves us of our complicity. Too often we make sustainable, healthy choices in one area of our lives and use those to make us feel good about ourselves. This doesn't mean we should stop trying to be whole—Andy works creatively to do the best he can with only one hand—but it does mean that though we may experience healing now, we will only truly be whole in the eschaton.

Andy thus embodies a difficult paradox. He learns to get by and make do with only one hand; as the title of one of Berry's essays has it, he "thinks little," patiently and creatively finding ways to serve the health of his place.[16] At the same time, however, he refuses to accept his maimed state as normal; his absent right hand reminds him of the wholeness toward which he yearns. Andy's fumbling efforts to tend his farm may not be what Heise considers a "viable path," but all too often those who propose large solutions are just looking for the next big technology that will magically make us whole.[17] They are like Andy in the early days after his accident, when his "mode . . . was force" and he insisted on "trying to piece himself whole by mechanical contrivances and devices." As Andy painfully learned, it is indeed impractical to farm with only one hand. And yet this is the difficult position in which Berry and those who would tend health find themselves.

Although Andy knows he will never be whole this side of heaven, he still longs for wholeness. It is this longing, a longing that permeates Berry's writing, that has been taken by some readers to be a nostalgic longing for a supposedly simpler past that was, in fact, oppressive and unjust.[18] This critique is articulated by authors such as Jack Kirby, who terms Berry a "sentimentalist," Tamara Hill Murphy who labels Port William "idyllic," and Lawrence Buell, who calls Berry's allegiance to family values . . . almost Norman Rockwellishly" mainstream.[19] In the words of another critic,

16. Berry, "Think Little," 71–85.

17. I offer an extended critique of this large-scale thinking in "Sublime Failure," 133–58.

18. In his essay in this volume, Jack Baker positions Berry's fiction within the *ubi sunt* tradition to provide a fuller response to those who see Berry's fiction as nostalgic.

19. Kirby, "Rural Culture," 592; Murphy, "The Hole in Wendell Berry's Gospel: Why the Agrarian Dream Is Not Enough"; Buell, *Writing for an Endangered World,* 159. Buell goes on to make the rather absurd claim that "Berry's beloved community is . . . homogenous . . . in every sense: culturally, religiously, economically" (*Writing,* 166). This is patently false, and Buell may have avoided this blunder if he engaged with Berry's fiction; both *Writing for an Endangered World* and *The Future of Environmental Criticism* cite only Berry's essays and (briefly) poetry. For my response to Murphy's essay—which is

"Berry's neo-Jeffersonian utopia" may be fine for white males, but it would likely generate an exodus of "escapees from oppressive rural communities, be they female, black, gay, Jewish, short on piety or keen on anonymity."[20] Such critics worry that Berry wants to sidestep the complex problems of our modern world by returning to some prior moment when things were better: if we could just return to the time before tractors, the time before freeways, the time before computers, the time before x, then everything would be right again.

After his wound, Andy initially succumbs to this simplistic nostalgia, believing that if he just had two hands again, everything would be all right. Yet he eventually realizes that his problems run deeper than the loss of his hand. His physical wound forces Andy to confront the wounds that had already dismembered his community, his family, and his soul. Rather than longing to return to his pre-accident state, he must learn to hope for an eschatological wholeness that can guide his efforts to make do with his broken body in a broken world.

Not only are we, like Andy, wounded, but we have never been whole. If many white Americans have been able to convince themselves that their communities were not seriously wounded, the black members of our communities are painfully aware of the injustices that maim our country. In his book *The Hidden Wound*, Berry traces how racism, like our infatuation with labor-saving technologies, stems from a dualism that devalues physical work. And not only the body politic, but each individual member is damaged by this "historical wound," a wound that Berry admits "is in me, as complex and deep in my flesh as blood and nerves."[21] In trying to live out the questions that surround this wound, Berry turns for guidance to the black people with whom he grew up. In spite of the unjust system in which they lived, they found creative ways to make do: "In the country, most blacks were skilled in the arts of make-do and subsistence. If most of them were poor, they were competently poor."[22] In her book recounting her return to Kentucky, bell hooks cites this passage approvingly and notes that

specifically about his fiction and yet relies on a selective misreading of it—see Bilbro, "Does Wendell Berry Have Rose-Colored Glasses?" For a defense of nostalgia as a longing that can lead to ethical action, see Ladino, *Reclaiming Nostalgia*, 55–56.

20. Garrard, *Ecocriticism*, 125. For more extended arguments responding to the charge that Berry's vision is inherently patriarchal, see Smith, "Wendell Berry's Feminist Agrarianism," 623–46; Bilbro, "The Eros of Child and Cupid," 287–308.

21. Berry, *The Hidden Wound*, 3–4.

22. Ibid., 115.

her grandparents had a similar view of competent, self-sufficient work as "humanizing." Like Andy, these black community members were maimed and wounded by an unjust system, and yet they found ways to cultivate health "on the margins."[23]

These African-Americans clearly have no simple, idyllic past to which they would want to return; as the negro spirituals have it, hope lies beyond the Jordan. Similarly, Berry's vision of shalom lies not in the past but in the eschaton. This is why Berry adamantly opposes sentimental portrayals of agrarian communities; they reduce the real complexity of rural life and render farmers passive. Berry responds to one critic who claims that advocates for small-scale farming are guilty "of a false nostalgia for an idyllic life never experienced" by arguing against all reductive stereotypes:

> The sentimental stereotype is just as damaging as the negative one. The image of the farmer as the salt of the earth, independent son of the soil, and child of nature is a sort of lantern slide projected over the image of the farmer as simpleton, hick, or redneck. Both images serve to obliterate any concept of farming as an ancient, useful, honorable vocation, requiring admirable intelligence and skill, a complex local culture, great patience and endurance, and moral responsibilities of the gravest kind.[24]

Similarly, Andy must struggle to avoid sentimentalizing his past, two-handed existence. Eventually, his once-whole body becomes a dim symbol of the wholeness he desires for his entire community. As Berry writes about Andy's development, "From the memory and a sort of foreknowledge of wholeness, after he had grown sick enough finally of his grieving over himself, he chose to heal." Andy longs for his body to be restored, but he also knows that will not happen in this life. Andy's healthy nostalgia longs for home, for wholeness, for shalom even while it knows such health is unrealizable this side of heaven.[25]

Berry depicts this "foreknowledge of wholeness" through Andy's heavenly visions of Port William as it will be, redeemed and made whole.[26]

23. hooks, *Belonging*, 180, 194.

24. Berry, "The Prejudice Against Country People," 109–110. Berry also responds to the charge that his work is nostalgic in "The Whole Horse," 119.

25. This healthy nostalgia seems akin to *saudades*, the Brazilian term that Eric Miller reflects on in his essay in this volume.

26. Andy is not the only member of Port William to receive a consoling vision of future wholeness. In her essay in this volume, Ingrid Pierce explores the significance of these visions at greater length.

Several of Berry's characters experience such visions, and Berry describes Andy's version of this dream in "Dismemberment":

> He saw a vision in a dream. It was much the same as Hannah Coulter's vision of Heaven, as she would come to tell him of it in her old age: "Port William with all its loved ones come home alive." In his dream he saw the past and the future of Port William, of what Burley Coulter had called its membership, struggling through time to belong together, all gathered into a presence of itself that was greater than itself. And he saw that this—in its utterly surprising greatness, utterly familiar—he had been given as a life. Within the abundance of the gift of it, he saw that he was small, almost nothing, almost lost, invisible to himself except as he had been visible to the others who have been with him.

Rather than locating his vision of health in some past state, Andy longs for a future wholeness that has not yet come. This is the heavenly vision that he witnesses at the end of *Remembering*, a vision of his community gathered and redeemed in divine love.[27] And Andy's body is itself made whole in this vision as he reaches out "the restored right hand of his joy" to reconnect himself with his beloved place and community.

This eschatological hope of redemption gives Andy strength to set about doing the small things he can do to tend the health of his community. When Andy experiences his heavenly vision at the end of *Remembering*, he doesn't want to stay. Rather, he desires to return to Port William as it is now and serve it as best he can in his brokenness; he senses that he "is not to stay. Grieved as he may be to leave them, he must leave. He *wants* to leave. He must go back with his help, such as it is, and offer it."[28] In this way, Andy's efforts to make do flow from his hope for a future redemption. Rooted in a love for the perfect shalom of his redeemed home, Andy and the other members of Port William learn to adapt to the wounded conditions of their real places.

By not immanentizing this vision and locating it in some particular historical moment, Andy resists the temptation to believe that he and his community have ever achieved this wholeness or can achieve it soon. They may be healed, but until the heavenly vision is realized they will not be made whole. As Hannah Coulter learns through the course of her many

---

27. For two excellent considerations of this divine, redemptive love in *Remembering*, see Donnelly, "Biblical Convocation," 275–96, and Kroeker, "Sexuality and the Sacramental Imagination," 119–36.

28. Berry, *Remembering*, 102.

disappointments, we must not allow "our hopes to become expectations."[29] Andy's example, then, calls us to practice hopeful work without any reasonable expectation of success. Andy is not optimistic, a feeling based on calculating odds of success, but rather hopeful, a virtue rooted in an eschatological faith whose consolation leads to good work done now. Optimism leads to expectations, and when these expectations are not fulfilled, despair follows. Hope, on the other hand, leads to faithful, patient work.[30] All too often, movements and organizations are based on expectations of success; while such movements may foster good work, if their members are motivated by optimistic expectations, they are almost certain to burn out in a few years.[31] John Leax fleshes out this important distinction between hope and optimism: "Hope is not optimism, for optimism is easy and hope is difficult. To imagine Port William as an ideal world or an agrarian paradise to be somehow established in suburban America is to misunderstand it entirely. It is to skip the suffering that every character in Port William endures."[32] Andy's maimed right arm will not allow him to

29. Berry, *Hannah Coulter*, 139. Jayber Crow professes a similar hope against hope when he concludes his parable of the "Man in the Well" by writing that a man of faith "believes that those who make their bed in Hell are not lost, or those who dwell in the uttermost parts of the sea, or the lame man at Bethesda Pool, or Lazarus in the grave, or those who pray, '*Eli, Eli, lama sabachthani.*'" *Jayber Crow*, 357.

30. This hope is akin to the faith and hope Kierkegaard ascribes to Abraham in *Fear and Trembling*. Abraham's hope was based not on any rational "calculation"—what Berry might call an expectation—but was rather a "faith by virtue of the absurd" that God would somehow rescue Isaac. Kierkegaard, *Fear and Trembling/Repetition*, 36. Alan Noble explores a related conjunction of absurd hope and gritty making do in his reading of *The Road*, "The Absurdity of Hope."

31. Thus, while I am sympathetic to Eric Freyfogle's desire for more rapid, systemic changes, I think Berry is right to insist on hope rather than optimistic expectations, on thinking little rather than joining movements. Freyfogle sees these tactics as fundamentally mistaken: "A common complaint against Berry and others is that they are nostalgic in wanting to restore a lost order. But the flaw here, again, is not chiefly in the aims they seek but rather in the means they propose to achieve them. Calls for individual moral reform are just not going to get us there, or anywhere close." "Wendell Berry and the Limits," 187–88. In his book, where he expands on his argument, he calls for "an activist community visionary" to apply Berry's ideas to making systemic changes (*Agrarianism and the Good Society*, 145). The community activists that Freyfogle envisions do important, necessary work, but they remain unlikely to defeat the multinational, big-money interests arrayed against them. So although Freyfogle seems to demand wholeness now, as Andy learns, such a demand dooms one to frustration and anger when change proves elusive. This is why Berry envisions a membership of neighbors creatively making do within a damaged system.

32. Leax, "Memory and Hope," 73.

forget the suffering that he and his community experience, and in the midst of this suffering he learns to practice the difficult virtue of hope and to work toward the re-membering of his community. Andy's eschatological hope orients his wounded life toward the difficult, slow work of shalom.

At the end of "Dismemberment," Berry articulates this movement from a hope without expectation to the patient, creative work of making do. While Andy and his friend Danny Branch may be the last of the Port William membership, they continue to shape the next generation through their stories and their work. They "secretly pray [that] they may be among the first of a time yet to come, when Port William will be renewed, again settled and flourishing. They anyhow are links between history and possibility, as they keep the old stories alive by telling them to their children." Like Hannah, they know better than to expect that another generation will make a living in their place, but they share the old stories in hope, keeping the redemptive vision of a Port William membership alive in the hearts of the next generation.

Andy and Danny don't just tell stories, however, they also set to work doing the best they can:

> Sometimes, glad to have their help needed, they go to work with their children. . . . But sometimes only the two old men work together, asking and needing no help but each other's. . . . And after so many years they know how to work together, the one-handed old man and the two-handed. They know as one what the next move needs to be. They are not swift, but they don't fumble. They don't waste time assling around, trying to make up their minds. They never make a mislick.
>
> "Between us," says Danny Branch, "we've got three hands. Everybody needs at least three. Nobody ever needed more."

Andy and Danny aren't whole—they don't have a full quota of four hands between them—but they don't let their old and compromised bodies prevent them from doing the good work they can do. In modeling the creative work of making do, they refuse to acquiesce passively either to their aging and wounded bodies or to the broken economy which has leeched the younger generation away from Port William. They resist the temptation to which Andy once succumbed when he hammered angrily and futilely at the industrial economy, insisting on making it whole. Rather, they find creative, inventive ways of making do within the constraints of this system.

This is the mode of making do that Certeau celebrates, a mode that works toward health in the midst of a broken system. In contrast to Michel

Foucault, who charts the ever-tightening grip of the disciplinary society, Certeau is interested in tracing the "tricky and stubborn procedures that elude discipline without being outside the field in which it is exercised, and which should lead us to a theory of everyday practices, of lived space."[33] These practices are not motivated by an expectation that the systems within which we are implicated will be made whole. Instead, Certeau explains, "The actual order of things is precisely what 'popular' tactics turn to their own ends, without any illusion that it will change any time soon. Though elsewhere it is exploited by a dominant power or simply denied by an ideological discourse, here order is *tricked* by an art."[34] Even if the system doesn't change, we can still find creative ways to work toward justice and health. Berry's stories are full of such creative tactics: think of Burley Coulter giving a lit dynamite stick to the game warden, who must then throw it into the pond, killing the fish himself in order to avoid being injured; or think of Tol Proudfoot getting back at the rude store owner by making a bet that authorizes him to jump on a basket of eggs; or think of the way the Port William membership foils Detective Kyle Bode and prevents him from finding evidence that Danny has "kidnapped" his father from the hospital.[35] Such episodes recall the trickster tradition in African-American stories and model a way of resisting a dominant, unjust culture. In fact, the image of Burley's friends standing together to foil Detective Bode may be inspired by Ernest Gaines's novel *A Gathering of Old Men*, in which the community subverts the efforts of Sheriff Mapes to identify the man who killed Beau Boutan.[36] In all of these examples, marginalized communities find ways to trick a rigged system. And these artful acts of subversion are simply the exclamation points on well-formed lives of creative opposition.

Certeau argues that such subversive practices require both artistic skill and a kind of hopeful joy: "People have to make do with what they have. In these combatants' stratagems, there is a certain art of placing one's blows, a pleasure in getting around the rules of a constraining space. We see the

---

33. Certeau, *The Practice of Everyday Life*, 96. Certeau's notion of making do shares some similarities with the hacking culture; both creatively subvert dominant structures to serve other ends. But whereas much hacking is done for personal gain, Andy and Danny make do for the good of the community, what Ivan Illich would call conviviality.

34. Ibid., 26.

35. Berry, *Nathan Coulter [Revised]*, 86–88; "The Lost Bet," in *That Distant Land*, 137–44; "Fidelity," in *That Distant Land*, 372–427.

36. Wendell Berry and Ernest Gaines were classmates together at Stanford, and Berry expresses his admiration for Gaines in several places. See, for example, "American Imagination and the Civil War," 36–38. See also hooks, *Belonging*, 186–187.

tactical and joyful dexterity of the mastery of a technique."[37] Certeau clarifies that these artistic tactics, these "diversionary practice[s]," do not come from "nostalgia" or "melancholy," which are alternative responses to an unjust, constraining system.[38] Those who, like Andy and Danny, find themselves within a broken economy may be tempted to passive melancholy or easy nostalgia, but Certeau and Berry point to more hopeful, joyful ways of making do. Such practices "introduce *artistic* tricks and competitions of *accomplices* into a system that reproduces and partitions through work or leisure. Sly as a fox and twice as quick: there are countless ways of 'making do.'"[39] Certeau's analogy here echoes, almost certainly unconsciously, the famous conclusion of Berry's "Manifesto: The Mad Farmer Liberation Front":

> As soon as the generals and the politicos
> can predict the motions of your mind,
> lose it. Leave it as a sign
> to mark the false trail, the way
> you didn't go. Be like the fox
> who makes more tracks than necessary,
> some in the wrong direction.
> Practice resurrection.[40]

The image of a wily fox—perhaps alluding to the medieval trickster Reynard—tracing unexpected paths calls for an artistic approach to life.[41] Making do is fundamentally an artistic tactic, creatively subverting a mechanized system that threatens to make us hopeless in the face of its "radical monopolies."[42]

If Andy learns to make do in the more common sense of the phrase—to get by with the use of only one hand, to make do with what he has—his friend Danny is the master of making do in Certeau's more particular sense. In his quiet, humorous way, Danny works to beat industrialism's

---

37. Certeau, *The Practice of Everyday Life*, 18.

38. Ibid., 27.

39. Ibid., 29.

40. Berry, *New Collected Poems*, 174.

41. While Br'er Fox is the antagonist of Br'er Rabbit in the African-American oral tradition, Reynard the Fox is the trickster figure in a medieval cycle of tales.

42. This is a phrase Ivan Illich coins to refer to the way that once a solution becomes industrialized, it's almost impossible to opt out. *Energy and Equity*, 46–47.

swords into plowshares, its spears into pruning hooks. Berry expands on Danny's methods in another recently published and as yet uncollected short story, "The Branch Way of Doing." This story begins where "Dismemberment" leaves off, with Andy and Danny working together in their old age. Andy reflects on Danny's life, remarking that Danny "has never been a conventional man."[43] Like his father Burley, whom Berry compares to "a well-running red fox," Danny leads a life that evades the expectations of an industrial economy. Danny and his wife "seem to have understood from the start that they would have to make a life together that would be determinedly marginal to the modern world and its economy." Yet in spite of their unconventional ways—or maybe because of them—their children and grandchildren have taken up residence around Port William, carrying on the family's creative, marginal mode of life.

The Branches are not disgruntled at having to lead marginal lives. They don't wish for better farms or more money. Rather, Andy perceives "some profound motive of good will, even of good cheer, that shows itself mainly in their practice of their kind of economy." They practice the "joyful dexterity" that Certeau identifies as the root of making do. Andy summarizes the principles of the Branch's economy in nine instructions, which include: "1 — Be happy with what you've got. Don't be always looking for something better. . . . 6 — If other people want to buy a lot of new stuff and fill up the country with junk, *use* the junk." Instead of passively purchasing and consuming the products of an industrial economy, the Branches find creative, inventive ways to make do along the margins of this system.

While many readers will find Berry's vision of hopefully making do inadequate to the scope of our environmental and economic problems, his fictional portrayal of Andy and Danny provides a response to the critiques some have posed to his agrarian vision. Andy's missing hand—and the analogous wounds it signifies both in Andy's life and, by extension, in Berry's and our own—reminds us that we are all wounded by the systemic problems of our modern economy; there is no escape into some idyllic wholeness. Thus, rather than desiring to return to some simpler past time, Andy and Danny find creative, marginal ways of doing good work where they are. Andy does not allow his wound to make him nostalgic for some easier past, and Danny does not allow the broken economy in which he finds himself to render him passive and discouraged. In this way, they each

43. Berry, "The Branch Way of Doing."

model ways of making do; they are wounded members who hopefully tend the health of a damaged place.

It may be easier to cast stones at Wendell Berry for not living up to the ideals he espouses than it is to recognize the ways in which we are all dependent on systems we oppose. But Berry's imaginative vision calls us first of all to stop trying to evade our wounded condition. Andy "maintain[s] a discomfort" with his wound and his dependence on an economy he opposes. From this recognition of our wounded state, we can work to practice the virtue of hope. Berry consistently resists the temptation to immanentize hope, to expect that the economic and political systems within which we live will somehow be made whole; rather, he envisions an eschatological hope, a vision of wholeness that orients our wounded lives toward shalom. Because Andy and Danny do not expect their marginal acts of making do to bring about radical systemic changes, they are free to continue hoping that they will. Such hope leads to the creative work of healing and re-membering, the marginal ways of making do. When we are threatened by discouragement or hopelessness and are tempted to seek a technological quick-fix—some new prosthetic that we can strap onto our maimed body— we need to remember that such strategies are doomed to failure because they distract our attention from the root problems. As Berry reminds us in one of his poems,

> [W]e pray, not
> for new earth or heaven, but to be
> quiet in heart, and in eye,
> clear. What we need is here. [44]

Bibliography

Baker, Bernard. "Responsibly at Home: Wendell Berry's Quest for the Simple Life." PhD diss., Case Western Reserve University, 1992.

Bawer, Bruce. "Civilized Pleasures." *The Hudson Review* 59, no. 1 (Spring 2006): 142–52.

Berry, Wendell. "American Imagination and the Civil War." In *Imagination in Place: Essays*, 17–38. Berkeley: Counterpoint, 2010.

———. "Feminism, the Body, and the Machine." In *What Are People For?* 178–96. New York: North Point, 1990.

———. *The Hidden Wound*. Second Edition. Berkeley: Counterpoint, 2010.

44. Berry, *New Collected Poems,* 180.

————. "Imagination in Place." In *Imagination in Place: Essays*, 1–16. Berkeley: Counterpoint, 2010.

————. "The Making of a Marginal Farm." In *Recollected Essays: 1965–1980*. New York: North Point, 1993.

————. "Letter to the Editor." *The Hudson Review* 59, no. 3 (Autumn 2006): 525.

————. "Nature as an Ally: An Interview with Wendell Berry." Interview by Sarah Leonard. *Dissent Magazine*, 2012. http://www.dissentmagazine.org/article/nature-as-an-ally-an-interview-with-wendell-berry.

————. *New Collected Poems*. Berkeley: Counterpoint, 2013.

————. "The Problem of Tobacco." In *Sex, Economy, Freedom & Community: Eight Essays*, 53–68. New York: Pantheon, 1993.

————. "The Prejudice Against Country People." In *Citizenship Papers*, 107–12. Washington, D.C.: Shoemaker & Hoard, 2003.

————. "Think Little." In *A Continuous Harmony: Essays Cultural and Agricultural*, 71–85. San Diego: Harcourt Brace & Co, 1972.

————. "The Whole Horse." In *Citizenship Papers*, 113–26. Washington, D.C.: Shoemaker & Hoard, 2003.

————. "Why I Am Not Going to Buy a Computer." In *What Are People For?: Essays*, 170–77. New York: North Point, 1990.

Bilbro, Jeffrey. "Does Wendell Berry Have Rose-Colored Glasses?" *Front Porch Republic*, December 31, 2016. http://www.frontporchrepublic.com/2016/12/does-wendell-berry-have-rose-colored-glasses/.

————. "Sublime Failure: Why We'd Better Start Seeing Our World as Beautiful." *South Atlantic Review* 80.1–2 (2015): 133–58.

————. "The Ecology of Memory: Augustine, Eliot, and the Form of Wendell Berry's Fiction." *Christianity & Literature* 65.3 (2016): 327–42.

————. "The Eros of Child and Cupid: Wendell Berry's Agrarian Engagement with Ecofeminism." *Mississippi Quarterly* 64.2 (2012): 287–308.

Buell, Lawrence. *The Future of Environmental Criticism: Environmental Crisis and Literary Imagination*. Blackwell Manifestos. Malden, MA: Blackwell, 2005.

————. *Writing for an Endangered World: Literature, Culture, and Environment in the U.S. and Beyond*. Cambridge: Belknap Press of Harvard University Press, 2001.

Castellano, Katey. "Romantic Conservatism in Burke, Wordsworth, and Wendell Berry." *SubStance* 40.2 (2011): 73–91.

Certeau, Michel de. *The Practice of Everyday Life*. Translated by Steven Rendall. Berkeley: University of California Press, 1988.

Crouch, Andy. "Eating the Supper of the Lamb in a Cool Whip Society." *Books and Culture*, 2004. http://www.booksandculture.com/articles/2004/janfeb/8.26.html.

Donnelly, Phillip. "Biblical Convocation in Wendell Berry's Remembering." *Christianity and Literature* 56.2 (2007): 275–96.

Freyfogle, Eric T. *Agrarianism and the Good Society: Land, Culture, Conflict, and Hope*. Culture of the Land. Lexington: University Press of Kentucky, 2007.

————. "Wendell Berry and the Limits of Populism." In *Wendell Berry: Life and Work*, edited by Jason Peters, 173–91. Lexington: University Press of Kentucky, 2010.

Garrard, Greg. *Ecocriticism*. 2nd edition. Abingdon, Oxon: Routledge, 2012.

Goodrich, Janet. *The Unforeseen Self in the Works of Wendell Berry*. Columbia: University of Missouri Press, 2001.

Heise, Ursula K. *Sense of Place and Sense of Planet: The Environmental Imagination of the Global*. Oxford: Oxford University Press, 2008.

hooks, bell. *Belonging: A Culture of Place*. New York: Routledge, 2008.

Illich, Ivan. *Energy and Equity*. Ideas in Progress. New York: Harper & Row, 1974.

Kierkegaard, Søren. *Fear and Trembling/Repetition: Kierkegaard's Writings, Vol. 6*. Translated by Edna H. Hong and Howard V. Hong. Revised ed. Princeton: Princeton University Press, 1983.

Kirby, Jack Temple. "Rural Culture in the American Middle West: Jefferson to Jane Smiley." *Agricultural History* 70.4 (1996): 581–97.

Kroeker, P. Travis. "Sexuality and the Sacramental Imagination: It All Turns on Affection." In *Wendell Berry: Life and Work*, edited by Jason Peters, 119–36. Lexington: University Press of Kentucky, 2010.

Ladino, Jennifer K. *Reclaiming Nostalgia: Longing for Nature in American Literature*. Under the Sign of Nature: Explorations in Ecocriticism. Charlottesville: University of Virginia Press, 2012.

Leax, John. "Memory and Hope in the World of Port William." In *Wendell Berry Life and Work*, edited by Jason Peters, 66–75. Lexington: University Press of Kentucky, 2010.

Mannon, Ethan. "Leisure and Technology in Port William: Wendell Berry's Revelatory Fiction." *Mississippi Quarterly* 67.2 (2014): 171–92.

McLuhan, Marshall. *Understanding Media: The Extensions of Man*. Reprint edition. Cambridge: The MIT Press, 1994.

Murphy, Tamara Hill. "The Hole in Wendell Berry's Gospel: Why the Agrarian Dream Is Not Enough." *Plough Quarterly*, December 2016. http://www.plough.com/en/topics/faith/discipleship/the-hole-in-wendell-berrys-gospel.

Noble, Alan. "The Absurdity of Hope in Cormac McCarthy's *The Road*." *South Atlantic Review* 76.3 (2011): 93–109.

Peters, Jason. "Imagination and the Limits of Fiction." *Sewanee Review* 115.4 (2007): lxxxiv–lxxxvii.

Smith, Kimberly K. "Wendell Berry's Feminist Agrarianism." *Women's Studies: An Interdisciplinary Journal* 30.5 (2001): 623–46.

White, Richard. "'Are You an Environmentalist or Do You Work For a Living?': Work and Nature." In *Uncommon Ground: Rethinking the Human Place in Nature*, edited by William Cronon, 171–85. New York: Norton, 2006.

6

The Gift of Good Death
Revising *Nathan Coulter*

Ethan Mannon

"I approve of death, when it comes in time to the old. . . ."[1]

WENDELL BERRY'S DECISIONS TO revise his novels indicate the importance
he places on the aesthetic form of his fiction. In the cases of *Nathan Coulter*
(1960), *A Place on Earth* (1967), and *The Memory of Old Jack* (1974),
Berry used republication as an opportunity to tell his stories right. For *The
Memory*, this involved, according to Berry's note, no substantial changes,
but only the correction of "'errors' of genealogy and geography" and changes that "improved [his] editing." In "A Form for Living in the Midst of Loss,"
Jeffrey Bilbro explains that with the revision of *A Place on Earth*, Berry's
"technique caught up with his subject."[2] That is, by "cutting about one third
of what [Berry] called a 'clumsy, overwritten, wasteful' book," the revision
places the reader in the same position of incomplete knowledge endured
by the characters.[3] Without the context provided in the first edition—
evaluations of scenes as well as explanations of a character's biography and
thinking—the revision implies much that the first edition made explicit.

1. Berry, *New Collected Poems*, 361.
2. Bilbro, "A Form for Living," 89–105.
3. Ibid., 89. See also, 101–03.

Finally, the scale of Berry's 1985 revision of *Nathan Coulter* falls between his work with the other two novels. Along with many minor emendations, Berry made one major change: the removal of the final twenty-plus pages of the 1960 edition. Berry's elimination of this material transforms the death-story of Dave Coulter, Nathan's grandfather. In the first edition Dave survives a major stroke and lives on, much diminished, for more than a week; in the revision, the novel concludes after Dave collapses in the field and Nathan, unable to revive his grandfather, carries him home. Berry's revisions of these three novels make clear that while the arguments layered into his fiction certainly matter, so too does the texture of words, voices, images, and figurative language. Exploring the differences between editions of the same novel—as the first half of this essay does with *Nathan Coulter*—demonstrates the high value Berry places on the style of his fiction.

The altered terms of Dave's death also underscore the importance of a good death to Berry—a subject he returns to again and again in his fictional history of Port William, Kentucky, and its people. Though Dave's grief over his own mortality remains, Berry's revision gives his character a cleaner death by removing the period of invalidism and, with it, Dave's adamant refusal to let go of life. In its second version, Dave's death comes as a timely and natural event. And in its revised form, Dave Coulter's revised death shares much in common with the deaths of several other Port William farmers: "Old Jack" Beechum (*The Memory of Old Jack*), Burley Coulter ("Fidelity"), and Nathan Coulter (*Hannah Coulter*). Together, these farmers and their deaths offer an extended commentary on an individual's and a community's interactions with the end of life. Thus, the second half of this essay will place Dave's two deaths alongside three other deaths through which Berry describes an ideal way to leave one's life.

"There on the hillside": Dave Coulter's Second Death

Berry's 1985 revision of *Nathan Coulter* closes with the title character, now grown, trying to resuscitate his grandfather after the older man collapses in the field: "I straightened him out and knelt beside him, rubbing his hands and speaking to him. But I couldn't bring him to . . . I called his name, but he didn't stir. I picked him up in my arms and I carried him home."[4] Ending the novel at this moment eliminates much of the drama present in the first edition. In that volume, Dave Coulter's death—which occurs many

4. Berry, *Three Short Novels*, 117.

days after his collapse—so distresses Nathan that he has a one-night affair with Mrs. Mandy Loyd. His carelessness leads to his discovery by Mandy's husband, Gander, who tries to kill Nathan. The entire episode prompts Nathan's father to call him a "damned disgrace," and Nathan leaves home.[5] Berry's revision, occurring some twenty-five years after the original publication, pares back Nathan's biography by eliminating this entire sequence of events. It erases both his tryst and his exodus, and thus cements his position within the membership of Port William.[6] Within his revised life-story, Nathan remains under the tutelage of his uncle Burley and of his father—an education that gives Nathan a more direct path toward his (eventual) steadfast marriage to Hannah Steadman Feltner as well as his own status as a respectable and respected farmer.

Along with cleansing Nathan of his mistakes, the revised edition strips away many of the conclusions he reaches, and thereby forces the reader to contemplate and interpret Dave Coulter's life and death. Covering Nathan's development from boyhood to maturity, the novel also chronicles his grandfather's old age and decline. After one particularly hard winter that takes an obvious toll on Dave, the old man begins occasionally talking about his death, but usually declares "I reckon another twenty years'll see me out."[7] In a line Berry removed from the revised edition, Nathan shares that he and the others "were proud of him" for that kind of statement, "and admired him for refusing to give up."[8] Nevertheless, everyone recognizes the reality. Even though Dave "tried to keep from showing that he grieved about [his own death]," his mortality occupies his own and others' minds:

> It seemed to us that we'd never thought of him before as a man who would die. He never had thought of himself in that way. Until that year, although he'd cursed his weakness and his age, he'd either ignored the idea of his death or had refused to believe in it. He'd only thought of himself as living. But now that he finally admitted that he would die we thought about it too.[9]

From his thinking about his grandfather's death, Nathan decides that "you could tell sometimes that he grieved because after he was dead Daddy would still be there"—a passage Berry trimmed to "you could tell sometimes that

5. Berry, *Nathan Coulter*, 202.

6. On "the membership," see Stanford III, "Membership and Its Privileges," 118–30.

7. Berry, *Nathan Coulter*, 172.

8. Ibid.

9. Ibid., 173.

he grieved."[10] Further, Nathan even imagines, in the first edition, that if his grandfather could have held "his weakness . . . enough in his mind to know what it was, he'd have killed it and gone on living forever."[11] Finally, just before Dave's collapse Nathan comes to a realization that Berry cut from the revised edition: "I realized then that he didn't grieve only because he would die. There was more to it than that. When he was dead, as far as he was concerned, the land that had used him up and killed him would be dead too."[12] Removing Nathan's thoughts and realizations opens the narrative to questions: why does Dave grieve about his impending death? Is his determination to go on living admirable? Without the pressure exerted by Nathan's answers to these questions, the revision gives the reader greater freedom to contemplate Dave.

After the older man slips into a coma in a chapter present only in the first edition, Nathan contemplates the meaning of Dave's life in a long passage:

> he'd worked . . . driven by the idea of owning a piece of land and living on it, until finally the driving and the work had got to be more important to him than anything else. That had been his loneliness, dividing him from his family . . . And I thought of him as he'd been when he was old, grieving because he had to die. I remembered him telling Uncle Burley that he was going to die and getting a joke for an answer, because he had set his loneliness between them and Uncle Burley couldn't impose on it. He'd made his dying as lonely as he'd lived.
>
> It seemed to me that it had to be a tragedy for a man like him to die, who'd had the will to live forever. We had to know that, and had to grieve for it; but none of us had been able to tell him so. Our grieving had to be as lonely as his own.[13]

Nathan's thinking here suggests that he would have made an excellent English major. He analyzes discrete pieces of evidence and from them synthesizes an interpretation of Dave's life—an interpretation not present in the revision. The removal of this passage exemplifies the way that the 1985 revision systematically provides the reader with less interpretive scaffolding; Berry shows Dave, Nathan, and the others thinking about mortality,

10. Berry, *Nathan Coulter*, 138–39; Berry, *Three Short Novels*, 90.

11. Berry, *Nathan Coulter*, 179.

12. Ibid., 180.

13. Ibid., 187–88.

but consistently removes their conclusions. The meaning of Dave's life and his death becomes less determined in the revision, and meaning-making becomes work assigned to the reader. Thus, Berry's emendations to *Nathan Coulter* closely resemble his work with *A Place on Earth*—the revision of each novel is more concise and more ambiguous than the original.

Taken together, the emendations to *Nathan Coulter* and *A Place on Earth* show Berry distancing his fiction from his nonfiction. By stripping away Nathan's realizations, *Nathan Coulter* becomes less like a narrow polemic that drives toward one particular set of conclusions (Nathan's). Instead of working to support a specific thesis (as an essay might do), the leaner, sparer revision multiplies the possible meanings of its narrative. In the original edition, Nathan tells his story *and its meaning* to a rather passive listener; in the revision, a more taciturn Nathan invites the reader to form an empathetic connection with him, to imagine Port William through his eyes, and to decide for himself or herself the meaning of this place and community. In short, the revision requires more thought from the reader. This technique shows that Berry, older by two decades, revised his fiction (this novel and prior ones) with a new sensibility of genre in mind. If his revision of *A Place on Earth* demonstrated that "his technique [had] caught up with his subject,"[14] Berry's work on that novel and on *Nathan Coulter* makes clear that he also wished to better fit his technique to his *genre*. While his essays utilize a singular voice and perspective (quite effectively, I might add), he revised his novels to create greater ambiguity and, in the process, to embrace multiplicity—of perspectives, interpretations, and responses. This is not to say that his work in any genre is superior or primary, but only to note that his techniques are genre-specific. In particular, his work with *Nathan Coulter* shows him refining his approach to fiction: the revision stresses the intrinsic value of an open-ended narrative and de-emphasizes any single interpretation of the story.

The revised edition of the novel also gives Dave Coulter a cleaner death. As several passages above indicate, Dave Coulter's mortality was a source of grief to him. The first edition translates this grief into a scene full of stubbornness and animosity where, after his stroke, he refuses to die:

> Grandpa lay in his room from one day to another, staring up at the ceiling. He quit trying to move or talk, as if it took all his strength to hold his eyes open and to stay alive . . . from the look in his eyes we knew that he felt [his death], and he was fighting it . . . His

14. Bilbro, "A Form," 103.

eyes held him between his life and his death, allowing nothing to happen.[15]

During this time Nathan and the others recall their earlier hope that Dave "could die without being sick."[16] Berry's revision makes that hope a reality. The removal of the final pages means that Dave dies "there on the hillside."[17] Berry likely found this death preferable because Dave passes without a period of what might be referred to today as "failed convalescence" or "terminal," "life-limiting" illness. Berry further validates Dave's clean exit from life by removing a line full of fear and hate from Nathan: "I was afraid he was dying, and I hated to think of it happening there on the hillside."[18] Twenty-five years after publishing those words, Berry decides that the hillside is a perfectly good place for Dave to die—better far than many other possibilities.

Patterns of Death among the Membership: Timeliness, Community, Autonomy, and Pain Management

The two deaths of Dave Coulter illuminate much of Berry's thinking about right ways to approach the end of life, especially when combined with the deaths of three other Port William farmers. When Jack Beechum, Dave Coulter, Burley Coulter, and Nathan Coulter reach the end of their respective lives, Berry's final arrangements—or rearrangement in the case of Dave Coulter—reveal the importance of acceptance, timeliness, and community, as well as the paradox of control that plays out between an individual, the natural forces of decay, and what has come to be called the healthcare industry.

In *The Memory of Old Jack*, first published in 1974 (fourteen years after the first edition of *Nathan Coulter*), the title character dies a fitting and dignified death. Jack Beechum knows that he has come to the end of his life, and he has no trepidation:

> He has no fear of death. It is coming, there is nothing to be done about it, and so he does not think about it much. . . . Anyhow, what would a man his age propose to do instead of die? He has been

15. Berry, *Nathan Coulter*, 185.

16. Ibid., 183.

17. Ibid., 181.

18. Ibid.

around long enough to know that death is the only perfect cure for what ails mortals. After you have stood enough you die, and that is all right.[19]

After a day spent remembering the most significant events of his life, Old Jack feels himself coming to "a quietness," and accepts it.[20] Restful, quiet, and private, his death is so subtle that, like a coupling in a Victorian novel, the reader must infer what has just occurred. Old Jack slips silently out of his life and looks "natural, very like himself" when Mat Feltner finds his body.[21] When Mat tells his wife that Old Jack has died peacefully, in his own room, they both understand that "it could not have happened better."[22] Both realize that to have died "in a harness of tubes in some hospital bed" would have been far, far worse.[23] With *The Memory of Old Jack*, then, Wendell Berry holds up a state of calm acceptance and composure as the ideal way to meet one's end. Compared to Old Jack's death and the revised version of Dave Coulter's death, Dave's first death is tinged by bitterness: the days he spends desperately fighting off death make his end more melancholy. In revising the novel and eliminating the struggle, Dave regains dignity and poise. Mat Feltner's statement to the preacher in *The Memory of Old Jack*—that "it's not a tragedy when a man dies at the end of his life"—applies with equal weight to the new terms of Dave's death.[24] In fact, Mat's statement corrects one of Nathan's pronouncements that Berry removed from the revised edition. While Nathan decides that "it had to be a tragedy for a man like him to die," Mat insists on exactly the opposite.

Danny Branch's kidnap-rescue of his father, Burley Coulter, in "Fidelity" shares much in common with Berry's own redemption of Dave Coulter through revision. Though Burley is calm and composed about the end of his life, others take control of his death. Acting out of their love for him, his friends and family take Burley to the hospital in Louisville where he is at first disoriented and "talking out of his head"—a condition the membership

19. Wendell Berry, *The Memory of Old Jack*, 24. Old Jack's attitude is reminiscent of Addie Bundren's in William Faulkner's *As I Lay Dying*— "the reason for living was to get ready to stay dead a long time," 169—and of Berry's "Mad Farmer" who says that "When a man's life is over / the decent thing is for him to die." *New Collected*, 148.

20. Berry, *The Memory*, 144.

21. Ibid., 147.

22. Ibid., 148.

23. Ibid., 129.

24. Ibid., 150.

diagnoses as being out of his "right mind" because "he was no longer in his right place."[25] When his condition worsens, he stops responding to even his own name. "Lying slack and still in the mechanical room, in the merciless light, with a tube in his nose and a tube needled into his arm and a tube draining his bladder," Burley occupies "the harness of tubes" mentioned in *The Memory of Old Jack*.[26] In this situation, his life "no longer included even itself," and his body has become "a mere passive addition to the complicated machines that kept it minimally alive."[27] Danny and others understand that Burley "is hostage to his own cure"—"all trussed up in a hospital, tied and tubed and doped and pierced," they all realize that he "will never draw another breath for his own benefit."[28] The interminability of Burley's treatment makes it a horror. Compared to their earlier wish for him—that he could "die in his sleep out at work with us or under a tree somewhere"—his actual situation strikes them as unnatural.[29]

Danny's decisive action—he removes his father from the hospital without authorization, brings him back to Port William, hides him in a barn, and lovingly buries him after he dies—returns Burley to his natural place. Burley testifies to as much himself. Asked if he knows where he is after waking in the barn, Burley responds with an old joke ("right here"), but Danny is still certain "that Burley did know where he was."[30] Later, after Danny finds that his father has died, Berry spells out the rightness of this death: "In the hospital, Burley's body had seemed to Danny to be off in another world . . . Here, the old body seemed to belong to this world absolutely, it was so accepting of all that had come to it, even its death."[31]

The in-placement of Burley's death and his acceptance of it echo that of Old Jack. The link between their deaths is strengthened by the secret grave that Danny digs for Burley—a final resting place that follows the blueprint of the one Mat Feltner imagined would suit Old Jack. Mat thinks that the ideal place to lay Old Jack to rest would be in a semi-secret, unmarked grave:

25. Berry, *That Distant Land*, 375.
26. Ibid., 372.
27. Ibid., 376.
28. Ibid., 417.
29. Ibid., 374.
30. Ibid., 392.
31. Ibid., 408.

He would be taken in secret to a place at the edge of one of his fields, and only the few who loved him best would be permitted to go that far with him. They would dig a grave there and lay him in. . . . They would leave no stone or marker. They would level the grave with the ground. When the last of them who knew its place had died, Old Jack's return would be complete. He would be lost to memory in that field, silently possessed by the earth on which he once established the work of his hands.[32]

Though this is not the protocol followed for Old Jack, Burley's entombment comes very close. Danny selects a burial plot near the abandoned barn and overgrown fields of Stepstone Hollow. He digs the grave himself and pieces together a casket out of large, flat flagstones. After filling the grave, Danny spreads and levels the excess dirt and scatters leaves over the area to conceal his work. His effort, along with time, will thoroughly camouflage Burley's gravesite: "From twenty feet, only a practiced and expectant eye would have noticed the disturbance. After the dewfall or frost of one night, it would be harder to see. After the leaves fell, there would be no trace."[33] Danny has thus completely extricated Burley from the world of modern medical care, and has returned him to his place.

The title Berry gives to the story of Burley's death and burial makes clear that the central focus of the story is community. Acting first out of love for Burley, all the other characters in the story—Danny and Lyda Branch, Nathan and Hannah, and Wheeler and Henry Catlett—eventually stand together against Detective Kyle Bode. Sent to investigate Burley's disappearance from the hospital, Bode confronts a wall of passive resistance as Danny and the rest of the membership claim their rights to Burley. "Fidelity," then, describes the community's role in death. In the story, bringing Burley to his proper end requires cooperation between friends and family who confront the industrial-medical complex and, in the process, strengthen their own bonds. As Burley himself liked to remark, the "membership" of Port William includes the living and the dead; in this case, the transition from living to dead required the combined efforts of the membership.

---

32. Berry, *The Memory*, 157. Mat returns to this idea in "The Boundary," when he (now eighty-two) has walked too far from home: "Perhaps it would be possible to hide and die, and never be found. It would be a clean, clear way for that business to be done, and the thought, in his weariness, comforts him, for he has feared that he might die a nuisance to Margaret and the others" (*That Distant Land*, 304).

33. Berry, *That Distant Land*, 418.

The lineage of deaths in Berry's fiction—Dave Coulter's in 1938, Jack Beechum's in 1952, and Burley Coulter's in 1977—culminates in the account of Nathan Coulter's death given by his wife, Hannah. Grandson of Dave, nephew of Burley, and survivor of the Pacific theatre of World War II, Nathan Coulter knew death. Combined with his thoughtfulness, the deaths he witnessed make Nathan's own death Berry's most complete treatment of the subject. That is, because Nathan's character has contemplated the deaths of Dave, Old Jack, and Burley (and no doubt many others), that succession of deaths provides context and precedent for his own. We know that Nathan has meditated over at least one of these deaths because the final line of Berry's revision of *Nathan Coulter*—"I picked him up in my arms and I carried him home"—also provides the first line of *Hannah Coulter* (2004), framed in that novel as the conclusion of the last story Nathan tells his own children about his childhood.[34] Echoing many of the characteristics discussed above, Nathan's death also reveals a paradox relating to control and outlines a role for the medical establishment.

To speak of maintaining "control" over one's death verges on a non-sequitur. At the end of life, human bodies begin their return to dust—an inevitable process, and one over which we have no real control. Nathan seems to understand and to accept this fact. In his old age he grows sick but refuses a doctor. As Hannah explains, Nathan avoids the doctor so that "he could be captured by his death before he could be captured by the doctors and the hospitals and the treatments and the tests and the rest of it."[35] When Nathan speaks of his plan and his desire, his metaphors emphasize wholeness: "I don't want to end up a carcass for a bunch of carrion crows, each one taking his piece, and nobody in charge. I don't want to be worn all to holes like an old shirt no good for rags."[36] The paradox here is that Nathan maintains control over his life and death by giving that control up, wholesale, to the same natural cycles he has witnessed and managed as a farmer.[37] Because he believes that "dying will have to take care of itself," Nathan is unwilling to put his death in the hands of doctors who will make it a "technological process." As he says, "I'm going to live right on"—a line

34. Berry, *Hannah Coulter*, 3.

35. Ibid., 160.

36. Ibid., 161.

37. Like the speaker of "The Man Born to Farming," Nathan understands that as a farmer, he "enters into death / yearly, and comes back rejoicing" (lines 3–4). See Berry, *The Mad Farmer*.

implying that *both* life and death are parts of a *natural process*.[38] Nathan does, however, find a simple role for medical science. Understanding that there will be pain, Nathan uses a prescription for "medication" from his doctor. This "dope" (as Lyda Branch calls it) fits in to Nathan's controlled submission to his own death: because he did not like what the medicine "did to his mind," he takes it only at night.[39]

Hannah says that at the end of Nathan's life, "Death had become his friend." Describing the moment of his passing, Hannah says, "when the time came to go, he went."[40] Though Hannah's and Nathan's love and marriage were profound, she also notes that "the death of an old man is not the same as the death of a young one. It is not wrong, it is not a surprise."[41] Hannah's thinking here echoes the Mad Farmer's sentiment in the epigraph, Mat's words about Old Jack's death not being a tragedy, and also provides a fitting gloss for all of the good deaths in Port William.[42] Having lived their lives and worked their work in their places and among the membership, their deaths are natural, and they are beautiful.[43]

Conclusion: Port William and Palliative Care

Viewing these four deaths as an interlocking set reveals Berry's efforts to outline the terms of a good death (as well as some of the major challenges to the same) and also hints at a possible motivation behind Berry's revision of *Nathan Coulter*. To begin with the latter, I find the chronology of Berry's work in fiction during the 1970s and 1980s very suggestive. After publishing *The Memory of Old Jack* in 1974, Berry's next published works in fiction were a revision of *A Place on Earth* in 1983 and a revision of *Nathan Coulter*

38. Berry, *Hannah*, 161.

39. Ibid., 162.

40. Ibid., 163.

41. Ibid., 165.

42. Including the death of her Grandmam Steadman: "When Grandmam died in her time in the spring of 1944 . . . it seemed almost too orderly and natural to be sad." Ibid., 46.

43. In this way their deaths stand in stark contrast to the many violent deaths in Port William's history: Ben Feltner's (shot to death by a friend; see "Pray without Ceasing" in *That Distant Land*), Ernest Finley's (suicide; see *A Place on Earth*), Andrew Catlett's (shot and killed; see *A World Lost*), Virgil Feltner and Tom Coulter (missing in action and killed in action during World War II; see *A Place on Earth* and *Hannah Coulter*), and Jimmy Chatham (killed in the Vietnam War; see *Jayber Crow*).

in 1985. Circumstantial though the evidence may be, it certainly appears that *The Memory*, with its story of Old Jack's ideal death, marked a turning point for Berry. After *The Memory*, something prompted him to return to his earliest novels. Perhaps he felt his style had matured and he wished to refashion old work to reflect his new sensibility. Perhaps the market for his fiction changed after the publication of *The Unsettling of America* in 1977. Or perhaps Old Jack's death sharpened Berry's sense of his own themes and, in turn, revealed Dave Coulter's bitter end as unfitting for a Port William farmer. In step with natural rhythms and understanding the contours of a good life, perhaps Berry decided that those in the membership must remain exemplary, even in death. The revised version of Dave's death does, after all, fill out the suite of deaths that indicate Berry's critique of a death-denying culture.

To attest to the reality of death, and its propriety, Berry provides four men who have lived more than the "three-score and ten" allotted human-kind: Old Jack dies in his early nineties, Dave and Nathan in their late seventies, and Burley in his early eighties. Thus they are no longer young men who would be likely to regain a great quality of life after a serious injury or illness. And as Mat Feltner thinks in "The Boundary," "if a man eighty-two years old has not seen enough, then nobody will ever see enough."[44] Part of the goodness of each man's death, then, comes from his own recognition (to varying degrees) of its imminence and of his satisfaction with what his life contained.[45] Old Jack represents the ideal: composed and prepared, his uncomplicated death occurs after more than ninety years of living and with-out sickness or physical pain. Dave, too, stops living at the right time, but his grief over his own mortality (even in the revision) clouds his death with a layer of remorse. With Burley's story Berry explores the "complications"

---

44. Berry, *That Distant*, 294.

45. Because Old Jack, Dave, Burley, and Nathan represent a fairly specific demographic, their deaths do not allow us to speculate regarding Berry's views of adolescent, young adult, or middle aged sickness and death. Those interested in pursuing that line of inquiry might begin with Mattie Keith Chatham from *Jayber Crow*, with Nathan and Tom's mother (*Nathan Coulter*, 25–34 and "The Brothers," *Carolina Quarterly* 8.3, 5–11), and with Elton Penn ("An Empty Jacket" in *A Place in Time*). Mat Feltner's death represents a middle ground. At age eighty-two, Mat dies after a period that Andy Catlett hesitates to call an "illness": "it was not like other illnesses that I had seen—it was quieter and more peaceable. It was, it would be truer to say, a great weariness that had come upon him, like the lesser weariness that comes with the day's end—a weariness that had been earned, and was therefore accepted" (Berry, *That Distant*, 310). Mat's death, then, has much in common with Big Ellis's (see "The Requirement" in *A Place in Time*).

that modern medicine can layer into one's death—a problem Berry returns to in the final chapter of Nathan's life story. Danny's decisive action in "Fidelity" and the support Nathan receives in *Hannah Coulter* drive home the importance of community; without the membership, Burley would have remained and Nathan would have become "hostages" of the healthcare industry—victims of their own deaths.

Though these stories reveal Berry's skepticism toward the healthcare industry, there is actually some agreement between the ideal death he outlines in his fiction and some of the thinking in the field of palliative care.[46] First of all, Berry is not alone in noting the complications one encounters at the end of life. In "A Good Death," John Dunlop—a medical doctor on staff at the Zion Clinic in Illinois—describes two trends that increase the number of "gradual deaths": developments in medicine that have "significantly decreased the incidence of sudden death" (including a national 911 system, emergency rooms, intensive care units, and trauma specialists) as well as "new life sustaining technologies becoming available at an unprecedented rate."[47] Dunlop explains that these systems and technologies have changed the dying process into "a quagmire of ethical issues" to which modern medicine responds, by default, with "one technological intervention . . . added to another."[48] He also notes that submitting to tests, treatments, and life support tends, over time, to rob the patient and the patient's family of autonomy, as well as dignity.[49] Recognizing these trends, Nathan responded by allowing his life to run its course towards its end rather than directing it toward treatment that he thought would wear him "all to holes like an old shirt no good for rags."

Nathan's decision parallels the increasing awareness within the field of medicine that "the tools that allow us to find meaning and purpose in old age and death are unlikely to be medical or scientific."[50] In "In Search of a Good Death," David P. Schenck and Lori A. Roscoe echo Dunlop by noting that in a world where "70% of those who die in an institutional setting will do so after a decision is made to withhold or withdraw treatment[,]

46. Those interested in Berry's treatment of the healthcare industry in his nonfiction should consult "Health is Membership."

47. Dunlop, "A Good Death," 69.

48. Ibid., 70.

49. In her editorial, Ann Gallagher (part of the Faculty of Health and Medical Sciences at the University of Surrey) also discusses "the meaning and role of concepts such as autonomy and dignity." "The Good Death," 243.

50. Schenck and Roscoe, "In Search of a Good Death," 62.

. . . dying has become a series of difficult decisions for patients and their families to navigate."[51] Schenck and Roscoe also emphasize the importance of "autonomy" and "control" as components of a good death, and suggest that one way to maintain them is through the use of personal narrative. That is, they describe storytelling as an act that helps bring about closure: "telling stories about one's imminent death may give voice to an experience that medicine cannot fully describe, or change."[52] And as a creative act in which a person constructs his or her story, personal narrative also offers autonomy and self-direction.

This scholarship reveals one final characteristic of the good death Berry describes in his fiction: storytelling. Schenck and Roscoe offer life writing as a complement to palliative care. But however valuable personal narrative might be, one cannot tell the story of one's death. To make meaning of a life and to pass that on requires a witness and a community: Nathan for Dave's death in *Nathan Coulter*, Mat for Old Jack's death in *The Memory*, Danny for Burley's death in "Fidelity," and Hannah for Nathan's death in *Hannah Coulter*. Each of these characters serves as a witness who forms and preserves the memory of a death and of the life it concluded. The membership of Port William is enriched by the living members, but also by their recital—and their habitual *re-visioning*—of past lives. In offering the membership and its stories to his readers, Berry offers a primer on what it means to live and die well. Both require a community that actively and thoughtfully collects the stories of its members.[53] His fiction outlines a good death as a gift that complements and concludes a good life. And that is a story worth repeating.

Bibliography

Berry, Wendell. *The Art of the Commonplace*. Berkeley: Counterpoint, 2002.
———. "Health Is Membership." In *Another Turn of the Crank: Essays*, 86–109. Washington, D.C.: Counterpoint, 1995.
———. *The Mad Farmer Poems*. New York: Counterpoint, 1998.
———. *New Collected Poems*. Berkeley: Counterpoint, 2012.
———. *What Are People For?* Berkeley: Counterpoint, 1990.
———. "The Work of Local Culture." In *What Are People For?: Essays*, 153–69. New York: North Point, 1990.

51. Ibid., 61.

52. Ibid., 66.

53. See Berry's "The Work of Local Culture."

Bilbro, Jeffrey. "A Form for Living in the Midst of Loss: Faithful Marriage in the Revisions of Wendell Berry's *A Place on Earth*," *Southern Literary Journal* 42.2 (2010): 89–105.

Dunlop, John. "A Good Death," *Ethics & Medicine* 23.2 (2007): 69–75.

Faulkner, William. *As I Lay Dying*. New York: Vintage, 1990 [1930].

Gallagher, Ann. "The Good Death," *Nursing Ethics* 20.3 (2013): 243–44.

Oehlschlaeger, Fritz. *The Achievement of Wendell Berry: The Hard History of Love*. Lexington: University Press of Kentucky, 2011.

Schenck, David P. and Lori A. Roscoe. "In Search of a Good Death," *Journal of Medical Humanities* 30 (2009): 61–72.

Stanford, Thomas W. III. "Membership and Its Privileges: The Vision of Family and Community in the Fiction of Wendell Berry," *Logos* 14.2 (2011): 118–30.

7

Living Faithfully in the Debt of Love in Wendell Berry's Port William

Fritz Oehlschlaeger

BURLEY COULTER IS WELL-KNOWN to readers of Wendell Berry for his
sense of the way all the living and dead of Port William belong together
in a "membership." Asked by Wheeler Catlett in "The Wild Birds (1967)"
whether his designating Danny Branch his heir is a way to apologize for
what he's "done wrong," Burley responds with an unequivocal "No," acknowledging that we need "to know what we ought to have been and ought
to be" but insisting that "we oughtn't to let that stand between us." Our
failures and even our cruelties—though Burley seems incapable of the latter—must not be allowed to divide us finally, for "we are members of each
other. All of us. Everything. The difference ain't in who is a member and
who is not, but in who knows it and who don't." Burley has felt the need to
acknowledge Danny as his son and Kate Helen Branch as his wife. Doing so
is simply a matter of "honesty," a way of coming out into the open, showing himself, and being cleansed of secret fault. He acts in response to a
requirement, one might say, and yet without feeling that requirement to
be burdensome or constraining. Instead acknowledging the requirement
opens the way to a freedom in knowing "the way we are," and "to *know* that
is the only chance we've got, dead and living, to be here together."[1]

How Burley comes to his sense of the membership is clarified by "The
Requirement," a story from *A Place in Time* devoted to his recollection of
Big Ellis's final sickness and death in 1970. "Well, you get older and you be-
gin to lose people, kinfolks and friends," Burley begins, "Or it *seems* to start

---

1. Berry, "The Wild Birds (1967)," In *That Distant Land: The Collected Stories*, 355–56.

when you're getting older. You wonder who was looking after such things when you were young. The people who died when I was young were about all old. Their deaths didn't interrupt me much, even when I missed them."[2] Of course it was those already older who were "looking after such things" while Burley was busy being his uninterrupted self. As Burley began himself to experience the loss of "people who mattered" to him, he began to "feel that something was required" of him:

> Sometimes something would be required that I could do, and I did it. Sometimes when I didn't know what was required, I still felt the requirement. Whatever I did never felt like enough. Something I knew was large and great would have happened. I would be aware of the great world that is always nearby, ever at hand, even within you, as the good book says. It's something you would maybe just as soon not know about, but finally you learn about it because you have to. (171)

Our own aging and decline, together with the loss of others, interrupts us with the knowledge that the world is fallen, that the price of sin is death, but suggests perhaps a fortunate dimension to that fall. For as we come to feel the inadequacy of what we yet feel required to do for those we lose, we can begin to understand ourselves as infinitely in debt, both for those among whom we have lived and for our own lives. Then, by something like a Kierkegaardian movement of the infinite, we change within, coming to rest in the debt of love and willing to remain so. We still gladly do what we feel required to do, knowing full well we can never discharge our debts but only "strive to accomplish the duty of being in love's debt to each other," as Kierkegaard puts it.[3]

Burley turns to the language of debt specifically in the last parts of his history with Big Ellis. He remembers sitting with Big, thinking again of the "requirement" and the inadequacy of any response he might make:

> What could you do? What could you do that would be anyways near enough? I could feel the greatness of life and death; and the great world endless as the sky swelling out beyond this little one. And I began again to hear from that requirement that seems to come from the larger world. The requirement was telling me, "*Do*

---

2. Berry, *A Place in Time,* 171. Further references to this volume will be given parenthetically.

3. Kierkegaard, *Works of Love,* 194.

something for him. Do more than you've ever done. Do more than
you *can* do. (179–80)

When Burley asks whether there is anything that he wants, Big answers
only "Not a thing. Not a thing in this world." Just as Burley is about to leave,
however, Big does think of something he would like Burley to do: to take
and care for a ".22 revolver," which "was the only really good thing Big had
ever owned" and which "he had taken care of" like "a king's crown" (180).
Receiving a gift, then, is what Burley can finally do for Big, an irony not lost
on Burley: "So I had come to do something for Big, if I could, and instead
Big had done something for me, and I was more in debt to the requirement than ever" (181). Willing to remain indebted to others, and lovingly
to acknowledge how that indebtedness is owed to the whole "great world,"
the membership of all things, is what Burley can finally do. It is both more
than he has ever done and more than he can do, for he could never do it by
himself. Even his ability to receive Big's gift is dependent on their whole history together. As the story ends, Burley does find "something" to do for Big,
even if "it wasn't enough." He fires Big's pistol at an "old dinner bell leaning
on its post," getting exactly the "grazing hit" he wants and sending the bell
ringing as if to sum "up all the dongs it had ever rung." That bell "filled the
day and the whole sky and brought the worlds together, the little and the
great." Burley knew "Big heard it and was pleased" and Burley was himself
"pleased." It was a "grand sound" and a "good shot" like those Burley and
Big had made and taken at life together (181). It was a fine tribute to their
friendship and to that wonderfully good-natured man, Big Ellis.

I find myself easily able to identify with Burley's sense that the deaths
of others require something of us, that our response will never be enough,
and that we must learn to live in grateful debt to the requirement itself as
that which presses us toward an ever widening awareness of our interconnectedness with all things. But I do not think these responses I describe
are simply givens. American individualism characteristically leads to our
thinking that freedom involves escape from restriction or limitation: requirements are something to be avoided, circumvented, or, at best, com-
pleted—that is, put behind one. Debt is increasingly becoming a discredited
concept as well—rightly so, in my view, as long as we are thinking of it in
monetary terms. There are good economic and national security reasons to
be troubled by our national debt, and we desperately need to become more
aware of the intergenerational consequences of debt. As of this moment,
however, I've not heard any politician articulate a condemnation of debt

worthy of Burley Coulter: one that argued the greatest evil of too much economic debt is to make the whole notion of debt so repugnant that one will never be able to experience being in debt in the Kierkegaardian way—as a matter of willing to remain in the debt of love forever. That's a politician I could happily vote for but do not expect to see.

These comments derive from my own sorting through my several experiences teaching Berry's works to graduate students at my institution, Virginia Tech. My students generally found Berry's writing very compelling, but they invariably preferred both his essays and his poetry to the fiction—and particularly to the short fiction. I think there are many reasons for this. First, as many of them are concerned about environmental matters, their engagement with much of the non-fiction is quite direct—that with the fiction less so. Moreover, Berry has a standing, for them, as perhaps the most eminent agrarian voice in today's environmental literature whereas his fiction occupies a smaller niche in the wide universe of fiction they read. The fiction also seems conventional in form and narration, particularly to young writers who are seeking new forms of story telling. Perhaps even more important are the cultural factors, starting with the difference between the experiences of today's mobile, urban-suburban, digitally accomplished students and the life of Port William. I can remember a particularly intelligent male student puzzling over the way the generations of Port William experience life essentially as repetition in a way that he could not imagine satisfying. Port William abounds, too, in deep, intelligent women, but they tend not to be mobile or in search of public power in ways my female students take for granted.

In the rest of this essay, then, I want to suggest, as if to my students, one of the things I see Berry doing in his fiction—and to do so by recalling Burley's language of the "requirement." My examples will come largely from two of Berry's collections of short stories abounding in rich intersections— his most recent one, *A Place in Time*, and the earlier *Fidelity*. My suggestion is that Berry is creating in Port William, through Andy's remembering and continual imaginative recasting, a context in which one can, like Burley, come to understand "requirement" not as something imposed on one and thus resented but rather as the chosen duty of remaining in the debt of love. Berry leads us to see how doing first what others "require"—the land and animals, perhaps, as well as people—can lead us out of ourselves, into habits of responsibility, and finally to gratitude for what we have been called to do. The language of "fidelity" can be used to put this point in a related way.

Berry's task has been one of social and cultural reconstruction, of weaving together again the fabric of a life torn asunder by "War and the Economy," to quote Jayber Crow. It is to recreate an order in which fidelity of all kinds is again imaginable and possible. I want to call this an order of presences, by way particularly of contrasting it with that tremendous power of negation Berry identifies especially with the Second World War. In our time, we live everywhere under that power capable of simply making things go away, as Berry makes clear in pointing to the way negation is evident in so much of our language as well as practice. Mountaintops are removed, our countryside becomes "deserted," rural peoples are "cleared," workers become obsolescent, disposable, displaced (to God knows where), or replaced by machinery. All of this in the name of "creative destruction."[4] Perhaps that power of making things go away has been brought to its zenith and even democratized through our digital technologies. A couple of clicks and what has been made falsely present is no more. No wonder Berry has resisted writing on the computer, with its reduction of the bodily effort of writing with a pen or pencil. For one whose ideas are in things as much as they are for Berry, the computer screen must seem at best a place of ghostly images.

Before turning to the stories, I want to make two points. First, I do not think that recreating an order of presences will involve all of us becoming agrarians or residents of towns like Port Royal, Kentucky. It's my hope that increasing numbers of Americans will be able to live lives devoted to sustainable agriculture within vibrant local economies, but to look for this kind of shift on a mass scale seems utopian. Most of us will have to engage Port William analogously, looking for ways to reinvent a culture of fidelity in the variety of places we now are.[5] Second, as should be obvious already, and will be so in the rest of this piece, I consider Berry's fiction to be everywhere interrelated with his work in other genres—particularly his essays on marriage, sexuality, community, economics, and sustainable agriculture. The restrictions of space, however, mean that these connections will have to remain largely implicit.

It seems appropriate to begin with some of the specific connections between *Fidelity* and *A Place in Time*. *Fidelity* begins with "Pray Without Ceasing," *A Place in Time* ends in prayer. The second story of *Fidelity*, "A

4. See "Our Deserted Country," 105–115.

5. For an excellent treatment of the ways in which we might find "creative ways to work toward justice and health," even while being implicated in a destructive economic system, see Jeffrey Bilbro, "Andy Catlett's Missing Hand: Making Do as Wounded Members," in this volume.

Jonquil for Mary Penn," recalls the early days of the Penns' marriage and includes the terrible story of Mary's family rejecting her for marrying Elton, who, in their view, is "nothing." The final story of *A Place in Time*, the title story, returns to a history of Elton and Mary's marriage, concluding with Andy's meditation on that very rejection of the Penns by Mary's parents, the Mountjoys. At the center of *Fidelity* is "Making It Home," the story of Art Rowanberry's return to Port William after his service and wounding in World War II. One of the last stories of *A Place in Time*, "At Home (1981)," comes back to Art, who still bears "in the back of his mind," as "a sort of comment on everything else, the clamor of the big gun he had served" (188). In the title story of *Fidelity*, Wheeler Catlett pronounces Burley "a faithful man," a description the membership of Port William itself attests to as they resist the encroaching world of people like detective Kyle Bode. In eulogizing Burley, Wheeler remembers his fondness for saying "I've never learned anything until I had to"—until it was required.[6]

Several stories in *A Place in Time* trace the process by which Burley "learned what he had to." These include "Burley Coulter's Fortunate Fall (1934)," "Stand By Me (1921–1944)," and "The Dark Country (1948)," as well as "The Requirement (1970)." If the opening story of *Fidelity*, "Pray Without Ceasing," points toward the latter stories of *A Place in Time*, so, too, does the final story of the earlier volume, "Are You All Right?" For in that simple story, Andy comes to recognize how Elton and his faithful going to check on the Rowanberrys during a time of flood was a way of placing the aging brothers "under the sign of mortality" (192). But Andy knows, too, that it was "neither of the Rowanberrys who was under the sign of mortality that night" but rather Elton, who "before another April came" would be in his "grave on the hill at Port William" (199). Andy's young son, Marcie, comes to a very beginning knowledge of the facts of "loss" and "absence" in *A Place in Time* through the death of his friend, Elton, taken in the very middle of life in "An Empty Jacket (1974)." Thus the awareness that no one knows the hour passes from generation to generation.

Miss Della Budge quotes Paul's letter to the Thessalonians when she comes to the Feltners' house after Ben's death in the opening story of *Fidelity*. "It'll come by surprise . . . It's a time appointed, but we'll not be notified," she says to her former student Jack Beechum, who says he knows it and does "know it." "So we must always be ready," she continues, "Pray

---

6. Berry, *Fidelity*, 186. Further references to this volume will be given parenthetically.

without ceasing" (54).[7] A possibly continual prayer is something Andy has seen in his Grandmother Feltner, whom he remembers sitting motionless in her rocking chair enduring the pain of arthritis and, as she would say, "occup[ying] her mind with thoughts." What Andy knew her to be doing—as surely "as if she had told me"—"was praying" (9–10). From her Andy hears the story of his great grandfather's death, a story that helps us to imagine what living out Paul's great exhortation might look like. It is a story of murder, of course, that oversimplification by which one seeks to annihilate time by making another as if he or she had never been. But it is also a story of fidelity: that of Jack Beechum, who holds Mat Feltner in the street, preventing him from pursuing Thad Coulter in murderous anger of his own; of Mat Feltner and his mother Nancy Beechum Feltner, who make what peace can still be made by defusing the righteous anger of the lynch mob; of Martha Elizabeth, Thad's daughter, who remains absolutely steadfast in her love of her father; and of Andy's grandmother Feltner, who remembers the story, sees its further workings in time, and brings all its members to her prayers.

The story begins with an infidelity of sorts when Thad Coulter mortgages his farm in order to finance his son Abner's going into the grocery business in Hargrave. Thad brags "in Port William of his son's new status as a merchant in the county seat," (12) thereby setting himself up for additional shame when Ab later fails. Berry's description suggests a kind of nothingness, a gap, that inserts itself between the generations living under our current version of the American dream as one in which each generation "does better" than that before it. Thad's "life and its entire effort" are offered as "hostage[s]" to Ab's possibilities as a merchant. What's eliminated is any creative way for the life and effort of the one to pass into the other. The father's life can only be "cashed out," as we say, and the son—freed of any lived sense of his parents' work—fritters away his inheritance through many small "derelictions" (12). The sense of his own foolish alienation from his own life and work lies at the heart of the intense shame and "self-condemnation" Thad brings to his meeting with his best friend Ben Feltner. What follows is a tragically missed moment. Ben responds to the drunken Thad in the only way possible, telling him he will have to "get sober and come back." Thad does "not have to take Ben's words as an insult," but "it was perhaps inevitable that he would." He has come to Ben hoping that somehow "Ben could release him from the solitary cage of his

7. I Thessalonians 5:17.

self-condemnation" (15). Indeed Ben's response should be read precisely as a way of doing this, for he tells him it will take time. Thad, however, wants to fix his fate once for all. In killing Ben, he destroys the one most likely to remember him as he had once been, executing judgment on himself as unworthy of redemption—a judgment he finalizes later in his jail cell.

As Mat Feltner settles upon revenging his father, he feels an "elation" (34) not unlike that "singular joy" (25) felt by Thad Coulter as he prepares to go to town to kill Ben Feltner. "New-created by rage," Mat feels that he and "his enemy" are "as clear of history as if newborn" (34–35). Mat would fix the difference between them once for all, in a way nothing in this place in time could ever change. Fortunately for Mat, Jack Beechum, who likes to describe himself as "born ready," is indeed ready to meet what is required of him in this unexpected hour. He literally holds Mat "in time," in both senses, "striv[ing]" together with him in the dust until Mat relents (36). What moves Jack is a complex fidelity to the whole life of his place: to his friend Ben Feltner and what he has learned of peace and patience from him; to Mat, whom he knows will return to himself; to those of his own family so abruptly and seemingly casually removed from time—his brothers killed in the War, his mother who dies in 1865, his own stillborn son; perhaps even to his own father, who kept "vigil" over Jack after the War as if in fear of losing another child. The strength that passes almost bodily from Jack to Mat, together with his mother's own grief-born faithfulness, no doubt contributes to Mat's own ability to be faithful to himself and to his people in quieting the crowd. By refusing to authorize the collective vengeance, Mat takes a first step toward an eventual reconciliation of all those torn apart by Thad's killing his father. Indeed Andy recognizes himself to be "the child" of his grandfather's "forgiveness," (59) for the lineages of Feltners and Coulters are joined in him.

We have seen how Jack Beechum's fidelity makes Mat Feltner's continuing life—and with it his fidelities—possible. In a similar way, Martha Elizabeth's fidelity to her father, and then to something like the goodness of being itself, enables Granny Feltner to hold the whole story in her "thoughts" with charity. "It's a hard story to have to know," she tells Andy, "the mercy of it was Martha Elizabeth" (50). Thad himself has felt his daughter's unwavering faithfulness as he goes toward Hargrave to turn himself in: "It seemed to him that she knew everything he knew, and loved him anyhow. She loved him, minute by minute, not only as he had been but as he had become. It was a wonderful and a fearful thing to him that he had caused such a love for himself to come into the world and then had failed it" (44). Martha Elizabeth continues to give faithful consent to being, as if witnessing to her father's continued goodness in her, throughout her life. Andy remembers her as an older woman "always near to smiling, sometimes to laughter," one whose face "assented wholly to the being of whatever and whomever she looked at" (48). That steadfast love of Martha Elizabeth's shapes the way Granny Feltner has come to understand the story of Mat's father and Thad Coulter. She comes to recognize that God's love is not always a "pleasant thing" for people, but that it can be "terrible" if one thinks of "all it includes." "It included Thad Coulter, drunk and mean and foolish, before he killed Mr. Feltner," she tells Andy, "and it included him afterwards." God's love has been terrible for Thad, who could not bear to see it standing "as near him as Martha Elizabeth" and wearing "her flesh" (49–50). Perhaps it has been terrible, too, for Granny herself, for it has meant that she must try, in her faithfulness, to come to love Thad himself. "If God loves the ones we can't," she reflects, "then finally maybe we can. All these years I've thought of him sitting in those shadows, with Martha Elizabeth standing there, and his work-sore old hands over his face" (50–51).

Perhaps in Granny Feltner's prayer we can come to an understanding of one way to "pray without ceasing." Her fidelity takes the form of remembering the story, of praying the story, we might say, with a charity that resists the fixing of easy unalterable differences between the good and evil, the worthy and unworthy. In language reminiscent of Burley's about the "membership," she says to Andy, "Thad Coulter was not a bad man . . . I believed then, and I believe now, that he was not a bad man. But we are all as little children. Some know it and some don't" (12). How could such a prayer, aimed at holding together in kindness the whole lives of all the people of her place, be anything but perpetual? Andy's own fidelity lies in his allowing "the very voice of her prayers" to "reproduce" itself in his mind and in his storytelling (10). That voice, together with the strong continuing presence of his grandfather, remembered so vividly by Andy at the beginning of the story, leads him down "into the interior of the present" where the "Now" of eternity meets "the now that is in time," leaving "reminders of Itself" for us to witness and remember—reminders like the fidelity of Jack Beechum and Martha Elizabeth, Mat and Margaret Feltner (4–5).

The opening moments of "Pray Without Ceasing" provide an extraordinarily appropriate frame for the second and third stories of *Fidelity*, "A Jonquil for Mary Penn" and "Making It Home." When he would return from a long absence, Andy remembers, his grandfather Mat would sit next to him, his hand "clap[ping] lightly" onto his "leg above the knee" in a way that said "Hello" as if "we had been together the day before." The very "shape of his hand" seems imprinted on Andy's thigh "as vividly as a birthmark" (4). His grandfather's remembered touch confirms the goodness of Andy's bodily existence, "moment to moment." That kind of confirmation is what life in the mystery of the family, assuming it is a good one, can provide. The goodness of being, and the moment to moment dependability of its endurance, seem what is at stake in both the story of the Penns and Art Rowanberry's war time experience. The power of negation enters the Penns' lives through the terrible judgments Mary's parents render on Elton—"He's nothing"—and on her when she marries: "She no longer belonged to that family. To them it would be as if she had never lived" (66–67). It is crucial not to read Elton simply in terms of his struggle with Mary's parents' judgment. He is an extraordinary man, one in love with Mary but also "with the world," with "their place in the world," and with farming (79). But the Mountjoys' "rejection" does "cost him dearly." Because he cannot forgive them, they continue to hold a "power over him that he could not shake off" (78) even in his defiance. In her own way, Mary too struggles between the light and the dark. For the most part, the story depicts the way in which she and Elton find a new and supporting family in their neighbors. As their lives take hold in a supporting context, "she learned to imagine where she was" and begins "to think of herself as living and working at the center of a wonderful provisioning" (74). But at times—significantly on the day of her bodily sickness—it can all seem to her "arbitrary and awry," vulnerable to negation. She can imagine the house in ruin, Elton and herself gone, and all their lovely neighbors "gone too" (75).

The tremendous power of negation, let loose by World War II, is well known to Art Rowanberry, whose walking the last part of his journey home is a step-by-step recovery of at least partial trust in the goodness of the world. Art has served the "big gun," (86) the power of will that seems intent on demonstrating its ability to reduce to nothing every created and cared-for thing. In such a world, the only remaining fidelity possible is to the big gun and the swarm that fires it, for nothing else can be expected to remain from one minute to another:

> There was nothing you could look at that was whole—man or beast or house or tree—that had the right to stay whole very long. There was nothing above the ground that was whole but you had

the measure of it and could separate its pieces and bring it down. You moved always in a landscape of death, wreckage, cinders, and snow. (88)

As he is sitting "one afternoon" talking to a boy named McBride, a "shell hit[s] right where they" are and McBride "just disappear[s]" (88). Art himself is wounded, leading to his later release. Art will never forget the "mighty power" he has known, the "anger beyond the power of any man," (100) but as he nears his own place and family, he does come to think, "If a fellow was to be dead now, and young, might be he would be missing this a long time" (96). As Art rejoins his father, brother, and young nephew, the story ends with his father's delight, expressed in his urging the young boy to run to the house and tell them "to set on another plate. For we have our own that was gone and has come again" (105). The echo of Luke's parable of the prodigal son seems curious, for Art seems very unlike the younger son of Jesus's story. Perhaps the reference must be applied to the experience of a whole generation, who found in war the possibility of something like a riot of prodigality, a way to use up all that it had inherited, all for which it was in debt to the past.

The degree to which Burley is indebted to his Port William community—and the community in turn indebted to him—is the subject of "Fidelity." The story can be read perhaps as indirect comment on a project Berry has attributed to Elton Penn in "A Jonquil for Mary Penn." Elton wants to "have to say thank you to nobody" (66); his dilemma lies in his claim, that of an "extraordinary creature," to "respect itself, a claim that no creature's life, of itself, could invariably support" (78). "Fidelity" shows just how fully respect depends upon mutual fidelities, the loving honoring of debt in community. It shows how much Burley has, at the last, to be thankful for and how much others have to be thankful for in him. The story's crisis is one of fidelity in Burley's lived bodily experience. The medical treatment he receives in the Louisville hospital separates his dying process—which is mostly a denial of his dying process—from the rest of his experience and from those with whom he has lived. Danny acts faithfully, and in response to Burley's faithfulness, in ensuring that Burley "makes it home" to die and be buried where he belongs, in the woods. Thus Burley receives another gift, much as he has earlier from Big Ellis, remaining in debt inextricably to the last for his very ability to die in a way faithful to his living. Others—Lyda, Nathan, Henry and Wheeler Catlett—exercise faithfulness both to Danny and Burley as they play their parts in helping Danny carry out what Burley requires of him. The community pays its respects to Burley in gathering and in affectionate story-telling. Wheeler honors Burley as "a faithful man" who "learned what he had to," "changed" to meet what was required of him, perhaps especially by the young Tom and Nathan Coulter, and "made himself exceptional." Wheeler remembers also the "pleasure" Burley "took in pleasurable things," the way "he looked at the world and found it good" (186). Perhaps we do not think of ourselves as being in-debted to others for finding pleasure in the world, but what better witness can they offer of the goodness of going on—a witness we all, at some time, require? Wheeler's eulogy voices the community's loving acknowledgment of its debt to Burley. Such debts can never be repaid, for no one can com-pensate another fully for a life laid down. What we can do is to learn to live faithfully in debt, so that debt can come to be seen as an inevitable part of life in the "membership"—the sign of a required and constant reciprocal acknowledgment and forgiveness.

The process of Burley Coulter's learning "what he had to" is suggested comically in "Burley Coulter's Fortunate Fall (1934)" from *A Place in Time*. After spending what "seemed like forty days and forty nights" (34) paint-ing the roof of a run-down, sprawling barn for Grover Gibbs, Burley and brother Jarrat approach the end of the job. Jarrat remains as serious about his work as ever while Burley begins to rush, at the same time needling Jarrat and becoming impatient to get on with his uninterrupted self. "I got places to go and things to do," Burley announces, just before standing up to light a cigarette while on the steepest part of the roof—where he knows a fall would lead to his not getting up till "resurrection morning" (34). When an airplane flies over, Burley looks up, steps back to see better, and begins to slide, like an ice skater, right off the edge of the roof, all the while think-ing, "Well, this is the end of you, old bud." Fortunately he is caught by an old cedar tree, left for no very good reason to grow by the side of the barn. Whether Burley's saving was providential or a matter of luck is something he can never decide, so, like a sensible man, he "split[s] the middle and thank[s] Providence" for "[his] luck" (35). For once he and Jarrat seem to recognize the depth and unbreakability of the bond between them: they look "back and forth at each other what seemed a long time, and it was aw-fully quiet." Jarrat breaks the silence with a line that points ironically to the shape of the rest of Burley's life: "Well, are you practicing up for something, or was that it?" Unknowingly Burley has just practiced being interrupted by the unexpected, the unwanted, and yet discovering something "saving" in it. "It came to me I was alive," (36) Burley remembers, perhaps for the first time in that peculiarly acute way we come to know this when it comes to us that we might just as easily be dead.

The "requirement" comes unexpectedly to Burley in the form of Tom and Nathan Coulter's need of him after their mother's death. Lettie and Jarrat are living happily with their young boys when she takes sick—"right in the midst of things going on the way they ought to have gone on forever"—and dies "without waiting for us to get ready," (99) as Burley puts it in "Stand By Me (1921–1944)." Jarrat responds with relentless work, and Burley and Jarrat's own mother is unable to be mother again to the boys. Burley finds he "belonged" to Tom and Nathan "because they needed" him; they "stuck to [him] like burrs" (99). Their requirements as children meant something was required of Burley:

> They were just little old boys. They needed their mother, was who they needed. But they didn't have her, and so they needed me. Sometimes I'd find one or the other of them off somewhere by himself, all sorrowful and little and lost, and there'd be nothing to do but try to *mother* him, just pick him up and hold him tight and carry him around a while. Their daddy couldn't do it, and it was up to me. (101)

Burley recognizes that the boys "changed" him, from one often "just on the loose, carefree as a dog fox, head as empty as a gourd," to one whose "heart was bigger inside than outside" (104). After Tom is killed in World War II, Burley comes to the further recognition that those now absent are "with you in a way they never were before," and this, too, has to do with the enlarging of the heart. Our remembering the dead is a sign of the way the "world gets bigger on the outside" for us as our hearts get "bigger on the inside" (110). As Burley puts it, we can remember the dead "because they always were living in the other, bigger world while they lived in this little one, and this one and the other one are the same." This is something "you can't see" with "your eyes looking straight ahead," but that you do, "with your side vision, so to speak" (110). There is hope, I believe, but no easy consolation in this vision. No one is "going to see" the dead "here anymore, ever." "Our separateness and our grief" do no less than "break the world in two" (110). After Tom's death, the requirement of love takes Burley to Jarrat. There was "mainly nobody" (111) to do the grieving but Jarrat and Burley, and so Burley does it. What helped them to go on was the requirement, what was asked of them, this time by the "good animals" on whom they "depended"—and who depended on them, in turn, for tending and care (112).

Burley's sense of the wideness of the world derives, too, from his love of the woods. Jarrat and Nathan belong to the farm and to work. Burley is a good enough farmer himself, but one who is "entirely happy" when he is "bone-tired, thirsty, hungry, [and] lost" (116) in the woods, as at the beginning of "The Dark Country (1948)." For Burley, there is joy in being lost, in moving about in the darkness in a way that reinforces one's sense of how wide and mysterious the great world is. At times he seems to think and even to know without the mediation of words. Yet he is also capable of precise remembrance of the animals whose lives he takes as a hunter and trapper and of the "spot[s] of the country" (120) from which they have come. As a woodsman, Burley knows that "no life lives but at the cost of other lives" (122)—or, to put this otherwise, none of us has any choice but to be in debt. When he does take the life of an animal, Burley responds first with "regret," but then second with what could be called "thanks, for the acquired good" (122). Burley's sense of gratitude emerges strongly in "The Dark Country." As he comes to the Proudfoot farm, he remembers his teacher Miss Minnie with gratitude for her undiscourageable insistence that he could and would learn and for her "remain[ing] interested in him" (124) in a way that surprised him. He is grateful to Old Marster for "com[ing] up with something as good as" the sexual love he has spent a good bit of his time hunting in his roaming about. Another surprising "revelation" to him has been Kate Helen's coming "along with him at night" and her ability to be, "just as much there, wherever they were, as he was" (128). They have been entirely happy together, particularly in a "certain big old hollow sycamore," (128) out of which their boy, Danny Branch, has come. Burley's gratitude finds its richest expression as he thinks of Danny and then of his worries about Tom and Nathan during the war—and of Nathan afterward. Hoping the restless Nathan is now "circling a place he wants to light," Burley says "aloud, 'Well, bless him!'"—following this, almost immediately, with "Bless 'em *all!*" "A tremor of love for the three boys, the dead and the living, had passed through" Burley and "shaken him" (129). Immeasurably blessed himself, he cannot help but ask for blessing on the boys—and perhaps, by extension, that whole larger world. This is what Burley has been practicing for: being surprised by a love that has grown with his heart as it responded to the requirements of his being in debt to the membership.

Andy Catlett, too, is surprised at the end of *A Place in Time* by a supposition that wells up from his own charity—a charity formed by his responses to what has been required of him. "A Place in Time (1938–2008)," the final story of the volume bearing its name, returns to the story of Elton and Mary Penn. It has been prepared for by "An Empty Jacket (1974)," in which young Marcie Catlett gets his own first taste of the "once for all" quality of life through the sudden death of his friend Elton. The gathering of the community at the Penns' house testifies to the respect Elton has earned, respect he once feared would never be his. As Marcie walks about the place, it seems "as though he had come into the inside of Elton's mind," for all about him "were the things that were Elton's thoughts and the order that Elton had made" (186). "A strange freedom" comes upon him as he can now "walk freely into the barn," touch "the handles of the tools," and even touch Elton's work jacket left hanging from a nail. Yet he hears "himself crying," for he has entered the "changed world" of absence and loss, that once-for-all world known to his elders—who know, too, that no one knows the hour (187). The question posed in all but words is how Marcie should now carry forth "the thoughts and the order" Elton has made within him. "Faithfully," of course, is the answer, though what that means specifically can only be gotten at by telling and retelling how Elton's life informs Marcie's own as both are interwoven into the lives of a whole membership.

The task of being faithful to Elton, of remaining lovingly in debt to him, is largely ahead for Marcie at the end of "An Empty Jacket (1974)." But it is ongoing work being carried to the end by Andy in "A Place in Time (1938–2008)." Andy remembers how he and Elton first met and how exacting his friend could be as they worked together. If Andy were to apologize after accidentally or carelessly cutting off a tobacco plant as they hoed, Elton might well say, "Too late." Apologies "do not undo mistakes" (230). Elton's care and discipline helped him and Mary to become the worthy successors to the Beechum place, and together the Penns made a life, "a success, even a triumph" (232) of sorts. Three emphases stand out, in particular, in the story as Andy seeks to get the Penns' stories right. First of these is that Elton's life is not simply to be understood only as reaction to the Mountjoys' judgment of him. He has not been merely about negating their negation, however much he has feared, at times, "that they had been right" (219). Andy knows that Elton "was driven also by a passion for farming as great as that of Jack Beechum and Marce Catlett," that he "loved offering himself to the work," and "loved the knowledge of what one man's skill and strength could do in a day" (228). He and Mary took "what had been given them" and brought something substantial, an "abundance"—a "new thing"—into being (232). Yet as the story also emphasizes, the kind of wholeness achieved by the Penns was already under remorseless pressure from the economy of industrialization by the time of Elton's death—something he knew very well and "raged against" (233). When Elton died, the world that he "had helped to make" was "ending" (233).

Andy's final emphasis carries the story beyond Elton's death while honoring the force of his phrase, "too late." Andy remembers something he had learned from the Penns' daughter Martha, long after her parents' deaths. When Martha moved to Cincinnati, her grandmother Mountjoy had tried to "get in touch" (235) with her but she had not returned her call. Now it occurs to Andy that perhaps Mrs. Mountjoy and her husband "had been sorry" for their rejection of Mary and Elton, that they had suffered a "too-late sorrow" for what could not be taken back or undone. The thought comes "to Andy as a command he could not refuse, for he had in the same instant obeyed it" (236). Andy is "required," to use Burley's language, to think of Mrs. Mountjoy no longer simply as "a wicked old woman in a tale learned in childhood" but rather as "only human, a fellow sufferer with Mary, her disclaimed child, and with Elton, her declared enemy" (236). Perhaps this is what Andy has been practicing for: an act of imaginative charity that allows him to be "filled suddenly with the apprehension of such hurt and sorrow as might overflow the capacity of the world"—all of it "too late" to be remedied or undone in the world's terms. It seems to Andy "almost a proof of immortality that nothing mortal could contain all its sorrow," and he imagines the "immensity" of "outcry" that would result if all the world's "sorrow could somehow be voiced, somehow heard" (236–237). In a way reminiscent of his grandmother Feltner, Andy sits "thinking of heavenly pity, heavenly forgiveness, and his thought" is a "confession of need. It was a prayer" (237). This, then, is what we are required to do for one another as we live in the debt of love: to "pray without ceasing" that the story might yet be gotten right for all. To do so is a burden, for it comes by knowing the weight of the "too late," but perhaps finally it is a requirement as light and as vital as thinking, or breathing, itself.

Bibliography

Berry, Wendell. "Our Deserted Country," In *Our Only World: Ten Essays*, 105–115. Berkeley: Counterpoint, 2015.

Kierkegaard, Søren. *Works of Love: Some Christian Reflections in the Form of Discourses.* Translated by Howard and Edna Hong. New York: Harper & Row, 1962.

8

Hiding in the Hedgerows
Wendell Berry's Treatment of Marginal Characters

Michael R. Stevens

MANY TIMES, AS I'VE entered the world of Berry's fiction, I've felt as though the stories or chapters comprise a set of glorious glimpses. His main characters become familiar, solid, approachable, whether as narrative voices, such as with Jayber Crow or Hannah Coulter or Andy Catlett, or as anchoring figures at the front of the stage, such as with Mat Feltner or Burley Coulter or Uncle Jack Beechum. They stand out starkly in the open fields of the story-lines, to be seen straight-on, or in sharp relief, and to be understood and learned from. Perhaps in defiance of Aristotle, perhaps in deference to the human scale, Berry seems to value character over plot, the evolution or devolution of human lives over the ordering of events. But in his art of portraiture, he also populates the backgrounds and margins with figures who are minor in scope but significant in augmenting his meaning, for Berry never diminishes or devalues personhood, even among the characters he merely glosses. Though not in the midst of the fields, and perhaps clinging only to the hedgerows, these minor characters offer 'hints and guesses' at the thick variations and incontrovertible connections, the web of meaning within which every person dwells.

As a hedgerow hides many different sorts of creatures, some benevolent and some not, so also Berry's minor characters bring a range of nuances, both blessings and curses, in among the host. Perhaps most compelling are the figures forced to the literal margins of the community by some flaw or bias or blight. They are the ones who 'fall into the cracks' of the community, and though the world of Port William sometimes has compassion enough in it to shout down the hole, to reach in a hand, to run for help, Berry often shows that the gaps are too wide and deep, the margins too shadowy to pierce. Conversely, several of the minor characters in Berry's imaginative landscape provide shafts of light, slivers of hope, some version of coherence in difficult or disordered moments. They 'fill the cracks' of the narrative, guiding the protagonists through dark hours and hard moments, providing a touch of levity, or normalcy, in the midst of strain. They complete a sort of dialectic among Berry's 'supporting cast,' those trapped in the hedges juxtaposed with those who leap free. But one other grouping remains, sharpening the taste of bitter in Berry's bittersweet world. These are the malefactors, those who do harm, who 'widen the cracks' and don't necessarily pay for the harm done, who get away. Though such characters drag pain and even betrayal in their wake, they have to be there, Berry seems to assert, to make us remember the fragility of the communal web, or maybe to remind us of our dependence, our own vulnerability. The hedgerow can hide the vicious creature, or the wounded, can be a place of ambush or of traps and tangles. So be it, Berry asserts by his characterizations, so it is and ever will be, in this world. But we have to look and see and know in order to learn.

Those Trapped in the Hedgerows

In the most traditional sense of the marginalized, Berry places into his community of Port William a few African-American characters, whose lives are deeply folded into the land, but who stay partially hidden, and who eventually disappear. At the center of this characterization is Joe Banion, the Feltner's hired man, the descendant of Smoke, who had lived on the Feltner place in the time of slavery and its aftermath. Joe and Nettie live among the Feltner's as employees and, ultimately friends, but in a cautious vein, in a world shaped by racism. In *A Place on Earth*, Joe is described as such: "His face is that of a man who has learned long ago to do what is necessary: to work, to take pleasure as he finds it, to make do, to be quiet."[1]

Likewise, at his Grandfather Catlett's home, Andy Catlett communes with Dick Watson, the hired hand and friend of Marce Catlett, and beloved companion of the boys Andy and Henry. Andy's narrative voice, across the veil of half a century, reflects that "now, when the two races are more divided than ever, this history has acquired a conventional oversimplification,

1. Berry, *A Place on Earth [Revised]*, 37.

implying that what we came to call 'segregation' was a highly generalized circumstance in which the two races disliked or hated each other, and which assured the happiness of the one race and the misery of the other. And so perhaps I offend current political etiquette, as I offend the racism to which it is opposed, by saying that, in and in spite of the old racial arrangement into which we both were born, I loved Dick Watson, and he treated me with affection and with perfect and unfailing kindness."[2] The margin in which Dick dwelt was sustaining, both for him and for his housemate Aunt Sarah Jane, but only barely, or perhaps wonderfully barely:

> Owning little, living day by day from his small daily wage, such provender as the farm by agreement furnished, and what he and Aunt Sarah Jane grew or found for themselves, he lived a life that was in some ways less dragged upon by past and future than my grandfather's. He did not live upon accumulations. It seems to me that he was capable, often enough, of life as contemporary as the daily sunlight.[3]

Even as Dick showed the kindness of a mentor, Sarah Jane chose to teach from the margins, about the margins, in a way that Andy never forgot:

> She also spoke that day, as she often did, of the rights that her people had been promised but had never been given. She was my first preceptor in the matters of race and civil rights . . . . Aunt Sarah Jane's plain talk of racial injustice as she knew it, thereby introducing the fester of it into the conscience of a small boy, who knew it only as the accepted way and a mandatory etiquette, was by the measure of that time remarkable. To the extent that her talk was a discomfort and an instruction, it was a service. To the extent that it was interesting and a part of conversation, it was hospitality.[4]

What Andy learned, or at least stored away, in her presence was truth that could come from nowhere else in his life, and at no other time so aptly into his life, in the cultural milieu of the pre-WWII South.

Perhaps most telling of their dwelling on the fringe, in the hedge of life, was the persistent emphasis of the Watson's on the coming 'Day,' full of apocalyptic ambiguity: "Like Grandma, Aunt Sarah Jane was thoughtful of the end of the world. But whereas Grandma regarded it with some deep disturbance of temporality and dread, Aunt Sarah Jane, who held it sufficiently

2. Berry, *Andy Catlett,* 26.

3. Ibid., 27.

4. Ibid., 75–76.

in fear, also looked down upon it with some approval as the time when justice would rain down at last."[5] So the instruction in social justice that Sarah Jane offered in her cabin to the young Andy was not without a certain potency and even threat.

Dick's vision was more temporal, more in the moment, such as he had learned to live in all aspects of his life, as Andy recalls: "In my hearing at least Dick did not pay much attention to the great mysteries and mystifications, nor was he preoccupied with doubts . . . . He lived, he pleased himself as he was able, he endured."[6] So for Dick, no apocalyptic foreboding or doomsday talk, but rather a long set of discourses on "an event that Dick and his people called 'The Big Day.' When Dick and I talked about it, I too called it The Big Day. The Big Day came every year on a Saturday in August. It was attended by the black people in Hargrave and from the farms for miles around. For the ones who had moved to the northern cities, it was a homecoming. It was for its participants the greatest, grandest day of the year."[7] Of the parade and picnic and conviviality and dancing, Dick lived in anticipation that became palpable to Andy, a sort of heavenly feast, a feast of possibility and deliverance and endurance at counterpoint to a 'Day' of judgment and reckoning.

> Dick Watson looked forward to The Big Day with all his mind and heart. He had to talk about it, and because I often was the only available listener he talked about it to me. Probably he could not have found a better listener, for I identified utterly with him in his anticipation. . . . Though we were living in the great tremor of the drouth and its betokening of the end of time, we also foresaw the coming of this merely local event that caused Dick's mind, and therefore my own, to tremble with a presentiment of joy.[8]

A sort of glimpse of the Kingdom coming, for Aunt Sarah Jane coming in justice and rectification, for Dick coming in conversation and an evening's mirth—ultimately, this manifold vision offered hope even at the very margins, and something more than just a distant hope. As Berry notes in his tremendous book on racism and its costs, *The Hidden Wound*, in giving account of his boyhood friendship with the real Nick Watson and Aunt Georgie who lived at his Grandfather Berry's farm:

5. Berry, "Drouth," in *A Place In Time,* 91.

6. Ibid., 92.

7. Ibid., 94.

8. Ibid.

I think it would be futile, and perhaps condescending as well, for me to remember Nick and Aunt Georgie only to pity them. There are times, I admit, when I am moved by a necessarily vague pondering over what they might have been. But I am, I think rightly, much more moved, much more clarified and instructed, by what they *were*, for what they were was far from inconsiderable.[9]

From that lived recognition, Berry suggests a broader truth for the real Nick Watson and the whole African-American experience in America, including the Joe Banions and Dick Watsons and Aunt Sarah Janes of his fictional re-imagining: "They have endured and survived the worst, and in the course of their long ordeal they have developed—as most of white society has not—the understanding and the means both of small private pleasures and communal grief and celebration and joy."[10]

As an addendum to the power of Dick Watson's small, marginalized hope, Berry offers the brief story "Not a Tear," Andy Catlett's rumination on Dick's funeral in late 1945, which the boy Andy did not attend: "I was in school. It occurred to nobody that I should have gone, but I should have. I wish I had."[11] But Andy's father and grandfather were there, and they came away awed by the power of the send-off offered in the small black church outside of town. Wheeler Catlett's reconstruction of the funeral sermon— "Well, sir, it was perfect, Andy. It was just right. . . . That preacher was splendid"—offers a sense of the loss and yet the gain of one who lived and died at the margins. In death, if not in life, Dick Watson was lauded; as Wheeler described the preacher's eulogy, "It was not a speech. . . . It was a song."[12] In what seems like poetic lines, Andy recounts his father's recounting of the 'song,' and it is a reconciliation beyond Dick's genial longing for The Big Day each August, stretching even to the bounds of Aunt Sarah Jane's 'Day of the Lord':

> Blessed are the poor / in spirit, for theirs / is the kingdom of heaven. / Blessed! / Blessed are they that mourn, / for they shall be comforted. / Children, / don't cry no more. / Sister Sarah Jane, / don't cry no more. / Our brother, / where he is, / he don't hear no crying. / For his burden is lifted. / For freedom / has come to him

9. Berry, *The Hidden Wound*, 62.

10. Ibid., 63.

11. Berry, "Not a Tear," in *A Place In Time*, 113.

12. Ibid.

/ and rest. / For where he is / ain't no crying there. / Not a sigh. / Not a tear.[13]

And so the account goes, the feeling of what happens when the invisible bonds have snapped that held Dick close and tight to his hedge of life: "While the preacher regarded the people with his hands still lifted, my father said, an immense quiet came upon them, and the freedom of Dick Watson in that moment was present to them all. They sang a hymn, they said a prayer, and then they let him go."[14] So Dick's endurance lives on through the love, not only of his own community, but of his separated brethren, of Marce Catlett the crusty farmer weeping in the crowd, Wheeler Catlett the rhetorician awed by the language of hope, and Andy Catlett, both the little boy left home and the old man now remembering, sensing that Dick's small mien of dignity now had full sway and purchase.

Those Walking in the Shadow of the Hedge

Nightlife Hample lives on a totally different margin within the web of Port William's people—he is mentally ill, given to 'spells,' in the parlance of a century ago, which cause his decisively shy, myopic demeanor to become "sad and angry and confused and maybe dangerous."[15] He is the central character in one of Berry's richest stories, "Watch with Me," set in 1916 and featuring the genial patriarch Tol Proudfoot and a cast of younger characters, including Sam Hanks, Walter Cotman, and Burley Coulter. It is the story of a vigil, enacted by Tol after Nightlife, in the throes of a 'spell,' snatches up Tol's loaded shotgun from an outbuilding and walks off into the woods.

It was Tol who had talked Nightlife down the night before, when Nightlife had crashed the annual revival meetings at Goforth Church with a demand to preach his own sermon. The continuation of his watchcare over the troubled neighbor, the long walk through two days and a night in the woods and pastures around Port William, gives ample time to reflect on Nightlife's inner plight:

> He was a Hample, plain enough, but it was as though when he
> was a baby his mechanically minded siblings had taken him apart

13. Ibid., 115.
14. Ibid.
15. Berry, "Watch with Me," in *That Distant Land*, 82.

and lost some of the pieces, which they then replaced with just whatever they found lying around. . . . His mind, which contained the lighted countryside of Katy's Branch and Cotman Ridge, had a leak in it somewhere, some little hole through which now and again would pour the whole darkness of the darkest night. . . . From there he would want to call out for rescue, and that was when nobody could tell what he was going to do next, and perhaps he could not tell either. Or that was what it looked like to Tol, who had thought much about it.[16]

And so the vigil is premeditated by Tol, as an act of mercy for one unable to ask for it, one who seems instead threatening, who is armed in deadly earnest.

The vigil is not without moments of helplessness—such as when Nightlife bursts into Uncle Othy and Aunt Cordie Dagget's kitchen (a few years before they adopt little Jonah, later Jayber, Crow) at dinnertime—and hopelessness, when they lose Nightlife, and themselves, in the darkness, only to have him appear amidst the ashes of their fire flailing with the shotgun; and yet Tol's vantage is that this painfully marginalized soul needs to be accompanied, tended, neighbored, whether he wants it or not, wherever he goes, to the ends of the earth and time, to the limits of their own lives. But there is doubt, there is strain in the conviction:

> It was not going to make sense, not yet, and maybe not for a long time, if ever. And for a while, maybe a longish while, there would not be food or rest or comfort either. When they got to the end of the story, he reckoned, they would at least eat. He said to himself, 'I reckon it would be better not to have got involved.' But he knew even so that, helpless or not, hopeless or not, he would go along with Nightlife until whatever happened that would allow him to cease to go along had happened.[17]

Not lost in Tol's ruminations is the sense that the community for Nightlife extends beyond just his immediate concerns, for "he knew that Walter and Sam and the Hardys would keep going as long as he did,"[18] and that the acerbic Walter Cotman, despite hazarding "'if the damned fool is going to shoot hisself, why don't he go on and do it, and let the rest of us get back to

16. Ibid., 88.
17. Ibid., 101.
18. Ibid.

work?'," was still committed: "But Walter did not leave, as Tol—and Walter himself—knew he would not."[19]

So, this tired, troubled group carries on, keeping Nightlife within the margins, if just barely, of his own existence, which they've made their existence as well. When Nightlife loops full circle back to Tol's farm the next morning, just as a vicious storm breaks on the wayfarers, there is one final moment of tension, as the men all stumble into a shed with Nightlife right behind them, shotgun in hand. And then the nurturing they've offered him from afar culminates in a most unexpected way, as Nightlife leads them in a worship service, complete with a hymn, and an extraordinary sermon.

From the story of the ninety-nine sheep and the one, Nightlife offers an account from the lost lamb's vantage point, "who could imagine fully the condition of being lost and even the hope of rescue, but could not imagine rescue itself." As Nightlife puts it, "And the shepherd comes a-looking and a-calling to his lost sheep, and the sheep knows the shepherd's voice and he wants to go to it, but he can't find the path, and he can't make it,"[20] a poignant declaration about absolute loneliness, but from a man who had not been allowed to remain alone. Indeed, his words are immediately met with empathy and understanding in that little shed: "The others knew that Nightlife knew what he was talking about. They knew he was telling what it was to be him. And they were moved." As Andy Catlett found out from Elton Penn, who had in turn asked Walter Cotman himself, even the skeptic Walter was moved: "'Me?' Walter said. '*Course* I felt for him! The son of a bitch could preach!'"[21] That openness to hear him, to walk with him, to swallow fear and confusion and belligerence to watch over him, allows Nightlife to come back from the margins, to emerge from darkness into light.

Those Who Bind Up the Tears in the Hedgerows

One of the harsher realities that the years reveal to us is that many of our connections and relationships are only for a season. Life is seasonal—there are jubilant spring times, certainly, but also winters, droughts that gouge the plenitude, even lovely summers whose "lease hath all too short a date."[22]

19. Ibid., 103.
20. Ibid., 121.
21. Ibid., 122.
22. Shakespeare, "Sonnet 18," 59.

This ephemerality often characterizes our bond to old people in our lives when we are young. We need them, they are central to our formation—but just when we recognize these truths, the grandparent or elderly neighbor is gone. But the early imprint is often deep, its resonance strong.

These are the hedges that protect the fledgling field—perhaps old, gnarled stumps and bracken, the first boundary that can be made. Thus, we see in Jayber Crow's life the presence of Aunt Cordie—Cordelia Quail Dagget. A great-aunt, a shoestring-relation, from the margins even of the consummately marginal Port William—a little store and farm on the river ferry at Squire's Landing.

In Jayber's dark confusion of losing his parents, Aunt Cordie arrives as a figure of simple consolation—"I can remember how she seemed to be trying to enclose me entirely in her arms."[23] The affection she poured out on young Jonah was an extraordinary contrast to the typical orphan stories of Dickens or the Brontës—extraordinary because it is without constraint or obligation—an elderly couple, bereft with three young children lost long before, who somehow "had a store of affection that they now brought out and applied to me. Later I would know how blessed I had been."[24] So the boy Jonah receives the unexpected gift—being totally abandoned, then totally belonging once again.

Aunt Cordie offers the surprise of total love, something to heal and nourish the orphan even in his hopelessness: "From start to finish, I was pretty much Aunt Cordie's boy. When she spoke of me to other people, she always called me 'my boy,' tenderly and proudly, for I was her helper."[25] Jonah discovers not just how to be wanted, but how to be useful, which makes his blessing manifold, as he finds not only a mother but a teacher: "Aunt Cordie was good company and always kind, but she saw to it that I did my work right. The best part of my education, and surely the most useful part, came from her."[26]

Jonah's happiness at Squire's Landing has a short half-life, and Uncle Othy's death began to end it, but Aunt Cordie's own grief did not eclipse her love for the boy, but rather seemed to purify and simplify it—Jonah stored up that abundance of love for the next decade of orphanhood and loneliness: "I could see that Aunt Cordie was grieving, and yet she took care to be

23. Berry, *Jayber Crow*, 14.
24. Ibid., 15.
25. Ibid., 23.
26. Ibid.

a good companion to me. She praised my work, calling me 'my boy,' and told me stories, and would sit with me by the hour after supper, playing Rook or Old Maid. We were, in a way, playmates."[27] What would have seemed a regression to juvenile play actually serves as a storehouse of friendship for a boy who will not have it again in his childhood. And so Aunt Cordie seemed to embody a gentle but thorough hedge of protection—a loving boundary, albeit one that withers almost as soon as it blooms.

For Hannah Coulter, or, in her youth, Hannah Steadman, her half-orphaning upon the death of her mother leads to a very stereotypical experience with stepmother and step-siblings who envy her and seek to win away her father's affections. But the presence of her paternal grandmother, Grandmam Steadman, provides a thin but resilient boundary within the farmhouse and constrained life they lead, within which Hannah could grow and ultimately thrive. Speaking of her father's struggles with the ill-founded blended family, the aging Hannah reflects back that "I think the house became a strange place to everybody. It surely did become strange to me, and my father too became strange to me. From the time he brought Ivy and her boys home with him, I owed everything, simply everything, to Grandmam."[28]

Like Aunt Cordie, Grandmam collapses the generations, crosses the divide of time, accepts the new weight of effort and sacrifice: "And so Grandmam came back from that distance in time that separates grandmothers from their grandchildren and made herself a mother to me."[29] In a sense, Hannah became Grandmam's shadow self, a kind of re-birth and re-living. Remembering her own youthful vigor and shapeliness, Grandmam would try to communicate her link to Hannah: "Looking me up and down as I began to grow toward womanhood, she would say, 'Do you know your old grandmam was like you once?'"[30]

Of their early mornings together in the house, even when still physically separated, Hannah in her private room above the kitchen, and Grandmam in her cot or seat beside the kitchen stove, some strong synchronicity is at work: "And then she would sit in her rocker to brush her hair and put it up in a bun for the day. As I dressed and made my own bed and brushed my own hair, I would listen to her, knowing by the sounds every move she

27. Ibid., 27.
28. Berry, *Hannah Coulter*, 9.
29. Ibid., 12.
30. Ibid., 10.

made."[31] This doubling and correlation, by which Grandmam both guarded and instructed Hannah, pouring herself into her younger self, created a sort of miracle of wholeness within a fractured household: "We had, you could say, everything but money—Grandmam and I did, anyhow. We had each other and our work, and not much time to think of what we didn't have."[32] Ultimately, Grandmam's greatest gift to Hannah was to give her away to the broader world, a young woman of skill and poise and gratitude.

By the time Hannah is engaged to Virgil Feltner, and they are intimate enough to visit Hannah's girlhood home in Shagbark, ten miles from Port William, Hannah is aware of the awkward world she must re-open so that Virgil can look inside, into her past and her heritage. Hannah, a self-conscious character as well as narrator, laments as they leave the farmstead: "'Well, it's not very grand, is it?' And Virgil said, 'Don't think of it. Your grandmother makes it lovely.'"[33] In that statement, Virgil pronounces an unexpected benediction on all that Hannah is, because he recognizes that she is the product of Grandmam's giving. Perhaps he intuited in that moment, during that visit, all that she had done for Hannah, all she had surrendered for her granddaughter's victory.

His vision is ramified after the wedding, at the Feltner's Christmas Feast of 1941, celebrated while the specter of war and the change to come in the world hovers ominous but still in the background. And the patriarch and matriarch of the feast, Uncle Jack Beechum and Grandmam Steadman, reveal the beauty and propriety of that old world, fast fading. Hannah notes that "To keep from embarrassing me, as I understood, she had bought a nice winter coat and a little suitcase. . . . Mr. and Mrs. Feltner were at the door to welcome her, and she thanked them with honest pleasure and with grace."[34] Uncle Jack's arrival has regal overtones, but without the pretension and pomp: "Uncle Jack didn't *try* to have dignity, he just had it. A man of great strength in his day, he walked now with a cane, bent a little at the hips but still straight-backed. He was a big man, work-brittle, and there was no foolishness about him."[35] Of Uncle Jack's echoing of everyone else's compliments with "'Ay, Lord, it is that!'," Hannah observes that "his word fell upon the table like a blessing," and yet it is not in their words, but in

31. Ibid., 19.
32. Ibid., 14.
33. Ibid., 33.
34. Ibid., 36.
35. Ibid., 38.

their silence, their presence, that he and Grandmam Steadman show the wealth they bring: "Beyond that, he said little, and Grandmam too had little to say, but whatever they said was gracious. To have the two of them there, at opposite corners of the table, with their long endurance in their faces, and their present affection and pleasure, was a blessing of another kind."[36]

That's the last appearance of Grandmam in Hannah's narrative, except for occasional memories—as her life moves from marriage and mother-hood, to widowhood, to re-marriage with Nathan Coulter, to the estab-lishment of a new life and fuller family on the ridge above Sand Ripple, Hannah lives out a life that is an elegy to her grandmother, a co-visioning of a life such as Grandmam envisioned for her when she helped her pack her bags in Shagbark to go out into the world.

Those Who Rend and Ruin, but Don't Destroy, the Hedgerows

I'd like to end these reflections among characters who evoke sadness, though not quite despair. There are few thorough-going villains in Berry's fiction, besides the faceless corporations and powers-that-be. Troy Chatham, the stylish and selfish rival to Jayber Crow, uses and destroys, but with a still pitiable mania for progress and arrival. We can still care for him as a man because Mattie his wife has somehow kept her care alive. The good-for-little hired man Lightning Berlew might invite our contempt, as he does the old but observant Uncle Jack Beechum's, but he never rises to the level of nem-esis or malefactor, beyond his own ignorance. A better candidate might be Uncle Jack's despised foe from his prime years, Old Man McGrothers, who exults in Jack's failures (and who, as no surprise, also did a turn as a masked Regulator in the vigilante days of the late nineteenth century, in the clownish cast of "Don't Send a Boy to Do a Man's Work"). But none of these characters really rises much above caricature, as they incarnate the selfishness, the lowness of the acquisitive urge that threatens all that mat-ters within Port William and the whole world.

But there are certainly characters that wound and tear at the fabric of the community, precisely because they are so thoroughly part of it, or should be. In this category, which underscores time and again the vulner-ability of the community, are several uncles, whose relationships to the main characters and actions are at just enough slant, just enough ambiguity

36. Ibid., 39.

and love and license, to profoundly affect the stories of those whose they are. Into this sphere falls Uncle Andrew Catlett, the namesake and boyhood hero of Berry's fictive voice, Andy Catlett. Though it's hard to call Uncle Andrew a minor character, since an entire novel, *A World Lost*, is devoted to his reckless life and harrowing death, nevertheless he dwells on the near periphery of many of Andy's reflections on *joie de vivre*, and dissatisfaction, and enduring loss. So also the figure of Uncle Ernest Finley, Andy's great-uncle, little brother of his Grandma Feltner, who, crippled in WWI, keeps a trim and ordered carpentry shop in Port William that is a source of awe and fascination to the young Andy. This same Uncle Ernest, who smiles a rare smile when he sees Hannah Feltner's little war-baby Margaret, cannot overcome a disappointment of the heart, in his quiet infatuation and sharp despair in *A Place on Earth*, which leaves him in the utter loneliness of suicide. His loss is doubled by, or itself doubles, the grievous loss of Virgil Feltner, another of Andy's beloved uncles, as an MIA in the war, the hope of whose return eventually declines into ashes for his aching parents and young wife Hannah and all who loved him.

Each of these uncles reflects tragedy and loss, all shaded in violence and blood. In the cataclysmic losses, the wounds remain, but are perhaps cauterized. The community reels, but eventually finds a new vantage. That all three die within the timeframe of WWII shows them as metonymies for that brutal, heartless logic consuming the whole world, from which, as Berry's fiction persistently shows, the world never recovers.

But then there is Uncle Peach, Andy's great-uncle and baby brother of his Grandma Catlett, the worst of the bunch in some ways, the longest lasting blight and burden upon his family, the closest, perhaps, to a permanent trespasser on the sanctity of the communal bonds. In his far reaching story of Uncle Peach's trajectory, "A Burden," Berry reveals a shiftless man, a boy in a man's body, boasting and trading cusses with his boy nephews Andrew and Wheeler Catlett back in 1907, with tall tales of his service in the Spanish-American War and roughing it in the Indian Territory of Oklahoma. Braggadocio aside, "Uncle Peach had about him the ease of a man who had never come hard up against anything. All his life he had been drifting," and at age seven, Wheeler is charmed, as "with a boy's love for even the appearance of freedom, he loved Uncle Peach for his drifting."[37] But his love grows conflicted, as it must in the face of Uncle Peach's persistent failures, his drunken escapades, his eternal adolescence. As Wheeler grows into an

---

37. Berry, "A Burden," in *A Place In Time*, 39.

exacting man, a man who understands the fragility of the community and the damage done by dead weight, his wayward uncle becomes a test case of love's capacity.

Wheeler finds himself often torn between the poles of his father's disdain for the dead-beat brother-in-law, and his mother's irrational nurturing of the prodigal, and indeed,

> as he grew in experience and self-knowledge, Wheeler also grew to recognize in himself a sort of replica of his mother's love and compassion. . . . The change was in Wheeler. When the moment came, usually in the midst of some extremity of Uncle Peach's drinking career, Wheeler would feel a sudden welling up of love, as if from his mother's heart to his own, and then he would pity Uncle Peach and, against the entire weight of history and probability, wish him well.[38]

Despite the damage, sometimes irreparable, done by the figure of Uncle Peach, and all those who dwell among us doing harm from motives either dark or delinquent, a miracle is made possible by their weakness, their offense. We can learn, like Wheeler, to love beyond ourselves, beyond all reasonable range. In a sense, this teaches us what love really is, what it can be—a stretching of our compassion to cover the wounds and the offenses.

So it is that this minor, and in his minor way malignant, character of Uncle Peach, tearing his holes in the hedgerows of community and obligation, actually and accidentally makes passageways for an unexpected flourishing of love. And when Wheeler, a young man recently married, immersed in the work of law that he loves, gets the call to head to the Stag Hotel in Louisville, the favorite denizen for Peach's benders and breakdowns, the nephew goes at once, angry and grousing, but buoyed by that strange compassion. The title of the story that contains this vignette, "Thicker Than Liquor," is also part of the mocking epithet that the teenaged Wheeler had needled his mother with regarding Uncle Peach: "Blood is thicker than liquor."[39] But when Wheeler repeats the phrase as a full adult, he no longer mocks. He faces the reality of a burden that can only be properly borne with love. Having cleaned up Uncle Peach, bought him a bit of bootlegger whiskey to take off the edge, and more or less carried him to the train, Wheeler nears Peach's home with a mixture of exhaustion and anger: "It seemed to him that he was still in his leap, still falling, still attached to Uncle Peach,

38. Ibid., 43.
39. Berry, "Thicker Than Liquor," in *That Distant Land*, 150.

134

who was still falling."[40] But Uncle Peach's sleep turns into nightmares, and Wheeler acts with the same boundless, thoughtless love that a father would show his sick child: "And Wheeler lay down beside him to quiet him. For a while he did sleep quietly, and then his dreams returned again. Wheeler was awake for hours, soothing and consoling Uncle Peach when he fretted and muttered and cried out, struggling with him when he fought."[41] This is a depth of love that is difficult to separate from wrestling, grappling with consequences, a love that is vulnerable and bleary-eyed and bone-weary.

And then Uncle Peach, the cause and consummation of all the troubles in this and scores of other stories of Wheeler's life, grows lucid and does an utterly unexpected thing—he returns the love, with his own words of consolation: "'Wheeler boy, this is a hell of a way for a young man just married to have to pass the night,'" and with that gesture this decrepit man-boy, the family's pariah and pain, shows why we love—because it can heal, even if just a little, any measure of woe. "'I thought of that,' Wheeler said. 'But it's all right.' And he patted Uncle Peach, who went back to sleep and for a while was quiet. Later, Wheeler himself went to sleep, his hand remaining on Uncle Peach's shoulder where it had come to rest."[42] A breakage that creates mending, a revulsion that ends in embrace—it's hard to reckon with this power, to make love not only strong but resonant—sometimes, like Wheeler, we can only say in wonder: "It's all right."[43]

These characters are all small on the narratological scale, bits and pieces of the grand tapestry, the patchwork quilt of Wendell Berry's world, of the membership of Port William and the common folk of this remarkable and hidden place. Small, but each of them is essential, both to make the stories move forward, to allow the central characters to become fuller and more powerful and dimensional in our eyes, but also essential simply insofar as they show glimpses of our own humanity. At the margins, in and out of the hedgerows, ebbing and flowing across this fictional landscape, Berry's minor characters, with their fragmentary lives, help create the stunning wholeness of Berry's vision for the world. These are glimpses that are more revealing than many a gaze, and we are privileged to see the aggregate whole.

40. Ibid., 162.
41. Ibid.
42. Ibid., 163.
43. Ibid.

Bibliography

Berry, Wendell. *The Hidden Wound*. Berkeley: Counterpoint, 2010.

Shakespeare, William. "Sonnet 18." In *Shakespeare's Sonnets,* 59. New York: American Book Co., 1905.

PART 3: Responding to the Stories

9

Kentucky River Journal

Eric Miller

THE RIVER IS BEAUTIFUL in a way only rivers can be. From its ridged bank I look down at a wide bend, water moving at the speed of peace. And I remember that a river can capture your heart. With the touch of soft epiphany I feel what the Brazilian artist Milton Nascimento yearns toward when in a poignant song about journey, "Clube da Esquina N°2," he imagines *o coração na curva de um rio*: your heart on the curve of a river.[1]

"Everything sad that ever happened to me / I have mourned beside a river," writes Maggie Anderson.[2] It's no wonder. Rivers absorb, carry, cleanse. Some say rivers drain the earth. I think they indwell it.

***

For two weeks this spring I'm dwelling beside the Kentucky River, camping. I spend the days in Frankfort, eight miles south—but, as it turns out, upriver—at the Kentucky Historical Society, reading letters written to Wendell Berry, trying to grasp the meaning of the turn toward localism in our time. At night, fireside, the letters stream back to me. They span decades and come from across the continent, across the globe, landing one by one in the tiny post office that sits in the town of Port Royal, at the top of the hill above the Berrys' farm.

Just below the farm the Kentucky River continues its winding course, flowing north to the Ohio, about thirty miles from where I'm camping. This

---

1. Nascimento, *Clube Da Esquina*.
2. Anderson, *A Space Filled with Moving*, 6.

river has long been, as Berry wrote in an early essay, "a place where a man, staying by himself, could become deeply quiet."[3] It is a good place to listen to what these localists, one by one, have to say.

***

I wanted you to know that you have in your audience people that have quietly been learning the land for 10 years or more and have never had an adequate spokesman until now. You bring the philosophy and the intellectualism of country life out so well that I applaud you. You articulate the things I have tried to live for. Thank you.

A Montana woman, self-identified as an "organic beef raiser," 1973.[4]

***

The longing for what Berry's fictional Andy Catlett calls a "truer world" courses through these letters, whether as gratitude, rage, or both.[5] That's what I hear in the correspondence. That's what they hear in Berry.

As a people we are, of course, infamously willing to fall for anything that promises the merest taste of *beyond*. Writers by the thousands appeal unashamedly to such longing; the millions of readers of J. K. Rowling—or for that matter E. L. James—are only the latest testament of our common yearning. So formal qualities aside, what marks Berry's appeal? What has set him apart, these past fifty years, as spokesperson and symbol of localists everywhere, in their quest for something beyond?

Berry's appeal begins, I think, with a distinctive moral vision directed forcefully at both history and us, we who have no choice but to live out our histories.

But which of our histories will we follow?

This is the decisive question, the one Berry, with elegance and wit, pressures us to answer. And he leaves no question about the path he believes we must take. A truer world does exist, he avers, and *has* existed, at least in

3. Berry, *The Long-Legged House*, 111.

4. All letters are cited anonymously and can be found in the Wendell Berry Collection, Kentucky Historical Society, Frankfort, KY.

5. Berry, *Andy Catlett*, 19.

part, despite our fatally misguided efforts to transcend it. In *Andy Catlett: Early Travels* an aging Andy Catlett, Berry's fictional alter ego—born in 1934, the year of Berry's own birth, and the narrator or central character of three of Berry's novels—sets forth his judgment in sharp strokes:

> The old world in which our people lived by the work of their hands, close to weather and earth, plants and animals, was the true world; . . . the new world of cheap energy and ever cheaper money, honored greed, and dreams of liberation from every restraint, is mostly theater. This new world seems a jumble of scenery and props never quite believable, an economy of fantasies and moods, in which it is hard to remember either the timely world of nature or the eternal world of the prophets and poets.[6]

Andy speaks in this story as one who for decades has worked to draw close to that "true world," a journey he begins following a crisis in his young adulthood. Living in Chicago in the 1960s and working as a journalist, Andy, we learn in *Remembering*, found himself forced into servitude to "the reign of a compunctionless national economy" that was by then "established everywhere," only a few daring to speak against it—certainly not the editor of the magazine that employed him. Brought painfully to a point of moral clarity, Andy quits his job and resolves to speak out, through practices as well as words, as he returns to Kentucky. "Something needed to be done, and he did not know what. He turned to his own place then—the Harford Place, as diminished by its history as any other—and began to ask what might be the best use of it. How might a family live there without reducing it?"[7] This became Berry's own enduring, questioning quest: to live on his farm as part of his native community, in good faith with, in Catlett's phrase, "the timely world of nature."

But Catlett, in this same passage, refers to another world, a linked world: "the eternal world of the prophets and poets." And here we come more directly into the mystery of Berry's appeal. Berry is of course a celebrated poet. And "prophet" may be the single word most employed to describe his vocation. But in his fiction Berry takes his readers into this "eternal world" through another path: not prophecy, nor poetry, but myth. It is from the ancient realm of myth that his poetry and prophecy surge. His fiction at its deepest is an instantiation of it.

---

6. Ibid., 93.

7. Berry, *Remembering*, 79–80.

Within *Andy Catlett: Early Travels*, a novel that serves as a kind of prologue to all of his fiction, Berry traces his fictional project's mythic fundament. This novel features Andy as an old man recalling a voyage of decisive import he made as a nine year old to visit his grandparents in Port William, Kentucky, a few days after the Christmas of 1943. Andy's own family lived in the county seat ten miles away, but trips to his grandparents were, to his delight, common. In this story his parents turn the ordinary into an adventure by sending him there on his own, by bus.

It is a heady moment. And it is quickened by Andy's recent immersion into an enchanted ancient world. Accompanying him on his journey, he recalls, was his "new copy of Sidney Lanier's *The Boy King Arthur*, imbued already with the voice of my mother, raptly reading it to me."[8] A dreamy child, Andy throughout the story finds the mythical world of Merlin speaking into his own tender experience of his grandparents' Port William. When his grandfather greets him at the bus station by wagon, Andy feels, joyously, a sense of being truly transported—that "the world the mules were drawing us into was a truer world than the world of Hargrave." "And I liked it better," he adds.[9] At his grandparents' unelectrified farm, Andy experiences the electricity of the past.

His encounter with the past takes place through the work he witnesses his grandfather and grandmother doing. But it also comes through the telling of tales, stories kept alive by his grandmother, especially. Together they would speak, Andy reflects, "of the absent and the dead. Our talk took on the charm of distance and history almost like the stories of King Arthur and the knights of the Round Table. But this was *our* history and these were *our* people. Their names and stories and pictures had a worth to us that was timely and bodily and never to be put in a book."[10]

Berry of course would go on to do just that in many books and stories, all centered around Port William. But in Port William it's not the presence of magic that authenticates the myth. Rather, it is the presence of love—the deeper magic—that fills and saturates his world. In this universe, love, whether his characters sense it or not, is the supremely encompassing reality, the efficient cause of their lives. And so their history, as Andy muses, must be "told by love's losses, and by the coming of love, and by love continuing in gratitude for what is lost. It is folded and enfolded and

8. *Andy Catlett*, 4.

9. Ibid., 18–19.

10. Ibid., 83.

unfolded forever and ever, the love by which the dead are alive and the unborn welcomed into the womb."[11]

At the end of *Andy Catlett*, Andy, overwhelmed by gratitude for the welcoming love he has so long known, confides that it was this Christmas journey that sealed his enduring sense of communion with his grandparents and their world. In the book's last scene, Berry has young Andy stumble into the card game that begins *A Place On Earth*, his early Port William novel. Berry's long effort to render the true world is about to begin, thanks to love's awakening effect.

Middle Earth meets Middle America. Some middling Americans rejoice. Some even write letters.

＊＊＊

Just last week-end, matter of fact, while stopping at a newly-discovered neighbor's farm to buy raw milk and pick strawberries, I whispered to my girlfriend (while in the patch)—"Bet she's read Wendell Berry's essays." Sure enough, we get to chatting in the kitchen, I mentioning that I'm a poet of sorts, etc., and the first things she asks me is—"Have you read any of Wendell Berry's work?" And so things keep returning to their delightful sources.

A Washington D. C. attorney, 1982

I think it's the most beautifully written book I've ever read. The truths are so intrinsic.

A South Carolina woman after reading *Remembering*, 1988

＊＊＊

After one night as the lone tenter at the RV-clogged campground a massive black Nissan pickup—a "Titan"—pulls in next to my site. A middle aged man with long, stylish gray hair jumps out and starts to set up camp. He's tall, thin, friendly, and alone. I take him for a high school social studies teacher or a real estate agent. We exchange greetings. I warn him about the floodlight that might keep him awake. We shake hands and I leave for the day.

11. Ibid., 119–120.

When I get back in the evening I wander over to his site. He's brought along two chairs; with elaborate but unfeigned Kentucky hospitality he gestures me toward the empty one. It's not long before he tells me he's on a "bucket-list tour." There's something about the wistfulness in his eyes, as he gazes toward the river, that makes me sense what's coming next. It's pancreatic cancer. He has refused chemotherapy. At fifty-four, he's dying, and quickly. He wanted to camp beside this river, he says, as the first stay of his final tour. All of this within fifteen minutes of conversation.

In quest of the new localists, I've met a local. To say the least. A native of southern Indiana, Don's lived in northern Kentucky since the early 1990s, most of that time building houses. A year and a half ago he began to experience symptoms that went undiagnosed; within a year he had lost seventy pounds and finally received the medical—the biological—verdict. Now there remain waiting, memories, pain. And conversation along a river.

Does the day destroy the myth? Or does the day demand it? This is the storyteller's test. And the listener's, too.

***

The afternoon I met Don he was lucid. By nightfall, sitting at the fire, he wasn't lucid so much as loose, tongue freed by spirits of, in his case, definite medicinal value. He only takes half of his dosage of pain-killers, he tells me, so as to remain on this side of comatose; he supplants the missing meds with alcohol. He wants to talk—loves to talk, in fact, to "bullshit"—and has a perfect campfire repertoire of stories and opinions on any number of topics. He's a true-blue Democrat, I learn, and will vote for Hillary; from the way he says it, I gather that in his circle this makes him a maverick. The Republicans cause wars, he preaches, and the Democrats get us out of them. "Look at the history." I, out of politeness, don't look too closely.

Just what am I doing in Kentucky, he wonders. I try to explain. He's old enough to remember the fading of the old, local way of life, for sure. But when I describe this new movement, there's no sense of a resonant chord being struck. He tells me about an autistic friend who is a talented sprinter, a Special Olympian, in fact. The young man's employer, a national grocery chain, sponsored his participation in the 2011 Games in Athens. *That's* something that never would have happened in the old world, he says.

The conversation moves on. "What did you want to do with your life?" he asks suddenly. When I stumble around for an answer, he volunteers that he "just wanted to build a good house. That's all I really wanted to do." It's a declaration he'll make twice this night. A high level of craftsmanship has gotten much harder to achieve, he says, due to the massive construction firms that now control the market. Disgusted with the state of affairs, he ended up leaving house-building and landing a government job.

That's exactly what the localists are after, I think, without trying to explain: to make possible the building of a good house—to ensure a satisfying vocation for the builder and a lasting abode for the owner. I do tell him about the master carpenter I went backpacking with who refused to build the kind of houses the market had come to require; he too quit his work. Don nods.

We talk a good deal about his illness over the two nights I'm fireside with him. An older sister, unbelievably, is this very moment dying of lung cancer. Had she been a smoker? Never. How does his family account for this grisly twin take-down? It's all speculation, of course. But in the rural part of Indiana where they were raised their house was downhill from neighboring farms, chemically-sustained farms. The family suspects contamination through well water. I tell him about Sandra Steingraber's story in *Living Downstream*, how the preponderance of cancer in her immediate family gives the notion of the "genetic fallacy" new meaning, since she, adopted, is no blood relation to her family.[12] Cancer's environmental origins, studiously understudied, remain shrouded by willful and shameful ignorance for the most part, she contends. Don nods in vigorous agreement.

It occurs to me that Don in just a couple of hours has shown me two things: why the old local ways finally failed. And why the new localism must succeed. We need good shelter, and we need real safety. We need a world that measures success by our ability to protect and nurture the deepest goods we know: bodily and spiritual health. If the old world was weakened in the end by its own corruption—by its neglect of and at times distaste for the wellbeing of all—what's replaced it hasn't, seventy-five years on, distinguished itself by resplendent moral achievement, whatever its pretensions. Quite the contrary. Shoddy housing shows. Feeble bodies fail. Our days as a civilization are precisely as numbered as Don's. At some point we will require—will *see* that we require—meaningful, enduring vocations and relations.

This, at least, is the localists' insistent cry. As seen in their letters.

---

12. Steingraber, *Living Downstream*.

***

I read "The Futility of Global Thinking" when I woke up at five this morning, and I nearly cried.

Some smart corporation ought to reprint it complete in a pamphlet . . . and circularize a million copies to the right people, and someone else ought to preach it as the gospel. Millions ought to preach it so that millions more can hear it.

A Frankfort resident, September 1989

***

Don tells me that he could be in hospice care. He wonders if he has thirty days to live. I don't doubt his assessment. He's barely able to eat. He suspects, wryly, that at any moment a family member will show up with a court order dragging him to a hospital, requiring that he get "treatment," care that he's convinced, after his own investigation, has no chance of returning him to health. He wants instead to sit by the river, for a few days, at least—just like, as it happens, a beloved Berry character, one "Burley Coulter," whose son rescues him from the hospital so that he might pass on in peace, at home.[13]

I ask Don if, with death staring him down, he finds himself thinking much about the afterlife, about faith, god. No, he claims, not at all. But we talk religion anyway. Raised and schooled Roman Catholic, he married young, to a "Wesleyan" of the serious variety. He gave it a try, but neither Catholic nor Protestant faith took. "Do you believe in God?" he asks me sharply—"that he's real, that he lives?" When I say I do, he states, simply, that he doesn't "have that blind faith." "Why does this kind of faith have to be 'blind'?" I reply. But in his mind it's a tautology: if it's faith, it's blind faith. He'd cried out in the past, he says, asking God to show himself. But no response. He moved on.

The fire dying, my spirit worn, I go to bed. Twenty feet away, I listen to him coughing through the night.

Early in *Walden* that trenchant if not quite charming forefather of the literary localists, Henry David Thoreau, asks a probing question in parallel form: "Who shall say what prospect life offers to another? Could a

13. Berry, "Fidelity," in *That Distant Land*.

greater miracle take place than for us to look through each other's eyes for an instant?"[14]

The presence of Don, a man whom life is offering no uncertain prospect, has pressed my pursuit of this miracle to the limit. Looking through his eyes, dimming by the hour, I ask myself, Is myth yet in sight? Or might myth, even in the midst of ultimate extremity, *sustain* sight—and so, perhaps, a politics of hope?

***

A World Lost, the second of the Andy Catlett novels, has at its center violent death: the murder of Andy's uncle, his father's older, loveable, but gently renegade brother Andrew, Andy's namesake, whom Andy regarded with sweet and fierce admiration. The death occurs in the summer of 1944, a half-year after nine-year-old Andy's Christmas journey to Port William. Present in town when the murder took place, Andy, now in his sixties, looks back, trying to piece together—and more importantly, understand—what happened. It's a story of acute sensitivity told in the spirit of inquiry, an inquiry factual and spiritual at once. By the story's end the facts about the murder come clearer. But not as clear as the spiritual resting place Andy finally achieves in the face of suffering, death, and love.

If eternal love is at the heart of Berry's mythical universe—if, as Andy says, "The order of time is shaped and held within the order of eternity," and if that order is founded upon love—what does this mean in the face of suffering and death?[15] Does such love amount to anything beyond mute consolation?

Berry's answer is a quiet, searching *yes*. In view of our painful, guilt-ridden plight, love knows one response: what Berry summarizes as, simply, redemption—redemption that makes movement possible, even in the midst of loss.

Redemption, Andy's maternal grandfather tells him as a boy, is "a little flowing stream"—and for the thirsty, it's "there all the time."[16] Andy, decades later, will in *Andy Catlett* echo this affirmation, describing time itself as "held and redeemed by love, which is always present."[17] Looking down at

14. Thoreau, *Walden*, 52–53.

15. Berry, *A World Lost*, 19.

16. *Remembering*, 49.

17. *Andy Catlett*, 119.

the earth from a plane, Andy in *Remembering* sees a world "that cannot be helped except by love."[18] Love, in these stories, is both the constituent element and the rescuing agent of our world—even when everything seems to defy it.

Accordingly, the most consequential moments in the Port William world center on whether the characters, as travail and loss afflict them, will align themselves with love—with *reality*—or not. In Andy's own story of crisis, *Remembering*, he struggles bitterly to reconcile himself to a devastating personal tragedy: the loss of his right hand due to a farming accident at a neighbor's place. In his rage, Andy finds himself in a state of desolation. It strikes most acutely as he withdraws from his wife and so wanders "outside whatever held them together"—precisely the position many moderns classify as "freedom." But "the little hell of himself alone," Andy discovers, "does not excite him." "All choice is around him," we're told. But "he knows nothing that he wants."[19]

What he most needs, we're made to see, is to surrender to the deep presence and active reality of love. But this is not emotional so much as structural surrender, a surrender that occurs at the intersection of ontology and the human will. It's a choosing, often tortured, to realign one's being in the midst of pain with a world that is nonetheless founded upon and defined by love.

And Andy does surrender—as he, humbled, corrects and recounts his understanding of his own life. "He has been wrong," he comes to see, troubled especially by the anguish he has caused his wife. "That she, entrusted to him, should ever have wept because of him is his sorrow and his wrong." The experience and apprehension of love have restored his vision and righted his heart. "He must have her forgiveness. He must forgive himself. He must forgive the world and his own suffering in it."[20]

Two decades later, Andy's crisis is different, as we learn in *A World Lost*, not existential so much as historical, swelling from the past: Who was his uncle? Why was he murdered? Most important, is it possible to assuage the grief that yet burdens him and his kin?

Andy reaches a point in which, after much inquiry, he recreates the murder; in the process he reconstructs his uncle's character, trying with all of the wisdom he can summon to look him in the eye. "Finally you must

18. *Remembering*, 86.
19. Ibid., 8, 38, 42.
20. Ibid., 93–94.

believe as your heart instructs," he declares. "If you are a gossip or a cynic or an apostle of realism"—all positioning themselves beyond the bonds of love—"you believe the worst you can imagine. If you follow the other way, accepting the bonds of faith and affection, you believe the best you can imagine in the face of the evidence."[21] Sight requires belief. Berry chooses to believe in love, and draws his uncle's portrait accordingly.

But make no mistake: he is serious about heeding "the evidence"; the portraits of both Andrew and his wife Judith are exacting in their depictions of the ways they failed the complex claims of love, even as each also yearned toward it. Berry's depictions give credence to Chesterton's maxim that "Love is not blind. That is the last thing it is. Love is bound; and the more it is bound the less it is blind."[22] Only eyes lighted by love see what is actually here.

But what of the pain, the grief, the sorrow? Whither redemption? Here, Andy rests in a redemption that transcends our tragic mortality. It's worth a meditative read.

> I imagine the dead waking, dazed into a shadowless light, in which they know themselves altogether for the first time. It is a light that is merciless until they can accept its mercy; by it they are at once condemned and redeemed. It is Hell until it is Heaven. Seeing themselves in that light, if they are willing, they see how far they have failed the only justice of loving one another; it punishes them with their own judgment. And yet, in suffering that light's awful clarity, in seeing themselves within it, they see its forgiveness and its beauty, and are consoled. In it they are loved completely, even as they have been, and so are changed into what they could not have been but what, if they could have imagined it, they would have wished to be.[23]

This life, with its sorrow and joy, ends. Love goes on, and takes our lives with it, as we are willing.

Such willingness is not easy to achieve. In the face of destruction and loss, affirming the ultimacy of love requires more than many can offer. But its reward, redemption, though costly, is an evident, undeniable good in Berry's world. Redemption brings—as story after story show—reconciliation, peace, flourishing, joy, even as distress and travail continue. By

21. *A World Lost*, 87.
22. Chesterton, *Orthodoxy*, 76.
23. *A World Lost*, 104.

narrating the world so, Berry offers a gritty, constructive hope to those suffering the world, as well as delighting in it.

It is of course hope that is Christian in source and shape, though Berry, to be sure, has been coy about the nature of his affirmation of orthodox Christian doctrine. But inasmuch as he professes Christian faith, it may be that Berry, like Chesterton, Tolkien, and others, finds its plausibility to be bound up precisely in its mythic quality. This myth features at its center what Chesterton calls "something more human than humanity": love in mystically incarnate, self-sacrificing, redeeming form acting in time.[24] It's love that re-builds old worlds and moves toward new ones.

If we dare take up Thoreau's challenge and peer through Berry's eyes, it's this—this apprehension of and surrender to cosmic love—that his eyes tell us we need.

But of course he's far from universally persuasive. Maybe reading Berry's fiction offers a kind of Rorschach test, revealing to us, finally, what we each think when we see the word *myth*.

***

We are one world, the Gulf war precipitates black snow in Kashmir, and the same with thoughts, so many of these too dark and deadly. Thank God Port Royal is there. I suppose there will always be Port Royals somewhere in the world, holy-men, good men and women in spite of all. But yours is a voice that carries far, and speaks to a sort of memory in our very blood. And one mossy stone speaks as eloquently as a whole river-gorge that forgotten native language.

An English poet and scholar, summer of 1991

I hope you can find the strength to reject the adulation of religious milk-sops—those who embarrass you by calling you a prophet. Spend some time in the camps of the enemy—spend a week in a chemistry lab, for example. You will be safer there. Or argue the meaning of good education in front of your local school board. Become frightened, as I have become, out of any belief system. Then real poetry will begin again.

An American farmer and writer, Fall 1989

24. Chesterton, *The Everlasting Man*, 185.

On my last day in Frankfort I head to Buddy's Pizza for a quick lunch. When I place my order I notice the tattoo on the attendant's arm, a single word emblazoned in black: *saudades*. It's the Portuguese word for longing, aching longing, that nonetheless marks absence with joy. It's a Brazilian go-to word, as distinctive in their psychic lexicon as *futebol* is in their athletic, showing up in all kinds of circumstances: song lyrics, at the close of a letter, in conversation. It conveys something like what Americans mean by "the blues." But it's blue tinged with yellow, heading toward green. In the midst of the absence, the longing, there's yet, somehow, presence: the grateful celebration of what was, of what is, of what might yet be. *Saudades.*

When, noting the tattoo, I ask the girl if she'd been to Brazil, she says no, and rapidly tells me her tattoo's back story. She'd discovered *saudades* in a book. "I looked it up and fell in love with the idea," she says. She's heard all kinds of pronunciations of it. But since I've lived in Brazil, she says she'll take mine as authoritative. (A gringo's dream—or joke.)

That night, my last in the campground, happens to be the Saturday of Memorial Day weekend, and the place has turned into a party spread over a dozen acres. Don is gone. He'd packed up Friday morning, heading to Indiana to be with his sister. I'm left alone with several hundred people, and eight days of letters saturating my mind.

The locals are rocking into the holiday. While waiting for a potato to bake I hear the music of Stillwater, the band playing at the pavilion on the other side of the campground. I wander over. It's a country-rock mood they're in, in a passable, pleasing Eagles vein. They're old enough to know how this sound hit in the mid-1970s, how it seemed to help reconcile us to the world we knew was being lost—the world of meadows, family reunions, horse-back riding, the old folks at home. When the band breaks into Fleetwood Mac's "Dreams" I find myself, not quite to my surprise, at tears-edge. *You say / You want your freedom / Well who am I to keep you down . . . But listen carefully to the sound / Of your loneliness . . . in the stillness of remembering what you had / And what you lost / Oh, thunder only happens when it's raining . . ."*

This is the blues. My mind roams and races, to my uncle battling leukemia, to my niece who this week got engaged, to Don and his big black "Titan," mocking with its hundreds of horse-power his utter loss of strength. Longing wells up. Tears flow down.

Is there yet a way, in this land of harsh loss, toward *saudades*? Toward a greener world? If there is, it might run alongside that stream of redemption, moving north to some great river and carrying our hearts along with it, curve by beautiful curve.

Bibliography

Anderson, Maggie. *A Space Filled with Moving*. Pittsburgh: University of Pittsburgh Press, 1992.

Berry, Wendell. *The Long-Legged House*. Washington, D.C.: Shoemaker & Hoard, 2004.

Chesterton, G. K. *The Everlasting Man*. San Francisco: Ignatius Press, 2008.

———. *Orthodoxy*. San Francisco: Ignatius P, 1995.

Nascimento, Milton. *Clube Da Esquina*. Audio CD. Blue Note, 1995.

Steingraber, Sandra. *Living Downstream: An Ecologist's Personal Investigation of Cancer and the Environment*. Philadelphia: Da Capo, 2010.

Thoreau, Henry David. *Walden and Civil Disobedience*. New York: Penguin Classics, 1983.

Wendell Berry Collection, Kentucky Historical Society, Frankfort, KY.

10

"The End of All Our Exploring"
Homecoming and Membership in *Remembering*

Gracy Olmstead

What we call the beginning is often the end
And to make an end is to make a beginning.
The end is where we start from.[1]

I READ WENDELL BERRY'S *Remembering* in exile. An Idaho girl attending college in Virginia, I had come to feel a sort of yearning for the past—for kith and kin, for the sprawling fields and winding country roads of my childhood. I remembered counting rows of corn on my way to piano lessons, breathing in the delicious scent of mint every late summer afternoon. My grandfathers were farmers, and my people were begat of farming folk: they practiced the patterns of early mornings and weekends spent doing chores, of eating food grown close to home, of warming bellies with home-cooked meals. Though I didn't grow up on the farm, the farm's legacy and rhythms were all around me, and I was deeply proud of my grandfathers and their work. Their vocation as farmers made me an Idahoan: their long legacy on the land tied me to it, bound me to its rhythms and history.

The autumn before reading *Remembering*, I'd written a piece for my college's literary journal on "home." In it, I told the tale of my fathers and

1. Eliot, *Four Quartets*, 46.

forefathers, considering people who had invested all their life and toil into the next generation. What, I asked, would be my work—what would be my first fruits, and how could I offer them up in thanks as my fathers had?

Berry's novella rose up to me in answer. In it, he describes Andy Catlett's journey from—and eventually back to—his home in Port William, Kentucky. As a young man, Andy left home in order to attend college and become a journalist. Yet in the midst of his new career, he began to tell stories that filled him with yearning for a place, and people, he knew and remembered. So he returned home, eager to embrace the work of his own forefathers. But as the story unfolds, we discover that Andy's return is far from perfect: there is much hardship he must overcome before his home-coming can be complete.

Perhaps because of its length (the novella is only 103 pages), *Remembering* reads with a lyrical grace more reminiscent of poetry than of prose. It is dense with metaphor, from its opening words to its closing sentences. The very title of the work—"Remembering"—is heavily allegorical, speaking not only of Andy's reminiscence throughout the story, but also of the meta-phorical and communal grafting-in that happens when Andy embraces his "membership" in Port William. He is literally re-membered. Throughout the novella, Berry explores biblical themes of creation, naming, and fall, his words echoing the cadences of Genesis's opening chapters. These fragments of biblical narrative help frame Andy's journey to and from his "Eden," and hint at the deeper spiritual meaning of his journey.

Remembering is also deeply reminiscent of T.S. Eliot's *Four Quartets*, particularly *Little Gidding*, both in its lyrical rhythms and in its overarch-ing themes. Berry, like Eliot, uses the allegory of flame and water, tree and flower, night and dawn to tell a story of sanctification and redemption. In what follows, I consider these connections between Berry and Eliot's works, noting the themes they borrow from Genesis and historical writers such as Dante, and proffering some lessons we can learn from both. Andy Catlett's profound journey showed me the beauty and meaning one can find, even in exile.

Creation and Fall

After Andy returns to Port William for the first time, he embraces the farm-ing lifestyle of his ancestors. But when he loses his right hand in a machine accident during harvest season, the loss threatens all Andy has invested in and learned thus far. The newfound helplessness results in an existential crisis, as Andy grapples with his loss. He withdraws from his home and people, forcing himself outward from the place he has begun to cultivate. This is how Berry starts *Remembering*: with a broken Andy, smarting from the pain of loss that's built up in him following his (literal and metaphorical) dismemberment. In a story that functions as an epilogue to *Remembering*, one that Berry wrote for *The Threepenny Review* in 2015, he describes Andy's journey thus: "He became so large in his own mind in his selfish suffering that he could not see the world or his place in it. He saw only himself, all else as secondary to himself. . . . Eventually, inevitably, he saw how his selfishness had belittled him, and he was ashamed, and was more than ever alone in his shame."[2]

Remembering begins with a dream Andy has while in exile, one which offers stark contrasts to the creation story of Genesis 1. Whereas God commands, "Let there be light,"[3] *Remembering* begins with the words "It is dark."[4] In Genesis, God clothes and gathers, fosters fruit and vegetation, births life and plenty. But in Andy's vision, "bulldozers pushed and trampled the loosened, disformed, denuded earth, working it like dough toward some new shape entirely human-conceived."[5] All throughout the first and second chapters of Genesis, there is a naming and a calling: God gives name and identity to everything—sun, moon, stars, earth, vegetation, animal—and he calls his work "good." But in his dream, Andy sees "the fields and their names, the farmsteads and the neighbors were gone; the graveyards and the names of the dead, all gone."[6] In the midst of this chaotic dismemberment, the modern farmer looks upon his work and declares it "*not* enough . . . I cannot *afford* to quit."[7] The farmer's words are the opposite of a benediction, the ultimate un-rendering of the creation account.

"Between melting and freezing / The soul's sap quivers. There is no earth smell / Or smell of living thing," writes T.S. Eliot in *Little Gidding*.[8] He opens his poem on a wintry day, in which everything is dead yet suffused with the sun's glow. In this beginning, we see the pale waiting and death

---

2. Berry, "Dismemberment," *The Threepenny Review*, Summer 2015.

3. Gen. 1:3, KJV.

4. Berry, *Remembering*, 3.

5. Ibid.

6. Ibid.

7. Berry, *Remembering*, 4.

8. Eliot, *The Four Quartets*, 49.

reflected in the first few pages of *Remembering*—but there is still hope of redemption and renewal. The *Four Quartets* are each a meditation on the importance of place and remembering: Little Gidding, a small village in Cambridgeshire, England, has a rich history of community and collective faith (much like Berry's Port William community). The members of Little Gidding formed themselves into a mutually supportive collective, focusing their work around the rhythms of religious discipline and neighborly rapport.

East Coker, an earlier poem in the *Quartets*, considers the disillusionment and despair met along life's journey, fostered by humankind's loss of limits. In the first line of the poem's fifth section, Eliot writes, "So here I am in the middle way"[9]—a reference back to Dante Alighieri's *Inferno*, in which he writes, "Midway in our life's journey, I went astray."[10] Here, too, we find Andy: midway through his life's journey, experiencing all the pain of disillusionment and exile.

But *Little Gidding*, the last poem in Eliot's *Quartets*, considers the importance of redemption: our salvation from the ravaging effects of mortality and sin. Eliot used *Little Gidding* to tell his own story of remembering and return: bringing us from a vision of creation marred and broken to a vision of all things restored. Yet before we get there—to that moment of redemption in which "all manner of things shall be well"[11]—we must first go through the fire.

Namelessness and Exile

Still smarting from the loss of his hand, Andy travels to San Francisco for an agriculture conference. As he listens to the various speakers, he becomes angered by their abstract, desensitized musings. For Andy, the scholars' words teem with the seeds of liberation from love of community and loyalty to place. Theirs is a theoretical, detached language in which the problems and pains of particular farmers are aggregated, reflected in numbers rather than faces or names. This is what he rejected as a young reporter.

And this was the temptation that met me in Washington, D.C. as a journalist. I entered an intellectual and academic world like none I'd yet experienced. I was paid to write my opinions, to read heady philosophical

9. Ibid., 30.
10. Dante, *The Divine Comedy*, 3.
11. Eliot, *The Four Quartets*, 56.

works, to attend lunches and happy hours at which some of the world's smartest people drank coffee and wine together. They would share their thoughts on society, culture, politics, economics—and I often read, or saw, their derision and frustration with the "other." When referencing those across the political aisle, or the unwashed masses they directed their words towards, many indulged in a sense of separation, utilizing stereotypes similar to the generalizations of Andy's ag experts. Among these people, I felt myself a faceless presence surrounded by people I did not know, who did not know me. There was a time when I could say my name, and people knew it: I was a "Howard," and they knew my father or grandfather. I could identify myself as much as "Wally's granddaughter" or "Rick's daughter" as with the name "Grace." But the city wiped this slate clean. It unfettered me from the past, from the identity and community Andy finds himself yearning for.

This cosmopolitan abstraction, which confronts and tempts Andy throughout his time in California, seems particularly dangerous to writers: it enables us to worship ideas and hold them up without reference to place or people. It tempts us to float in the realm of the ideal, without seeking groundedness. There is comfort and security in this lack of knowing: an ability to be alone, and in that aloneness, to be selfish and self-worshiping: to set oneself on a pedestal, unfettered by the obligations and needs that we face when we are tied to people and place. It enables us to separate from the particular pains and needs of a specific place and prescribe universal (and thus useless) solutions to particular, complicated problems.

When his turn comes to speak at the conference, Andy recites the names of his loved ones, longing to put flesh and sinew to the ideas tossed about emptily in his midst. "I speak for Dorie Catlett and Marce Catlett," he says. "I speak for Mat and Margaret Feltner, for Jack Beechum, for Jarrat and Burley Coulter, for Nathan Coulter and Hannah, for Danny and Lyda Branch, for Martin and Arthur Rowanberry, for Elton and Mary and Jack Penn."[12] But even as he names his kith and kin, "they departed from him, leaving him empty, shaking, wet with sweat."[13]

Why does this happen—why do these names, spoken in earnest love, desert Andy after he utters them? Berry suggests the answer earlier in the chapter, when Andy muses on his own namelessness in exile: "A man could go so far from home, he thinks, that his own name would become

12. Berry, *Remembering*, 21.
13. Ibid.

unspeakable by him, unanswerable by anyone, so that if he dared to speak it, it would escape him utterly, a bird out an open window, leaving him untongued in some boundless amplitude of mere absence."[14] When Andy names his Port William neighbors at the agriculture conference, they "escape them utterly"—separated from him by all the physical and spiritual distance he's put between them.

Throughout the Bible, names are more than mere monikers. They indicate the intimacy of relationship ("O Israel, Fear not: for I have redeemed thee, I have called thee by thy name; thou art mine"[15]); the vocation of the name-bearer ("thou shalt call his name Isaac: and I will establish my covenant with him for an everlasting covenant, and with his seed after him"[16]); and our relationship with our forebears ("he called their names after the names by which his father had called them"[17]). After all, we do not choose our names: they are given to us. Andy has wandered from home, and in doing so, has lost his place—has lost his connection to the people who mean so much to him. He's dismembered himself from his community, and his namelessness reflects this condition. Later, Berry tells us that "When [Andy] lost his hand he lost his hold. . . . He remembered with longing the events of his body's wholeness, grieving over them, as Adam remembered Paradise."[18]

Stillness and Wandering

After waking from his haunting dream, Andy emerges from his San Francisco hotel room and begins to wander aimlessly through the streets. He is without purpose, without context. As he wanders, he watches the faces of the people he passes: noting their quiet distance, their anonymity. He considers the loss of limits (and thus of specificity or intimacy) that sin and brokenness have brought into the world. Urban existence often separates human beings from each other: fostering distrust rather than love, individualism rather than collectivism. When a woman passes him, "something in

14. Ibid., 5.
15. Isaiah 43:1.
16. Genesis 17:19.
17. Genesis 26:18.
18. Berry, *Remembering*, 23–24.

him for which he has no word cries out toward her, for the world between them fails in their silence, who are alone and heavy laden and without rest."[19]

Berry here references Jesus Christ's promise in the Gospel of Matthew: "Come unto me, all ye that labour and are heavy laden, and I will give you rest."[20] Rest is also a key theme in the opening chapter of Genesis. It is the pinnacle and climax of God's created work: "And on the seventh day God ended his work which he had made; and he rested on the seventh day from all his work which he had made."[21] But here, as in Andy's opening dream, there is only loneliness and restlessness. Andy continues to note the "night walkers" surrounding him, all of them hurried and huddled in the hours before the dawn. He's tempted to envision an alternate version of himself living in this city: rich and comfortable, living alone in gentility and grandeur. It's another temptation to dis-member himself: to distance himself even further from his community, while indulging in all the selfish pleasures of cosmopolitan abstraction. But already, Andy is beginning to turn from exile toward the love of place and people. In this particular moment of temptation, Berry writes, Andy "reminds himself of himself. . . . And he says then lucidly to his mind, 'Yes, you sorry fool, be still!' For the flaw in all that dream is himself, the little hell of himself alone."[22]

In this way, Berry suggests that our greatest temptations to selfishness can (and should) be refuted through remembering: in both an intellectual and physical sense. The words "Be still" reference a famous Psalm: "Be still, and know that I am God: I will be exalted among the heathen, I will be exalted in the earth."[23] But Eliot also uses the phrase "be still" in the *Four Quartet's* second poem, *East Coker*:

> I said to my soul, be still, and wait without hope
> For hope would be hope for the wrong thing; wait without love
> For love would be love of the wrong thing; there is yet faith
> But the faith and the love and the hope are all in the waiting.
> Wait without thought, for you are not ready for thought:
> So the darkness shall be the light, and the stillness the dancing.[24]

19. Ibid., 35.
20. Matthew 11:28.
21. Genesis 2:2.
22. Berry, *Remembering*, 38.
23. Psalm 46:10.
24. Eliot, *Four Quartets*, 28.

Here too, the poet engages in an act of self-remonstration, as Andy does. In his moment of despair, he seeks out the promise of rebirth and redemption. *East Coker* focuses more on disorder and decay in the world than *Little Gidding*—in it, Eliot references the upheaval brought about by humanity's reliance on science and technology, rather than on the divine. But *Remembering* is also a consideration of this theme: in losing his hand to a piece of farm equipment, Andy literally as well as figuratively suffers the consequences of an industrialized age. As Jeffrey Bilbro notes in this volume's essay on Andy Catlett's lost hand, "Andy's maimed arm makes visible a wound that he and his community already carried—their dependence on industrial technologies that exacerbate their 'native imperfection[s].'"[25]

In the midst of his temptation toward otherness and dismemberment, however, Andy remembers (or re-members) himself—reminding himself to "be still," reminding himself that the "flaw" in this tempting dream of isolation is "the little hell of himself alone." This also hearkens back to Genesis 2, in which God himself says, "it is not good for man to be alone."[26] Membership—in marriage, in church, in community—is where virtue and vocation are found. Isolation and individualism cannot offer the same eternal goods.

Beauty and Light

Andy wanders over to a church and "reads the legend engraved across its face: La gloria di colui che tutto move per l'universo penetra, e risplende."[27] It's a line from Dante's *Paradiso*, and it means "The glory of Him who moveth everything / Doth penetrate the universe, and shine."[28] What's missing is the third line of Dante's verse: "in una parte più e meno altrove," which means in English, "in one part more and in another less."[29]

This was a portion of the novella I hadn't noticed until writing this essay—and its situation in the midst of Andy's wandering, in the midst of his difficulty finding "stillness," brought to mind a new facet of the story I hadn't previously considered. Berry portrays Andy as the archetypal sojourner, the character divorced from homeland who is seeking a sense of

25. See Jeffrey Bilbro's essay in this volume, "Andy Catlett's Missing Hand."
26. Genesis 2:18.
27. Berry, *Remembering*, 39.
28. Dante, *The Divine Comedy*, 493.
29. Ibid.

belonging. Like Dante, he depicts a wanderer in the midst of crisis, wandering a dark road in search of answers. In *Paradiso*, Dante has already journeyed through the depths of hell, and is about to embark upon the ultimate "homecoming": he stands at the threshold of heaven. Yet the assurance of Dante's "la gloria" passage is that God's glory penetrates the *entire* universe: he is resplendent in both good moments and bad, in both the haunted places and the glorified ones. (Eliot suggests this in the opening lines of *Burnt Norton*, the first poem in his *Quartets*: "Time past and time future / What might have been and what has been / Point to one end, which is always present."[30])

How does this fit into *Remembering*? Berry's work is always focused on the sphere of community, urging us to embrace our roots and our homelands. Andy is about to discover, as he continues to wander through this shadowy land, that there is a place where (at least for him) God's glory shines "in one part more": where a sort of earthly paradise or Eden exists for him. He's called to Port William, and finds blessedness by returning to it. Yet this line also assures us that in the midst of our wanderings, there is also glory. There are still visions of the divine and of beauty left to uncover—and each of these moments offer a sort of awakening, a call to further communion, an opportunity to proceed "further up and further in."[31] If we turn again to Eliot's *East Coker*, we see a perfect description of this aspect of Andy's journey in the final lines of the poem:

> Old men ought to be explorers
> Here and there does not matter
> We must be still and still moving
> Into another intensity
> For a further union, a deeper communion
> Through the dark cold and empty desolation,
> The wave cry, the wind cry, the vast waters
> Of the petrel and the porpoise. In my end is my beginning.[32]

It is at this point in *Remembering* that Andy emerges from the streets of the city, and finds himself surveying the San Francisco bay. Shadows fall away as the dawn grows steadily around him. Outside the network of man-made machinery and edifice, creation beckons: sky and water, seagulls and

---

30. Eliot, *Four Quartets*, 14.

31. Lewis, *The Last Battle*, 203.

32. Eliot, *Four Quartets*, 32.

eucalyptus trees. Andy has ventured "through the dark cold and empty desolation" of the city, and here meets "the wave cry, the wind cry, the vast waters" (to quote Eliot's lines above). And here comes the turning point in Andy's wandering: it begins with an ending, a limit—the point at which Andy is standing at the end of the pier. He watches a sea lion lift its head above the water, and then slip back under the waves without a sound. In his book *The Achievement of Wendell Berry*, Fritz Oehlschlaeger describes the scene thus:

> Nobody knows he is here; no communication could find him. He could slip under the waves into an absence as complete as that of the sea lion. "He wants nothing that he has," and "all choice is around him" (161). But to want nothing, to be able to choose anything, is to be nothing in particular, to experience oneself as nonbeing. It is not even to be lost, for one is lost only in relation to somewhere where one could be found. But at this point, the beauty of the San Francisco bay, of the great bridge reaching into the fog, and of the Marin Hills beyond penetrates Andy, and he is recalled to particular loves, first in the passionate cry of the Psalmist, heard, though he is not thinking of her, in "his grandmother's voice": 'Out of the depths I have cried unto thee, O Lord.'" (162).[33]

Here we see again the temptation of dismemberment and nonbeing from *Remembering's* beginning. But this time, Andy is no longer shrouded in darkness. He's surrounded by light. Shining glory reaches out in birdsong, the sound of the waves, the light of the dawn—and Andy remembers. He thinks back over a series of memories: some of his forefathers, some from his childhood, each sweet and tender and full of meaning. "He thinks of the long dance of men and women behind him, most of whom he never knew, some he knew, two he yet knows, who, choosing one another, chose him."[34] This pattern, this dance of membership, reaches out to Andy and beckons to him in his solitude. And in this moment, Andy chooses the ones who chose him.

As the sun rises, Berry writes, "the whole bay is shining now, the islands, the city on its hills, the wooden houses and the towers, the green treetops, the flashing waves and wings, the glory that moves all things resplendent everywhere."[35] In this last sentence, Berry returns to the line from

---

33. Oehlschlaeger, *The Achievement of Wendell Berry*, 180.

34. *Remembering*, 50.

35. *Remembering*, 49.

Paradiso that was inscribed on the church. He reveals the work divine glory and beauty have done in pulling Andy back to his calling and homeland. "Andy has been prepared for penetration by that glory by a long history of particular loves, and that glory has, in turn, moved him to remember those loves that have made him who he is," Oehlschlaeger writes.[36]

Redemption & Membership

In *Little Gidding* the poet meets with a collective ghost, whom he refers to as the "dead master."[37] This ghost represents the tutors, artists, and counselors that Eliot identifies with and seeks to emulate. Eliot's "dead master" is a sort of collective Virgil, if we are to again reference Dante's *The Divine Comedy*. The poet meets thus with his own membership, "in the uncertain house before the morning / near the ending of interminable night"[38]

> I met one walking, loitering and hurried
> As if blown towards me like the metal leaves
> Before the urban dawn wind unresisting.
> And as I fixed upon the down-turned face
> That pointed scrutiny with which we challenge
> The first-met stranger in the waning dusk
> I caught the sudden look of some dead master
> Whom I had known, forgotten, half recalled
> Both one and many; in the brown baked features
> The eyes of a familiar compound ghost
> Both intimate and unidentifiable.[39]

It's difficult not to associate Andy's morning vigil with this encounter in the "urban dawn." The ghost shares three lessons with the poet, the last of which speaks to Andy's own experience as he "treads the pavement" in San Francisco. The ghost tells Eliot of "the rending pain of re-enactment / Of all that you have done, and been; the shame / Of things ill done and done to

---

36. Oehlschlaeger, *The Achievement of Wendell Berry*, 181.

37. Eliot, *Four Quartets*, 53.

38. Ibid., 52.

39. Eliot, *Four Quartets*, 53.

others' harm / Which once you took for exercise of virtue."[40] He ends with the following words:

> 'From wrong to wrong the exasperated spirit
> Proceeds, unless restored by that refining fire
> Where you must move in measure, like a dancer.'
> The day was breaking. In the disfigured street
> He left me, with a kind of valediction,
> And faded on the blowing of the horn.[41]

The poet, like Andy, has erred—has chosen wrong paths, and experienced the "shame of things ill done." But the hope offered by the ghost is "refining fire," the emergence from exasperated wrongs by spiritual awakening. Both Eliot and Andy receive answers and hope from past counselors, from the "membership" that stretches behind and before them: "We die with the dying / See, they depart, and we go with them. / We are born with the dead: / See, they return, and bring us with them."[42] This vision of the dead will factor in later, in Andy's vision of Port William at the end of *Remembering*—but even here, Andy is beginning to remember his home. The membership of Port William continues to hold and keep him, even in the midst of his exile and desertion. He realizes that "he is held, though he does not hold."[43]

One crisp fall day in Virginia, I was running along a leaf-laden trail. It was a particularly difficult semester at college, one full of solitude and longing. But as I jogged along that lonely trail, the smell of woodsmoke wafted over to me—and with it, a whole swath of memories swept over me. I remembered sitting beside my great-grandfather, shucking corn while he recited poetry and Psalms. I remembered his familiar black and red gingham shirt, his snowy hair tufting thick and soft around his head, his velvety voice and twinkling eyes. I remembered how his back was crooked and bent from years spent digging ditches—how his hands were rough, work-worn, and strong. I remembered the way he spoke my name like a benediction, or a song. How much had he sacrificed in order to give life and sustenance to his family? He had passed on years before, but in this moment, he was as real and alive as the entire world of autumn around me.

---

40. Ibid., 54.
41. Ibid., 55.
42. Ibid., 58.
43. Berry, *Remembering*, 48.

Remembering gave me a vision of homecoming and place: it showed me the burden we owe to those who came before us, and demonstrated the importance of keeping their rhythms alive. As Eliot writes in *Little Gidding*, "history is a pattern of timeless moments."[44] Those who come before us, who make us who we are—my great-grandfather, for instance—do not just fade into nothingness as time proceeds. Their memory is timeless as their tradition is preserved, and the hope of reunion with them in a heavenly kingdom continues to breathe life into our vision of cultivation and creation. After reading *Remembering*, I felt in my soul a calling to place and its cultivation—to no longer be a nameless face on the subway or crowded city streets, to no longer bury my head in abstractions, but to name myself to others and to finally name others—to be neighborly, and known. This would not involve an abstraction of loved ones—Andy's academic lecture illustrates the dangers of such a practice. I wanted to pursue the opposite: particularized fellowship, the naming of real presences, giving meaning and depth to everyday life.

Our connection to a past collective is more than mere sentiment. It is about a love, a kinship that requires our allegiance and service. It's about keeping the membership alive, and continuing the work of creation that's been handed down to us. As Oehlschlaeger writes in his essay for this volume, Berry displays "'requirement' not as something imposed on one and thus resented but rather as the chosen duty of remaining in the debt of love."[45] After Andy remembers his "requirement" in San Francisco, he embraces this "debt of love," following it away from exile and toward his homeland. His second homecoming echoes Eliot's language when he describes the journey of the "broken king" in *Little Gidding*:

> And what you thought you came for
> Is only a shell, a husk of meaning
> From which the purpose breaks only when it is fulfilled
> If at all. Either you had no purpose
> Or the purpose is beyond the end you figured
> And is altered in fulfilment.[46]

44. Eliot, *Four Quartets*, 58.

45. See Fritz Oehlschlaeger's essay in this volume, "Living Faithfully in the Debt of Love."

46. Eliot, *Four Quartets*, 50.

In his first homecoming, Andy's purpose was good—but not perfect. It was "a shell, a husk of meaning." In this second homecoming, distinguished by brokenness and humility, the journey is fulfilled—the purpose stretching beyond Andy's original vision, altered by the suffering and anguish of the journey.

Imperfection and Homecoming

Two years ago, I returned home to Idaho because my grandmother was dying. I trod through the busy airports, flew on airplanes across the country. I stared out the window as patchwork quilts of Midwest farmland faded into the majesty of the Rockies, which faded into the familiar hills and valleys of home. The words of *Remembering* came to mind, as Andy served as my own guide on this journey:

> He makes his way among them, in the hold of a direction now, stepping, alone and among strangers, in the first steps of a long journey that, by nightfall, will bring him back where he cannot step but where he has stepped before, where people of his lineage and history have stepped for a hundred and seventy-five years or more in an indecipherable pattern of entrances, minds into minds, minds into place, places into minds: the worn and wasted, sorrow-salted ground, familiar to him as if both known and dreamed, that owns him in a membership that he did not make, but has chosen, and that is death and life and hope to him.[47]

My grandmother's impending death drew us all together, from the corners of the earth to which we had strayed. Aunts and uncles and cousins, fathers and mothers, brothers and sisters, we came and ate the familiar meals, told the familiar tales from our collective childhoods. We ate my great-aunt's peach pie, made according to her mother's recipe. My grandpa tossed together a salad made with greens and peppers and tomatoes from his garden, offering it to us as we slipped to and from the house. I curled up on the bed next to my grandmother and stroked her soft hands as she told me stories. I asked her forgiveness for those times—many times—when we gathered at the house, and I would slip into a quiet corner and read my books, fascinated more by the fictions and tales of unknown worlds than by the sweet reality of kith and kin spread before me.

47. Berry, *Remembering*, 54.

She smiled. A bookworm herself, my grandmother understood the enchantment—though as my cousin noted at her funeral, "she didn't want to travel the world and see all the wonders beyond Idaho; we know she had a great imagination and loved exploring through her books. However, she was a woman of contentment. Family was everything to her, being surrounded always by those she loved meant more than any new adventure could." Grandma understood the temptation of separation and isolation, but she had rejected it. Her childhood was not free from suffering: she was forced to become leader and mother to her siblings long before her time. But she chose to model herself after the women of courage and contentment who came before her. Thus the traditions of the dead, the cadences and dance of the membership, were not lost.

But much is lost, as time progresses. When I returned to Idaho, I saw new subdivisions and shopping centers rising across the old swaths of farm fields, the acres that used to go through cycles of planting and harvest when I was little. "In succession / Houses rise and fall, crumble, are extended, / Are removed, destroyed, restored, or in their place / Is an open field, or a factory, or a by-pass," writes Eliot in *East Coker*.[48]

Could it be that the old rhythms of my homeland could be forgotten, supplanted by new ones? "It was a country, he saw, that he and his people had known how to use and abuse, but not how to preserve," writes Berry. "Andy began to foresee a time when everything in the country would be marketable and everything marketable would be sold, when not one freestanding tree or household or man or woman would remain. . . . Something needed to be done, and he did not know what."[49]

Rest and Remembering

During his first homecoming, following his journalistic pursuits in the city, Andy returns to Port William with his wife Flora, and they begin their work of stewardship and cultivation. In Genesis, God looks upon the world he's created and blesses its beauty by calling it "good."[50] So too, when Flora sees the home she's called to help cultivate, she offers her own benediction: "Oh, good!"[51] But it isn't until Andy's final homecoming that he receives the full

48. Eliot, *Four Quartets*, 23.
49. Berry, *Remembering*, 79.
50. Gen. 1:4.
51. Berry, *Remembering*, 97.

benediction of his work. As Andy enters his woods, Berry writes that "finally he comes to rest."[52] In Genesis, once he's finished creating everything, God rests from his labor on the seventh day (the biblical number of completion, or perfection). Andy's return results from a humbling of self and its incompleteness, its restlessness. This enables him to embrace the proper rhythms of creation and community, and in doing so, to receive peace and rest. Andy lies beneath the trees, and falls asleep. When he does, he experiences a new vision—one entirely different from the vision which opened *Remembering*. It starts with darkness and nothingness, as the first vision did, but then proceeds into a vision of resurrection:

> Now from outside his hopeless dark sleep a touch is laid upon his shoulder, a pressure like that of a hand grasping, and his form shivers and forks out into the darkness, and is shaped again in sense. Breath and light come into him. He feels his flesh enter into mind, mind into flesh. He turns, puts his knee under him, stands, and, though dark to himself, is whole.[53]

This is the resurrection, with language that mimics the creation of Adam: "The Lord God formed man . . . and breathed into his nostrils the breath of life; and man became a living soul."[54] But this resurrection only happens after returning to our first love—in journeying along the prodigal's path, away from the "far country" and back to our homeland.[55]

After Andy is awoken by the touch of healing and restoration, he's led out by a shadowy figure—a type of Virgil, perhaps, or a vision of Christ—and encounters a vision of Port William as he's never seen it before. He sees it perfect, "clean and white . . . each field more beautiful than the rest. Over town and fields the one great song sings, and is answered everywhere; every leaf and flower and grass blade sings."[56] But more than the outward loveliness of the Port William he sees, it's the membership that makes this vision particularly beautiful and meaningful: "In the fields and the town, walking, standing, or sitting under the trees, resting and talking together in the peace of a sabbath profound and bright, are people of such beauty that he weeps to see them," writes Berry. "He sees that these are the membership of one another and of the place and of the song or light in which they live

52. Ibid., 100.

53. Ibid.

54. Gen. 2:7.

55. Luke 15:11–32.

56. Berry, *Remembering*, 102.

and move. He sees that they are the dead, and they are alive. He sees that he lives in eternity as he lives in time, and nothing is lost."[57]

This is the vision of the creation work complete, a particularized vision of Paradise, and it gives Andy the strength and grace he needs to continue his earthly work of cultivation, imperfect though it may be. "From wrong to wrong the exasperated spirit / Proceeds, unless restored by that refining fire / Where you must move in measure, like a dancer," the ghost tells Eliot.[58] Berry, too, describes our membership as a form of dance. Belonging to a place and a people involves limitation: following pattern and tradition in a way that restricts the self. But in these limits, there is beauty. The song's very boundaries, its requirement to "move in measure," brings greater beauty. Andy's vision of what his place ought to be—what it *is*, in eternal light— breaths new life into his stewardship. "The world sings," Berry writes. "The sky sings back. It is one song, the song of the many members of one love, the whole song sung and to be sung resounding, in each of its moments. And it is light."[59] And this final blessing, this declaring of all things to be *good*, brings the novella full-circle from its beginnings in disorder, chaos, and discontent—back into the light.

T.S. Eliot also finishes his *Four Quartets* with a benediction: an old benediction, one that envisions the grace beyond the fires of sin and de- cay: "Sin is Behovely, but / All shall be well, and / All manner of thing shall be well," he writes.[60] The lines are borrowed from Julian of Norwich, a Christian mystic and theologian who lived in the 14th century. The quote is a part of her deeper quest into uncovering the reasons for suffering and pain in our world. In response to her quest, God gives her a vision not of explanation, but of assurance. In *Remembering*, the loss of Andy's hand is never fully explained or solved—he isn't physically re-membered in this book. But the assurance that "all shall be well" resonates in Berry's closing sentence, when he writes that Andy "lifts . . . the restored right hand of his joy."[61]

The Bible speaks of a Savior who came to earth to live as an alien and sojourner, suffering all the pains and distresses of membership with the human race. His homecoming was not left unmarred—but rather, the

57. Ibid.
58. Eliot, *Four Quartets*, 54.
59. Berry, *Remembering*, 101.
60. Eliot, *Four Quartets*, 56.
61. Berry, *Remembering*, 103.

physical emblems of his suffering signaled his victory. His pierced side and nail-marked hands told a story of redemption that a perfect, unmarred body could not. So too, our homecoming is never perfect: marred by the imperfections of human nature, the stained history of sin, and the dissonant rhythm of the machine. T.S. Eliot believed that our present sufferings would result in future redemption and beauty; and *Remembering* explores the imperfections inherent in our homecoming—and offers up the vision needed in order to overcome all the blemishes of the past and present.

I came to *Remembering* as if to my own tale, in a sense: seeing in it the patterns of exile and return, love and kinship that laced through my own life. As Eliot writes near the end of *Little Gidding*, "We shall not cease from exploration / And the end of all our exploring / Will be to arrive where we started / And know the place for the first time."[62] I have not yet—not permanently, not physically—"arrived where I started." For reasons both practical (my husband, a military man, is stationed in Virginia) and philosophical, I have remained in my new home, just outside Washington, D.C. There was a time when I was determined to return to Idaho, to buy up farmland near where my grandfathers tilled the soil. Perhaps that will still happen: sometimes I still hope for it. But my journey thus far has been more philosophical: seeking to shake off the façade of elitism and disdain that would keep me from embracing the people of my homeland, the legacy I hold so dear. We are not cosmopolitans; we are not scholars. We are rural folk, passionate about family and faith. Such grounded allegiances help prevent aloofness and prejudice in my journalistic work.

But my journey has also involved a conscious, deliberate decision to love my place: my in-laws, my church, the neighbors who hail from Mexico and Honduras, the military family up the street. It has involved an ongoing effort to foster the ethos of my grandmother's home—the beauty, the hospitality, the grace—even from afar. It's involved, perhaps most importantly, a realization that our longing for "home" harkens to a vision beyond our immediate reality, never fully encapsulated in an earthly dwelling or community. It's a vision we can carry in our hearts and seek to achieve, wherever God might plant us.

Here, for Andy—and for all of us—the "last of earth left to discover / Is that which was the beginning."[63] We return to our homeland not as perfect specimens of humanity, but rather as flawed and broken ves-

---

62. Eliot, *Four Quartets*, 59.
63. Ibid.

sels: able to see with larger, deeper vision because of our brokenness and humility, able to understand our origin and purpose because of the journey and its hardships. Thus, we pass together "through the unknown, unremembered gate,"[64] into a vision of the beginning as we've never seen it before: a vision of delight and wonder and perfection that was not known, but which we now know, and in which we are fully known.

Bibliography

Caspar, Ruth. "'All Shall Be Well': Prototypical Symbols of Hope." *Journal of the History of Ideas* (January–March 1981).

Dante Alighieri. *The Divine Comedy.* Translated by Henry Wadsworth Longfellow. New York: Fall River, 2008.

Eliot, T.S. *The Four Quartets.* Orlando: Harcourt, 1971.

Oehlschlaeger, Fritz. *The Achievement of Wendell Berry: The Hard History of Love.* Lexington: University Press of Kentucky, 2011.

Lewis, C.S. *The Last Battle.* New York: Harper Collins, 1998.

64. Ibid.

11

I've Got To Get To My People
Returning Home with Jayber Crow

Jake Meador

Sometimes I knew in all my mind and heart why I had done what I had done, and I welcomed the sacrifice. But there were times too when I lived in a desert and felt no joy and saw no hope and could not remember my old feelings. Then I lived by faith alone, faith without hope. What good did I get from it? I got to have love in my heart.[1]

NEAR THE END OF *Jayber Crow*, the rural Kentucky barber is reflecting on his life in the small community of Port William. The woman he has loved for years is dying. The town itself is dying. He has buried many of the townspeople himself. The town's children, now adults, have left. Some, like Jimmy Chatham, are dead, killed in a war whose point is still not known to the members of Port William. Others whom we meet in Wendell Berry's fiction, such as Margaret Settlemyer, desire to return but don't know what kind of life the place can offer them and so they stay away. In the midst of this loss, Jayber is thinking about the sacrifices he has made, the forfeiture of the things he once dreamt of as a young man who aspired to the ministry, the possibility of marriage, of being highly regarded in his community, and obtaining an education that the world would respect. And he is wondering if it was worth it. What did he get in exchange for giving his life to this membership and particularly for pledging himself to Mattie Chatham? His

---

1. Berry, *Jayber Crow*, 247.

answer is that he "got to have love in [his] heart." In many ways, that's his final word on the matter. Love is what Jayber received.

But this answer, if we are not careful, can come off as something of a truism or a cop-out. Ours is a day where "love wins" is a bumper sticker, in which an undefined conception of love that seems to mean little more than some sort of intense emotional attachment has become one of our god words. How can something that has become as hackneyed and clichéd as "love," let alone "love in [his] heart," justify the things Jayber gave up? If anything, today's conception of love might be inimical to the sort of extreme sacrifices Jayber has made. So what's going on in that passage? If we are going to understand Jayber and understand how this thing he received justified his life of sacrifice, then we must understand what it means to have love in one's heart, what it means to be free, and how love transforms the way we see our lives and our neighbors.

***

In *The Little Way of Ruthie Leming*, Rod Dreher talks about the difficulties of growing up in small-town America as a bookish, academically inclined young man.[2] For someone like Rod, growing up in a place like that is a classic example of what the business world calls a bad culture fit. Dreher loved books and dreaming of far-off places; his family loved hunting, the land, and had no use for imagination or even, really, dreams of anything other than southern Louisiana. In other words, Dreher and his neighbors were confronted with the same problem: How can you know someone who is utterly different from you and still love them?

In one of the book's most painful scenes, he talks about a day where he was made to go hunting with his father and tomboy sister rather than being allowed to stay home and read a book or visit his cosmopolitan, world-traveling aunts who lived nearby. While they were out, Rod saw a squirrel in a tree and fired. When he approached the squirrel, he saw that he had actually hit *two* squirrels and the second was only a baby that was spasming on the ground as it died. Rod broke down and started crying over the dying squirrel. Then his father and sister approached. His sister laughed at him. His dad called him a sissy. And that was the end of it.

2. Dreher, *The Little Way of Ruthie Leming*.

No doubt, many young people with inclinations similar to Rod's and from similar parts of the country can tell similar stories. I know I can. I remember vividly a time when I was in high school at a youth group event with my church, a fundamentalist congregation in Lincoln, NE. I was carrying a thick, paperback version of *Les Miserables* in my pocket. Before youth group started, I was sitting alone when one of the youth workers approached me and saw me reading. At first they were excited, thinking I must be reading my Bible or a commentary or some suitably "spiritual" book. When they saw I was reading a novel, they scoffed. "Why would you waste your time with *that*?" they sneered.

I couldn't tell them that reading that book was one of the best things I'd ever done. I couldn't tell them that I'd learned more from that book than I had from all their lecturing and "leadership" over my time in their youth ministry. And I couldn't tell them that I was deeply lonely and my best "friends" at that time were old dead authors whose books had an ability to grab me more profoundly than anything I had encountered up to that point at church.

Instead, I remained quiet and became resentful toward my place, toward the people in it, and toward the way of life that I saw practiced there. Knowledge of neighbor, in this case, seemed inevitably to lead to hostility to them, or perhaps apathy. I withdrew into myself, developing "friendships" with my books and isolating myself from the people I bumped into on a daily basis, telling myself (often with good reason) that these people were not really my friends, not really my neighbors.

Though there are some small points that make it unique, this is mostly a familiar story, particularly in an era of rural brain drain and the hollowing out of middle America. It's also a generational story as millennials look at their own family and often feel isolated from them. In a painfully overwrought piece for the Daily Beast, one younger writer bemoans how Fox News made her dad crazy.[3]

Increasingly, Americans simply do not know how to live with each other and particularly how to live with people whose income, education, and personal affinities are unlike their own. Misunderstanding and resentment breeds more misunderstanding and resentment. So, like the residents of Hell in C. S. Lewis's *The Great Divorce*, we choose to move further and further from each other, both psychologically and, quite often, geographically. If there is a piercing question about community life in America, it may

3. Yen, "How Fox News Made My Dad Crazy."

well be the same one confronting Dreher and his family during Dreher's youth in rural Louisiana: How can we know our neighbors and love them?

The consequences of this inability to love our neighbors and our place are many. According to a piece in *The New York Times*,[4] crippling loneliness afflicts no small number of people in both the United States and the UK. One study cited in the article found that 43% of all adults over age 60 in the United States report feeling lonely. An older piece in the *Times* reporting on a 2006 study[5] looked at a larger slice of the population and found that the majority of American adults have only two confidants with whom they can discuss life's most pressing questions, such as serious health problems or who would have guardianship of their children were they to die. More alarming still, 25% reported that they did not have even one such person in their life.

These studies shouldn't necessarily surprise us. It has now been 21 years since Bill Putnam made his name with a journal article titled "Bowling Alone" on declining social capital in America. It's been 16 years since his famous book of the same title was published. Loneliness in America is, at this point, a widely observed epidemic.

Of course, what is striking about this is how so many of us continue to define the problem. The *Times* piece from 2016 begins by telling the story of an 81-year-old British woman calling a hotline established by the National Health Service to provide lonely seniors with a person to talk to. Likewise, many of Putnam's proposals for dealing with the breakdown of social capital terminate in some version of government action. It is no coincidence that the politician who gave us the Life of Julia ad[6] is a huge fan of Putnam's work, after all. When many of our neighbors and peers confront the epidemic of loneliness, the only resource they have to draw upon is the power of the state, a power backed by coercion, which is inimical to love.

This epidemic of loneliness we are experiencing today is, in large part, the result of many traditional sources of community failing in the latter half of the 20th century and the early years of the 21st. The lesson many millennials have taken from the divorce epidemic of the 1980s is that marriage is an unreliable, outdated institution. This is why most of us delay marriage until our late 20s or early 30s and why such absurd ideas as a

---

4. Hafner, "Epidemic of Loneliness."
5. Fountain, "The Lonely American."
6. Douthat, "The Party of Julia."

"marriage lease" are enjoying a surprising and alarming popularity[7] with younger Americans. In what will likely go down as a strong candidate for "least self-aware sentence ever written," one 20-something living in Silicon Valley wrote:

> As a child of divorce and an aspiring designer-entrepreneur in Silicon Valley, I was suspicious of marriage. Out here, we're data-positive and solution-oriented and if your product (i.e. marriage) is failing for 50% of your customers, then you need to fix it or offer something better. So when I discovered polyamory and non-monogamy as I headed to Burning Man in 2013, I realized I'd stumbled onto another way.[8]

It isn't just marriage that is failing as a social institution, however. Neighborhoods and small towns are as well. To take only one example, in my home state of Nebraska 83% of all counties saw their populations decline from 2000 to 2010.[9] The 17% that grew are exclusively in eastern Nebraska near the urban hubs of Lincoln and Omaha or are located along interstate 80. This phenomenon is, like the rise of loneliness, well-studied at this point. To take only one example, sociologists Patrick Carr and Maria Kefalas analyzed the issue of rural brain drain in their book *Hollowing Out the Middle*.[10]

Yet if we focus exclusively on rural areas, we will miss an important point: Urban neighborhoods are often failing in similar ways as a source of social capital for their members. Charles Murray's *Coming Apart* looked at how this phenomenon played itself out in white America from the 1960s to 2013. What Murray found is not particularly surprising: There was a 45% drop in times that people entertained friends at home from 1975 to 1997. When asked if their whole family eats dinner together, 69% more Americans answered "disagree" in 1999 than did in 1977. These are across-the-board statistics, rather than isolated stats looking at distinctly rural problems. Any way you slice it, it's hard to avoid the conclusion that both Murray and Putnam have come to: "America's social capital has seriously eroded."[11]

---

7. Rampell, "A High Divorce Rate."
8. Messina, "Why I Choose Non-Monogamy."
9. Young, "Some Rural Nebraska Residents."
10. Carr and Kefalas, *Hollowing Out the Middle*.
11. Murray, *Coming Apart*, 245.

That said, Murray's book is a helpful corrective in some ways for how it takes a more granular look at the problem of social capital in America and makes an important point: While it's true to say that community life has simply disappeared for many Americans, there is a small sub-set for whom this new economy has actually enriched their experience of community. These are the residents of what Murray calls the Super ZIPs, the wealthiest ZIP codes in America where a disproportionately high percentage of residents have top educations and make very good money.

These new elites are less likely to divorce, less likely to have children outside of marriage, and tend to live stable, successful lives. To tie this back to our previous discussion, this is where many of the emigrants from rural America end up. As Carr and Kefalas note in their book, the most talented members of rural communities often move to what Murray calls the Super ZIPs after a lifetime of being told they are too good for their small town or even for their state. "To make something of themselves," they must leave and find a major coastal city that can draw out their best qualities and aid them in their personal success. Murray himself, a native of small-town Iowa who has lived and worked in Washington DC for much of his adult life, is in fact an excellent example of this phenomenon. Dreher would be still another. After growing up in rural Louisiana, he went on to live in Washington DC, New York, Dallas, and Philadelphia.[12]

The resulting picture, then, is more complex than a simple and unambiguous decline of communal life. What we have instead is something more like the failure of most traditional local economies which then led to the failure of traditional communal life in those places. Buoyed by technology and a spirit of individualism, things Berry identifies with the "boomer" spirit of American life, we have been cut free from the older sources of community in the United States. What has replaced them is a new form of community that is inaccessible to the masses but deeply rewarding to a privileged few. For those with the skills, wherewithal, and (often) the personal connections to turn that autonomy to good effect, this economy can offer great rewards (although likely not rewards large enough to justify what must be given up to obtain them). Yet for those who lack these resources, the contemporary economy and its premium on "knowledge workers," has been a curse. If justice demands that each person receive what they ought as image bearers of God, then this economy is failing, even if it has made a select few quite wealthy.

12. Dreher, it is worth noting, eventually returned home.

Here we must return to *Jayber Crow*. There are two loves and two freedoms discussed in Berry's novel. The love we spoke of at the beginning and which we will attend to later is the greater. But the lesser "love," which actually does not even rise to the level of love, is what we find in Troy Chatham. Troy is by some margin Berry's greatest antagonist; in him we find the most expansive summation of the vices that Berry's non-fiction writing has been addressing for nearly 50 years. The first thing we might note about Troy is this: He's one of the only Port William characters of his generation with no known family ties to others in the Port William membership. The other novel from the same period, *Hannah Coulter*, concerns many of the characters whose roots in Port William are deep and span generations—Mat Feltner, whose father and grandfather are known to us from other stories, Nathan Coulter, whose uncle, father, and brother are known to us from other stories, Danny Branch, whose family is known from other stories, and so on. Though Hannah herself does not have the same story ties to Port William, Berry dedicates much of the novel's opening pages to telling us where Hannah comes from and who her people are. The same applies to another adopted Port Williamite, Jayber himself.

But we are told nothing about Troy's family. We know they have been in Port William long enough to own a family farm. But we don't even know the names of his parents. In the world of Port William, such a lack of knowledge about one's roots is anomalous and, in Troy's case, telling. For Berry, love is driven, or perhaps more accurately, constrained, by narrative. We must know the people we have come from and we must know the ends toward which we love our place and our people. Love is thus always realized in the place that exists between our roots and our *telos*, to use the technical term. We are free within that framework, but we must not be separated from it. If we are separated from it, love fails. And so we have summarized Troy Chatham.

When you don't know where you come from, it's hard to know where you're going to. Rather than arising out of the love and affection of people in a place that belongs to them (and to which they belong), Troy seemingly arises out of nothing. There is no mention of him in any of Berry's other narratives. He simply shows up in *Jayber Crow*, already fully formed in many ways, a kind of projection of the lonely individuals that our world has created. Near the end of *Breaking Bad*'s run, actor Bryan Cranston (who played main character Walter White) said that by the final season White has "expanded beyond the cavity of his chest, so he's bursting out of his skin with pride."[13] Troy is, in many ways, much like Walter, only with very different skills and resources at his unfortunate disposal. Cut off from his roots, the only *telos* that can shape and define Troy's use of his freedom is his own ambition, which inevitably leads to the expansion of his self as it radiates out into Port William and consumes what it touches, ultimately and tragically destroying a suggestively named forest called the Nest Egg. Elsewhere in *Jayber Crow*, Berry says that Athey Keith, Troy's father-in-law, knew that he belonged to the farm as much as his farm belonged to him—and of the two, his life would be the shorter. Troy is what happens when one lacks this knowledge. The person is still tied to creation, for one can't help but be as a human creature, but as a person "expands beyond the cavity of (their) chest," they expand out over creation as well. They come to think that their life is the longer and more significant and they come to act much as Troy does in *Jayber Crow*.

✳✳✳

Of course, up to this point we are only halfway to an answer of how to live with our neighbors in the midst of deep difference and disagreement. We understand more fully, thanks to Troy Chatham and Walter White, why our world has become as lonely as it has. It's not simply that we are "men without chests," to borrow a phrase from C. S. Lewis. It's that in the absence of a chest, which is Lewis's way of describing the part of ourselves that helps us order ourselves toward the natural order and to restrain and focus our appetites, we inevitably expand beyond ourselves and devour all that is around us. When we add to this deeply disordered way of being human the remarkable technological tools available to modern humans, it is perhaps remarkable that we are not worse off than we are. Even so, we have seen the fact of our loneliness and the erosion of neighborliness. We have seen how that has come about through the magnification of the self in the absence of anything to frame or explain the self. Now we must, finally, turn to Jayber. This also involves turning toward Mattie since Mattie is, as Anthony Esolen has elsewhere noted, the Beatrice to Jayber's Dante.[14]

If Troy's defining characteristic is his lack of roots and his inability to place himself within a narrative or a place larger than he is, then Mattie's

13. "Off the Cuff."
14. Esolen, "If Dante Were a Kentucky Barber," 225–47.

defining quality is how thoroughly integrated she is into the story of the Keiths and the membership of Port William. In one passage Jayber says of her that

> She was going about her life, taking her pleasures as she found them, suffering what was hers to suffer, doing what she had to do. She had about her no air of self-pity or complaint. And this could only have been because, in her own heart, she was not pitying herself or complaining. It was as though her very difficulties had confirmed her in her sense of herself and her capabilities.[15]

It is rather a short walk from such a description of Mattie to C. S. Lewis's words in *The Abolition of Man*: "For the wise men of old the cardinal problem had been how to conform the soul to reality, and the solution had been knowledge, self-discipline, and virtue."[16]

When Jayber first comes to Port William he lacks this sort of virtue. That is hardly a surprise, of course. Much of our knowledge of virtue, according to Berry, is derived from our knowledge and love for the physical creation as well as a love of our own roots—and Jayber had been carefully schooled in an agnostic kind of disdain for the world via his education in the Good Shepherd boarding school and as an orphan with minimal knowledge or memory of his family. Very little about Jayber's childhood had equipped him to love what he ought to love, this despite the fact that his education came from ostensibly Christian people.

Jayber comes to Port William with a longing for home and yet an inability to identify what home is or what obligations he might owe to it. He's guided to Port William by the only home he has ever had, the old house at Squire's Landing where he lived briefly with Uncle Othy and Aunt Cordie. That experience has given him *just* enough to know that he needs a home and that Port William might offer it. It causes him to see, even as a young man, that his people are in Port William, even if he doesn't know why or what that will mean for his future. Even so, he takes many years to give himself fully to the people and the place there in Port William, choosing for some time to hold over a part of himself and keep it separate from his membership in Port William.

He doesn't quite come to Port William as Troy Chatham does, but he is also not yet seeing it as Mattie would. Like all of us, he is *simul iustus et pecator*, simultaneously saint and sinner. He is alarmingly vulnerable to

15. Berry, *Jayber Crow*, 189.
16. Lewis, *Abolition of Man*, 77.

the siren song of self-realization, but also deeply vulnerable to the world created by too many people dedicated to precisely that end—which is to say he has a need for something different, even if he is not remotely able to define what that something is or to lay hold of that good in his own life. This virtue, to borrow and slightly adapt the words of one of Jayber's seminary professors, is not a thing he can be given; it must be lived out a little at a time. So Jayber comes to Port William in search of a place where he belongs. He does find that.

But he is not yet ready to recognize that belonging to a place means that a place can make demands upon you. So as he lives in Port William and "takes hold" of it, to use Burley Coulter's phrase, he also divides himself from it. He buys a car and spends many weekend evenings in the larger nearby town of Hargrave, taking up with a woman from Hargrave, and they carry on an on-again, off-again sexual relationship as Jayber gives himself in part to Port William and keeps back part of himself to use in whatever way he prefers. It is not until a night when Jayber is in Hargrave and sees Troy at the same bar that he is struck down. He realizes that, despite his hatred for Troy, they may not be that different. Both are living in Port William and receiving many benefits from it while simultaneously withholding much of themselves from the place. They are relating to home on their own terms, saying, in effect, "This far you can go and no further. This part is mine." In a powerful scene in which Jayber sits in the bathroom at the Hargrave tavern, he writes a note to Clydie, his Hargrave girlfriend, in which he says he is sick and that he doesn't know when he will be well again. And he says he has to leave. He leaves the car, that symbol of his final, desperate claim to autonomy from Port William. He walks home, passing through a dark and bleak night that Berry goes out of his way to note is a Saturday. When Jayber arrives home he tells us that,

> The sky had lightened a little by the time I reached the top of the Port William hill. It was Sunday morning again. I left the road and more or less felt my way home over the fences and through the fields, at considerable further expense to my clothes and shoes. I climbed into my frozen garden, went up the stairs, and let myself into my room. There was still some warmth from the coal fire I had left burning down in the shop. I sat in my chair and let the cold, slow daylight come around me.[17]

17. Berry, *Jayber Crow*, 243.

It is a Sunday morning. He walks through a garden. His old clothes are worn away by the walk. This is a resurrection. But note how it ends: "I sat in my chair and let the cold, slow daylight come around me." Jayber's is a stumbling, faltering resurrection. He could likely say, with C. S. Lewis, that he was a reluctant convert.

What does Jayber's post-resurrection life look like? It looks much like Mattie's in all the important ways. He gives up the parts of himself he withheld from his place, he lays down deeper roots in his barbershop but also with the people of the place, developing close friendships with Athey and Della Keith as well as Burley Coulter's son, Danny Branch, and his wife Lyda. Jayber remains very much himself; he is still a reader, he still has his odd habit of reclining in his barbering chair during slow times in the shop. He still keeps the odd $20 bill tucked away in a book, just as he once kept all his money in his shoe or in the lining of his coat. But he learns the thing that Troy never did despite his considerable advantages compared to Jayber. He learns to anchor his story in the story of Port William. And he learns that love is not simply a sort of strong feeling or emotional attachment to an individual or a place. It is a decision to lay down one's own life to serve the good of the people and place in which one has been placed, independent of one's own choosing or preference. Jayber realizes in the book's final chapters that we are free so that we can love and the end of our love is death, but a death we embrace with the hope of resurrection. Indeed, one of the great emphases of the final third of the novel, after Jayber's conversion, is on death. We lose Athey and Della and Jimmy Chatham. Finally, we lose Mattie herself. But, like Beatrice in Dante's *Comedy*, her death gives to the novel's protagonist a beatific vision. As Mattie dies she looks at Jayber and her smile "cover[s] [him] all over with light."[18] To love is to die, but to die covered all over with light in anticipation of the resurrection to come.

⁎⁎⁎

We are a lonely people. Like Troy, we do not know where we come from or where we are going. We are thus left with no vision for life larger than seeing it as a quest for self-fulfillment or, wretchedly euphemistic phrase, "self-actualization," as if human beings are no more than machines that must be activated before they can function. Jayber Crow's story offers us an alternative to this loneliness. But it is a hard and demanding

18. Berry, *Jayber Crow*, 363.

alternative. If we are condemned to be free in late modernity, as Sartre once said, than our resurrection must be *into* something. This is precisely what happens to Jayber. On his evening walk he passes through darkness, tearing his old clothes and washing himself in the cold snow of a Kentucky winter. He enters Port William as the sun is dawning on a bright Sunday morning. He has left behind Hargrave, left behind his car, left behind Clydie. He has left behind all the things he holds for himself—and he has done it to be spared the condemnation that Chatham will suffer. He has been called to death and sacrifice so that when his death comes he would stand in the light unashamed, wholly himself, just like his Beatrice. For Jayber Crow the call to neighborliness is not concerned with a list of to-dos or large-scale bureaucratic solutions. It is not a technique or a solution. It is, instead, a call to die. But what do we get in exchange for our dying? We get to have love in our hearts.

Five years ago I made a similar walk. I am writing this in the basement of a home my wife and I have bought that is about seven miles from the home I grew up in. I could walk there in about two hours. This is not the life I had planned for myself prior to grabbing *Jayber Crow* off a metal shelf on the first floor of the downtown Lincoln public library. At that point in my life, I was ready to leave Lincoln, to turn my back on those snobbish fundamentalists, and make a life for myself in a big city. My plan was to be one of those bright students described in Patrick Carr's *Hollowing Out the Middle* and get out of my rural home state and never return. Specifically, I had plans to take a year off in Minnesota living near some friends before applying to graduate school in 20th century history. My thesis advisor told me he could get me into Northwestern if I wanted. Even in a depressed job market, a Northwestern PhD would likely have been the ticket to a decent academic job and certainly toward a certain cultural prestige that, at the time, appealed to me greatly even if I tried not to admit it. But then I met Jayber. And the meeting of him was the undoing of me.

Within 18 months of reading the book, I had gotten married to a girl I met in Minnesota who had also once called Lincoln home. Together we moved back here and a year and a half after that we started a family—and my daughter became fifth-generation Nebraskan. Two years later my son was born, another fifth-generation Nebraskan. We named him Robert Wendell. The first name goes back in our family six generations, all the way back to Norway prior to my ancestors' arrival on the Great Plains. The middle name explains *why* he was able to be a fifth-generation Nebraskan at all.

Bibliography

Carr, Patrick J., and Maria J. Kefalas. *Hollowing Out the Middle: The Rural Brain Drain and What It Means for America.* Boston: Beacon, 2010.

Douthat, Ross. "The Party of Julia." *The New York Times.* 5 May 2012. http://www.nytimes.com/2012/05/06/opinion/sunday/douthat-the-party-of-julia.html.

Dreher, Rod. *The Little Way of Ruthie Leming: A Southern Girl, a Small Town, and the Secret of a Good Life.* New York: Grand Central, 2013.

Esolen, Anthony. "If Dante Were a Kentucky Barber." In *The Humane Vision of Wendell Berry,* edited by Mark Mitchell and Nathan Schlueter, 255–74. Wilmington: ISI Books, 2011.

Fountain, Henry. "The Lonely American Just Got a Bit Lonelier." *The New York Times.* 2 July 2006. http://www.nytimes.com/2006/07/02/weekinreview/02fountain.html.

Hafner, Katie. "Researchers Confront an Epidemic of Loneliness." *The New York Times.* 5 Sept. 2016. https://www.nytimes.com/2016/09/06/health/lonliness-aging-health-effects.html?_r=0.

Lewis, C.S. *The Abolition of Man,* 77. New York: Harper Collins, 1974.

Messina, Chris. "Why I Choose Non-Monogamy." *CNN.* 29 Jan. 2015. http://money.cnn.com/2015/01/29/technology/chris-messina-non-monogamy.

Murray, Charles. *Coming Apart: The State of White America, 1960–2010.* New York: Crown Forum, 2013.

"Off the Cuff: Bryan Cranston Previews the Final Season of 'Breaking Bad.'" *Rolling Stone.* 13 July 2012. http://www.rollingstone.com/movies/videos/off-the-cuff-bryan-cranston-previews-the-final-season-of-breaking-bad-20120713.

Rampell, Paul. "A High Divorce Rate Means It's Time to Try 'Wedleases.'" *The Washington Post.* 4 August 2013. https://www.washingtonpost.com/opinions/a-high-divorce-rate-means-its-time-to-try-wedleases/2013/08/04/f2221c1c-f89e-11e2-b0185b8251f0c56e_story.html?utm_term=.cc9b80273c71.

Yamato, Jen. "How Fox New Made My Dad Crazy." *The Daily Beast.* 31 July 2015. http://www.thedailybeast.com/articles/2015/07/31/how-fox-news-made-my-dad-crazy.html.

Young, JoAnne. "Some Rural Nebraska Residents Optimistic Despite Population Declines." *Lincoln Journal Star.* 12 Nov. 2010. http://journalstar.com/news/local/some-rural-nebraska-residents-optimistic-despite-population-declines/article_5b8107a4-eec0-11df-b3dc-001cc4c03286.html.

12

On Resurrection and Other Agrarian Matters

How the Barber of Port William Changed my Life

Andrew Peterson

I'M SITTING IN A little writing cabin on my property in Nashville. A few feet away a corked wine bottle lies on its side. The bottle is on a bookshelf, and the books on that high shelf are loosely categorized under the heading Agrarian Matters. That's where you'll find Peterson's *Field Guide to the Birds*, James Herriot's *All Creatures Great and Small*, some Thoreau, James Rebanks's *The Shepherd's Life*, a few books on beekeeping, *The Country Diary of an Edwardian Lady*, and some backyard homesteading manuals. Also on the shelf, in a space I made by parting the books like the Red Sea, is a communion chalice, handmade by a potter friend of mine. Those books, the wine bottle, and the chalice are a part of my life because of one person—and that person is a fictional character from a fictional town who cut fictional hair in his little fictional barber shop.

The Books

First, let me tell you about the books. I should point out right away that I'm no academic (not that there's anything wrong with that). I'm a smart enough guy, though my test scores and grades would never give that away. I grew up reading the wrong kinds of books, you see. What little I knew of the classics came by way of illustrated and abridged versions of books like

Moby Dick and *A Tale of Two Cities* and *The Count of Monte Cristo* and *Treasure Island*. The illustrations were terrible. I knew that even then. The abridgements were more like rewrites, which means I got next to nothing of the authors' prose, and only the simplest distillation of each story. Still, I read and reread them, and understood something I now know is tremendously important, which is that just because something is old doesn't mean it's boring. I soon graduated from abridged classics to pulp fantasy novels about dragons and dwarves and bards and quests for magical items that would either save or destroy the world. Those books were badly written, but they more or less rescued me from the boredom of a town that I was sure would trap me forever.

You should know that my childhood was spent mostly in the Deep South of North Florida. If you don't think of that part of Florida as culturally southern, it can only be because you've never been there, or, more likely, you've driven through on the way to Disney and never got off the interstate at the Lake Butler exit. Lake Butler was like Port William with alligators. That meant that everybody was somebody's cousin, all the other kids were way into F.F.A. and showing their cows at the State Fair, and that there were five bars and only one restaurant, which was a Hardee's, which didn't show up until my sophomore year of high school. Before Hardee's, we had to go all the way up the road past the prison about fifteen miles to Starke to get Pizza Hut on special occasions.

Because Dad was the preacher, some generous family gave us a half a cow every year, and our chest freezer would spill over with t-bones and ribeyes and ground beef wrapped in white paper. Sometimes I'd come home from school and an old guy in overalls would be on the porch talking to my parents, handing over a basket of corn from his crop. Sometimes a sweet old lady would deliver a cardboard box of canned green beans from her garden. This was the way of it in Lake Butler. People farmed. They raised cattle. I helped my buddy Darrell bottle feed his calves after school sometimes and he enjoyed making me gag when he let the slobbery calves suck on his fingers. My parents kept a garden, which they made us kids weed. I groaned and moaned and hurried through it because I hated it, truly and deeply, with relish, and because I had books to read and songs to write. I rode my skateboard and mocked my friends who listened to country music and cared about the difference between a heifer and a cow.

We moved to this little town when I was ten or so, which meant I was an outsider from day one. Everybody else was kin. Everybody else knew the rules. Everybody else moved to the rhythm of small town life, and I didn't know the dance moves. That was fine with me, though, because I wasn't staying for long. I planned to get out of Dodge as soon as I turned eighteen, before if I could manage it, and that's exactly what I did. I joined a rock band and hit the road. After the band died I went to college elsewhere. I got married and moved to Nashville and only went back for holidays, and if we're being completely honest here (and why wouldn't we be?) I confess that I looked right down my nose at all those people who stayed behind. They were still slow dancing to that small town rhythm, just the same as when I left, but I had found a better song in the big city.

Or so I thought.

There I was, a grown up singer-songwriter, making a decent career out of telling stories. Like my father before me, I preached, but instead of standing behind a pulpit I sat behind a piano. Again and again, stories proved to be the most effective way to tell the truth. High concept songs appealed to a few people, sure, but if I could tell them about what happened that time I went to Arizona, or write a song that mentioned my buddy Ben's name, effectively moving the lyric from concept to concrete, the whole crowd would lean in. They snapped to attention. It's no exaggeration to say that I can still feel the quality of the air change in the room when a story has connected to an audience. The same thing happened when my dad preached. Exposition was fine, and comprised most of the sermons, but when he paused, chuckled, and said, "Let me tell you what happened at the feed store the other day," even my squirmy little eleven-year-old self suddenly thought the feed store was the most interesting place in the world. And maybe it was. So I carried that idea into my music: sing pretty and craft a song well and they might give you the time of day; tell them a good story and they'll give you their *time*.

A musician friend had mentioned Wendell Berry the poet, but I wasn't into poetry at the time so I didn't care. Later that year after I played at a college in Wichita I heard a literature professor in a hallway talking about Wendell Berry the novelist, specifically about a new book called *Jayber Crow*. The professor was standing at his office door, shouting a joke down the hall to another professor. "I'm telling you, Jim, *Jayber Crow* is so good, it's the *new* New Testament." The professors laughed and moved on. That was most definitely the most heretical book review I'd ever heard, but it also most definitely made me want to read this Wendell Berry guy.

The day I finished *Jayber Crow* (and I've told Wendell and Tanya this story in their living room), it hit me so hard that I lay on the floor of my little subdivision home in Nashville and wept. After I got up and washed my face, I immediately started looking for property in Kentucky. I determined to be a Kentucky farmer forever. That faded pretty quickly, thanks to my lovely and reasonable wife, who gently reminded me that a songwriter could not just decide one day to be a farmer. So instead I drove to our local Home Depot, rented a tiller, and dug up four square feet of my backyard. I planted tomatoes, and got exactly one—one tiny, glorious cherry tomato, the taste of which was so good that I had no choice but to call my parents with the news. They laughed and reminded me how much I hated gardening when I was a kid.

Something, you see, had changed. Something definable. One day, I didn't want to grow things. I didn't care what the names of the trees on my street were. I didn't care where my food came from. I looked down on my roots, on the townspeople of my youth, on small town folks in general. Then, because of a story—because of a fictional barber whose struggle with God, with his place in the world, with love and loneliness, with the wanton destruction of the good and beautiful and ancient things that grew in the old forest where he wandered, with the fracturing of his community by the greedy hammer of industrial farming—I was changed. All at once I knew I wanted to live in the world in a way that honored my community, my family, and God's creation. I wanted to live in a place where I could watch the trees grow, where my children were familiar with not just the limestone under the cedars and the coming and going of birds and the way the sun casts shadows at different times of year, but also with their neighbors and friends as the years sang on like verses to a song.

We moved. Not far—just a few miles away—but far enough into the hills that we might have a few acres to tend. We got chickens. We tilled up the grass around the house and planted much more than just tomatoes: cucumbers, pumpkins, watermelon, corn, spinach, kale, zinnias and mums and foxgloves. We cut trails through the woods and all manner of adventures were had while our children grew. One day, our neighbors drove down the hill with a bag full of their surplus Better Boy tomatoes, and we offered them an armful of our corn. My life had come full circle. "What *happened*?" my parents wanted to know. "I read this story," I replied, "about a barber."

And so that bookshelf labeled Agrarian Matters is heavy with stories and essays and photographs of birds and bees and garden plans. Every spring, something ancient in me wakes up and I study the pages of those books, learning all over again what to do next, how to pay attention to this miraculous world, when to put the right seeds into the ground where I live, where the best place is for the new bee boxes. I am reminded, in the words of the Mad Farmer, to "every day do something that does not compute."[1]

The Bottle

The wine bottle next to the books does not contain wine. It contains blueberry melomel, which is mead infused with blueberries. The mead was made with honey from my bees. The blueberries came from a neighbor's blueberry farm. I made the stuff three years ago, but I can't bring myself to open the bottle. No occasion seems special enough. Part of it is that there's a good chance that it'll taste awful and I'll have to either gulp it down on principle like bad medicine or pour it down the drain. But the greater part is that the bottle represents something precious: the hard work and patience it took to make it, to tend the bees, to harvest the honey, to pick the berries, to crush them, to add the yeast and stir it every day for a week, to monitor the bubbling as it fermented, to siphon the good stuff from the must, to bottle it, and then to wait for a year while it aged. Whatever the mead tastes like when I finally open that bottle, no one will experience it like I will, knowing what I know about what it took to make it, knowing what I know of the blossoms all around my property from which the bees worked so hard to gather nectar, the care with which my human hands mixed and strained and stored the liquid that changed by some holy alchemy from one thing into another—into "wine to gladden the heart,"[2] according to Solomon. When I drink that mead, I will be connected with the earth in a profound way, ingesting the world around me, taking into myself a sweetness bought by long hours of work and years of patience. Ordinarily, I am not a patient man. But that day I will drink the fruits of patience. And my heart will be gladdened, reminded of that night when Burley Coulter poured his moonshine and the jug said, "Good-good-good."[3]

When bees swarm in the spring, it's because they've decided the hive is too crowded. At some point, a signal is given, a pheromone is released, word spreads to half the colony that it's time to start packing, and then one

1. Berry, "Manifesto," 173.
2. Psalm 104:15, ESV.
3. Berry, *Jayber Crow*, 113.

day the queen abandons her kingdom with half her court. It's an amazing thing to see if you happen to be there when they vacate the premises. Thousands of bees pour out of the hive entrance like moonshine out of a jug ("good-good-good-good-good"[4]) and they form a laughing, buzzing, whirling cloud of life. They're dancing, having ditched the old hive like the Hebrew children singing their way out of Egypt. The queen can't fly very far, so she lumbers off to a low hanging branch and sets up camp. The worker bees in her party cloud the air until they find her, then before you know it they've clustered around her, bearding from the branch in a basketball-sized cluster. This isn't home. They're just squatting till the scout bees sneak into Canaan and report back that they've found a suitable new home in a hollow tree. That can take a few days, so I've got time to catch them if I want and introduce them into a new, empty bee box. (In keeping with the analogy, I'm just a mean old Pharaoh, I suppose. As a side note, I've heard that edible honey has been discovered in Egyptian tombs. Honey, it turns out, never goes bad. Now you know.)

Last year all three of my hives swarmed, and I happened to be home each time it happened. The first two swarms were clouding when I walked outside. If you've ever wondered what twenty thousand swarming bees sounds like, it's like a distant chainsaw, or a stadium full of chanting Tibetan monks, or trees snoring, or the drone note on a bagpipe tuned an octave higher. It's like a combination of music, rain, and breathing.

The third swarm was special. I knew it was going to happen about five minutes before it did. I had walked out that morning to see what the bees were up to, and there was something subtly different about the sound of the hive. I still can't explain what I heard, but I knew that something was different. There was nothing odd about the bees' behavior, but I stopped in my tracks and watched them for ten minutes the way a dog, hackles raised, stares into the night at some unseen varmint. Then it happened. About ten feet in front of the hive, there seemed to be more bees than usual. "They're swarming," I thought. I yelled for my wife and kids, but it was pointless because no one else in our house finds any of this business half as interesting as I do. The cloud of bees grew, and then I watched, awestruck, as thousands and thousands of bees poured out of the box and into the air, as if someone had turned a tap. They spewed forth, but it was a joyous and orderly spewing. I remember laughing out loud, then I stepped out into the center of the whirl of life and held out my arms. Bees aren't aggressive when

4. Ibid., 114.

they're swarming, so I knew I was in no danger of being stung. They flew in an enlarging circle, those thousands of wings stirring up a sizzling rush of energy, and I stood in the center, arms raised like a wizard calling forth the elements. I was laughing because of the sheer exuberance of it all, and also because I knew that I had learned something without knowing it. My years of watching the bees had given me an intimate and intuitive knowledge of their behavior, not enough to articulate the change but just enough to know when it was time to stand still and to watch because the world was about to unfold one of its wonders for those willing to pay attention. Creation had set a table and I was invited to the feast. That day, I was a member of the community of life in my corner of creation.

It was over in about ten minutes. The bees gathered around their queen's branch and the sky grew still once again. Someone asked me how I got into beekeeping. After a moment's thought about the bees, the property, the garden, the jarring realization that the world is beautiful beyond telling and that it is passing away, about the slow work of learning to listen and watch, I said, "I read this book about a barber."

The Chalice

"Christ's blood, shed for you."

Those were the words my friend said as he offered the chalice of wine to my family and me. We stood in our house on a Sunday afternoon and prayed together, solemnly remembering the story that set the world on a course for its renewal. We drank the wine from the cup my friend Eddie made last year with his own hands, the cup he gave to me and mine as a thank you for some grace he believed he had received from our community. It was a precious gift. I placed the chalice on the shelf of Agrarian Matters because the Eucharist is, among other things, a tactile reminder that the world matters, that matter itself is sacred. Grapes—grown in a vineyard, tended by their gardener to produce good fruit, fermented and bottled and aged until that holy feast calls for their consumption by members of a community—those grapes are changed from small and simple things to eternal and sacramental elements, pointing us to something holy, which is God most of all, but also his world, which includes those of us keeping the feast: my wife, my children, my friends. In communion, the fruit of the vine is sanctified, elevating the loveliness of wine everywhere. "*This* matters," the priest tells us, "and so everything does." The world and all that is in it—dirt, seeds, compost, grapes, clay, fire, honey, books, humans, rain—is more beautiful, more substantive than we can imagine. Will we watch it, work with it, harvest it responsibly, listen to its music, so that when the moment comes we'll realize we've been changing imperceptibly into better creatures, miles from perfection but more perfect nonetheless, ready at last to stop in our tracks, attuned to some mystic change in the hive, that we might behold that whirring cyclone of freedom and jubilee? Will we stand in the center of the swarm and laugh because we have been shown some mystery all are invited to but few are willing to see?

There is grief in the ruination of the world, but the world is also being made new, so there is cause for celebration. *Jayber Crow*, according to the barber himself, is a book about heaven. It is a book about the awful destruction of what is good and beautiful, but it is also a book that opens a wound that opens a door to the healing that can only come from longing. Longing is the light that falls through the gash in Jayber's broken heart and spills around him and his story. One can live in the world hardened to its destruction, or one can join with the groaning that all creation voices, a groaning as of a woman in labor. There's a German word for that ache: *sehnsucht*, or "inconsolable longing,"[5] a word C. S. Lewis explores in his memoir *Surprised by Joy. Sehnsucht* is a gift, if a heavy one. To love the world, Jayber says, is not a terrible thing. "To love anything good, at any cost, is a bargain."[6] And what is the immeasurable gift that comes from loving something that is dying? An inconsolable longing. A longing for what? Resurrection.

A few years ago I was overcome by grief. Call it a midlife crisis if you want. The long, dark winter of Nashville had frozen any hope I had that my heart would ever heal. But then one day the daffodils pushed through the cold mud. I told my wife I was going out to work in the garden, and when I plunged my hands into the soil in order to plant the seeds I was reminded of Jayber's bitter sleep by the fallen log. He had lain down in grief, woke in grief, and went in grief to Mattie's hospital bed. Then with a single word from her he was awash with joy. In grief I knelt at the edge of my sleeping garden, and in grief I placed a dead-looking seed in the furrow, covered it over like a grave, and watched every day for the seedling to appear. I longed for it, waiting for that single word.

5. Lewis, *Surprised by Joy*, 68.
6. Berry, *Jayber Crow*, 329.

This, I believe, is what it means to practice resurrection. It is to re-hearse the movement from grief to glory. It is to love the good world even though it's dying, even though our hearts can hardly bear love's weight, even though we're dying along with the world, because love overcomes death by welcoming it, by looking it in the eye. Love lies down in grief but always hopes, always watches the mud for the resurrection of the seedling, always listens for the subtle change that signals the pouring forth of that joyful swarm. Love waits patiently for the feast that calls for the uncorking of the bottle, when the good-good-good blueberry mead is poured into the chalice and the toast is raised and all men and women give praise for the consummation of all stories, all songs, all harvests and weddings and winters into the eternal springtime of a new and unbroken creation.

That is why the books, the mead, and the chalice all rest on one shelf. These are all Agrarian Matters.

So if you ask me why I weep over the folly of war, or the sullying of the creek near my house by careless industry, or the casual waste of human life, or why my wife and I work to make our own few acres in Tennessee a place of peace and restoration and beauty, a part of the answer will always be, "I read a book about a barber."

Bibliography

Berry, Wendell. "Manifesto: The Mad Farmer Liberation Front." In *New Collected Poems*, 173. Berkeley: Counterpoint, 2012.

Lewis, Clive Staples. *Surprised by Joy: The Shape of My Early Life*. Orlando: Harcourt Brace & Co., 1955.

Index